Observing Agriculture in Early Twentieth-Century Italy

Observing Agriculture in Early Twentieth-Century Italy describes how Italian agricultural economists collected information about the economy of Italy between the Giolittian and the Fascist era. Practices of observation developed together with agricultural economics as a discipline and as a profession during this period and the study of these forms of investigation sheds light on the constitution of a coherent and self-conscious group of agricultural economists in Italy, and the scientific and methodological alliances they forged with agricultural economists elsewhere in Europe. Thanks to ambitious research projects Ghino Valenti in the Giolittian period, and Arrigo Serpieri after the First World War, led the transformation of Italian agricultural economists from agents of estate owners, to social and economic experts in the service of the Italian state.

The group of agricultural economists who gathered around Serpieri played an important role in supplying the ideology of agricultural elites with economic content, especially after the First World War, along lines that resemble the development of agrarian ideologies in other countries of Central Europe. Three main forms of economic observation – enquiries, statistics, and farm surveys – are investigated to demonstrate the two-way relationship between the observer and the observed in the co-production of observational knowledge.

Federico D'Onofrio, Ph.D. Utrecht University, has held post-doctoral fellowships at the Department of Political Science, Yale University, and the Paris School of Economics.

Rural Worlds: Economic, Social and Cultural Histories of Agricultures and Rural Societies

Series Editor: Richard W. Hoyle, University of Reading, UK

We like to forget that agriculture is one of the core human activities. In historic societies most people lived in the countryside: a high, if falling proportion of the population were engaged in the production and processing of foodstuffs. The possession of land was a key form of wealth: it brought not only income from tenants but prestige, access to a rural lifestyle and often political power. Nor could government ever be disinterested in the countryside, whether to maintain urban food supply, as a source of taxation, or to maintain social peace. Increasingly it managed every aspect of the countryside. Agriculture itself and the social relations within the countryside were in constant flux as farmers reacted to new or changing opportunities, and landlords sought to maintain or increase their incomes. Moreover, urban attitudes to the landscape and its inhabitants were constantly shifting.

These questions of competition and change, production, power and perception are the primary themes of the series. It looks at change and competition in the countryside: social relations within it and between urban and rural societies. The series offers a forum for the publication of the best work on all of these issues, straddling the economic, social and cultural, concentrating on the rural history of Britain and Ireland, Europe and its colonial empires, and North America over the past millennium.

www.routledge.com/history/series/RW

Observing Agriculture in Early Twentieth-Century Italy

Agricultural economists and statistics

Federico D'Onofrio

Routledge
Taylor & Francis Group
LONDON AND NEW YORK

First published 2016
by Routledge
2 Park Square, Milton Park, Abingdon, Oxon OX14 4RN

and by Routledge
605 Third Avenue, New York, NY 10017

First issued in paperback 2022

Routledge is an imprint of the Taylor & Francis Group, an informa business

Library of Congress Cataloging in Publication Data
A catalog record for this book has been requested

ISBN: 978-1-03-240248-2 (pbk)
ISBN: 978-1-4724-4358-8 (hbk)
ISBN: 978-1-315-56625-2 (ebk)

DOI: 10.4324/9781315566252

Typeset in Bembo
by Swales & Willis Ltd, Exeter, Devon, UK

Contents

Acknowledgements vi
List of abbreviations viii
Main investigations and surveys ix
Dramatis personae x
List of organizations xiii

1 Three forms of observation 1

2 Agrarian landscapes 23

3 Packaging agricultural variety 47

4 Measuring stocks, conjecturing flows 70

5 Stakeholder statistics 91

6 Observing typicality 112

7 Budget studies 133

8 Epilogue 155

Bibliography 167
Index 184

Acknowledgements

When I was appointed by Dr Harro Maas as a graduate student at the University of Amsterdam, he explained to me that I would take part in a project that consisted of three parts, each of them dedicated to a specific site from which economists observed the economy. My colleague Andrej Svorenčik would take up the study of economic laboratories, while Dr Maas himself would focus on economists as 'armchair observers'. The object of my investigations would be the economic observatory. This book stems out of my dissertation.

I want to thank, therefore, my supervisors at the Universiteit van Amsterdam and the Universiteit Utrecht, Prof. Mary Morgan and Dr Harro Maas. I am really glad to have been Harro's first Ph.D. student. He dedicated more attention to me than most supervisors would have done, and I hope the experience was a positive one for him as well. My colleagues at both universities made my days there a pleasure. Andrej Svorenčik and Dr Tiago Mata have been great sparring partners over the years. Dr Marcel Boumans has always been very supportive. I want to thank Prof. Richard Hoyle, the Rural World Series editor, for his encouragement and suggestions.

Prof. Giovanni Favero, Prof. Maria Malatesta, Niccolò Mignemi, and Dr Katja Bruisch have been extremely generous with their suggestions. Peter Howlett and Gerardo Serra made my stay at LSE particularly profitable. The Max Planck Institute for the History of Science offered me the opportunity to enjoy two very intense months of study in Berlin, among very clever and creative scholars. My visit to the Agrarian Studies Program at Yale University was also invaluable.

The personnel of Italian, British and Dutch archives and libraries have been invaluable. I have to thank the Archivio Centrale dello Stato in Rome, the Archivio di Stato in Rome, the archive and library of ISTAT (in particular dottoressa M. L. D'Autilia), the library of the Ministry of Agriculture and Forests in Rome, the Archive of the United Nations Food and Agriculture Organization in Rome (in particular dott. F. Ciccarello), the Biblioteca Nazionale Centrale di Firenze, the library of the London School of Economics, the British Library in London, the library of the Statistical Service of the Netherlands in Voorburg (Mr Alfred Moest).

Dott. R. Gaidano of the Società Agraria di Lombardia deserves a special acknowledgement for his kindness, and so does the staff of the Royal Institute of the Netherlands in Rome (KNIR) who hosted me twice. The readability of this book has been very significantly improved by the very professional work of Catherine Glover, whom I really thank for her tenacious patience.

Among many friends who contributed, in different ways, to this research, dott. A. De Santis must be mentioned not only because our conversations added many ideas to this work, but also because of his hospitality in Rome. Margherita Farina, Raffaele Nencini and Alessandro Poggio provided an invaluable support in the final stages of the writing of this text.

The dissertation on which this book is based was funded by the NWO (Dutch organisation of scientific research), VIDI GRANT 276-53-004.

Abbreviations

ACS:	Archivio Centrale dello Stato, Roma
CA:	Catasto Agrario
CT:	Catasto dei Terreni e dei Fabbricati (Land and Buildings *Cadastre*)
FAO:	United Nations Food and Agriculture Organization
Feder consorzi:	Federazione Italiana dei Consorzi Agrari
ICS:	Istituto Centrale di Statistica (Central Statistical Office, now ISTAT)
IGM:	Istituto Geografico Militare (Army Ordnance Survey)
IIA:	International Institute of Agriculture
ISI:	International Statistical Institute
INEA:	Istituto Nazionale di Economia Agraria (National Institute of Agricultural Economics)
MAIC:	Ministero di Agricoltura, Industria e Commercio (Ministry of Agriculture, Industry, and Trade)
SAI:	Società degli Agricoltori Italiani (Association of Italian Agriculturalists)
SAL:	Società Agraria di Lombardia
SUM:	Società Umanitaria di Milano
SBV:	Schweizerischer Bauernverband

Main investigations and surveys

Inchiesta Jacini: Giunta parlamentare per l'inchiesta agraria e sulle condizioni della classe agricola in Italia (Parliamentary Enquiry on the condition of agriculturalists in Italy), 1877–85.

Catasto dei Terreni e dei Fabbricati: a complete mapping of properties for fiscal reasons, beginning in 1886 and ending in the 1950s.

Inchiesta Zanardelli sulla Basilicata, 1902.

Inchiesta Faina: Inchiesta Parlamentare sulle condizioni dei contadini nelle Province Meridioniali e nella Sicilia (Parliamentary Enquiry on the conditions of peasants in the southern Provinces and Sicily), 1906–11.

Catasto Agrario 1910 (CA): a survey of Italian land by crop and average yield per hectare which served as the basis of statistics of agricultural output, 1907–10.

Inchiesta sulla formazione della piccola proprietà nel dopo guerra (Enquiry on the formation of smallholdings after the War), 1929–31.

Catasto Agrario 1929 (CA): a second survey of Italian land by crop and average yield per hectare, which updated the CA 1910.

World Agricultural Census: a collection of data provided by national statistical offices on the number, size, and productivity of properties, 1930.

Dramatis personae

Azimonti, Eugenio (1878–1960): born in Lombardy into a wealthy family, Azimonti graduated from the Scuola Superiore d'Agricoltura in Milan together with Arrigo Serpieri. He took the itinerant chair of agriculture, first in Sondrio (near Milan) and then in Basilicata, in the far south. After giving up the itinerant chair, he served as chief of the office of Federconsorzi for southern Italy and Sicily, and established a farm on his own in Basilicata. His writings reveal a long-standing interest for the agricultural modernization of the Mezzogiorno.

Coletti, Francesco (1866–1940): a statistician and sociologist, he succeeded to Ghino Valenti as Secretary-General of the Association of Italian agriculturalists (SAI) in 1898. In 1906 he became secretary of the Faina Enquiry. Between 1910 and 1926 he was a member of the High Council of Statistics.

Giolitti, Giovanni (1842–1928): five times President of the Council of Ministers of the Kingdom of Italy, he dominated the political scene between 1902 and the First World War, and this period is named the 'Giolittian age' after him. His politics was characterized by the concessions granted to the trade unions. He opposed the war in 1914, but initially supported Mussolini in his rise to power.

Faina, Eugenio (1846–1926): the owner of large estates in central Italy, he studied agriculture with Raffaello Antinori. In 1905 he became the first president of the International Institute of Agriculture. A member of the Italian Senate from 1892, between 1906 and 1910 he was the president of the parliamentary committee for the enquiry on the conditions of peasants of the southern Provinces and Sicily (Faina Enquiry).

Jacini, Stefano (1826–91): born into a family of silk industrialists and agriculturalists, he studied in Germany, at the famous agricultural school of Hofwyl. His statistical survey of Lombardy, published in 1854, was considered one of the best statistical works of the 1850s in the Italian-speaking world. He was a right-wing liberal, and in 1870 he joined the Senate. In 1877, he was elected the president of the parliamentary enquiry into agriculture.

Laur Ernst (1871–1966): the most important agricultural economist in Switzerland in the first decades of the twentieth century. After graduating from the Federal Polytechnic School in Zurich, he became professor at the same university and Secretary of the Union of Swiss Peasants.

Lorenzoni, Giovanni (1873–1944): a subject of Austria-Hungary, he graduated in Innsbruck, with a thesis on the cooperative movement in Germany. He also studied in Berlin with Gustav Schmoller and Max Sering. After taking part in the Faina Enquiry, as the technical delegate for Sicily, he held the post of Secretary-General at the International Institute of Agriculture between 1912 and 1917. In 1929, he was director of the enquiry on the conditions of smallholders for INEA.

Marenghi, Ernesto (1874–1925): after graduating with Niccoli from the Scuola Superiore d'Agricoltura in Milan, he collaborated with Giovanni Raineri's journal *L'Italia Agricola* and was technical delegate for Calabria in the Faina Enquiry. Before World War I, he wrote a long report on accounting offices in different European countries for the IIA. He eventually taught agricultural economics, land valuation, and accounting in Perugia and then Milan until his early death. He was considered one of the major Italian expert in land valuation and was nicknamed the Italian 'Aereboe' because he shared with the famous German economist a stance in favour of synthetic methods of valuation.

Niccoli, Vittorio (1859–1917): after his studies at the engineering school of Padua, he moved to Pisa to teach land valuation. Since 1890, he added to his teaching in Pisa a course in land valuation at the Scuola Superiore d'Agricoltura in Milan, decisively contributing to the education of a generation of agricultural economics. From 1902 he held the chair of land valuation at the University of Pisa, while also practising agriculture engineering in Florence.

Nitti Francesco Saverio (1868–1953): a well-known economist in his own time, he published several books on the structure of Italian capitalism and north-south imbalances. He was director of the economic journal *La riforma sociale*. He was elected to parliament in 1904 to represent the left-wing opposition to Giolitti. This did not prevent him from joining Giolitti's fourth cabinet in 1911 as Minister of Agriculture, Industry, and Trade. He served as prime minister in the aftermath of the Great War, facing international tensions and a difficult economic and social situation. When Mussolini came to power, Nitti went into opposition and soon left for exile in France.

Raineri, Giovanni (1858–1944): he graduated in 1879 from the Scuola Superiore di Agricoltura in Milan, and moved to Piacenza, where in 1892 he took part in the establishment of the Federazione Italiana dei Consorzi Agrari. Elected to parliament for the first time in 1905, with the support of the right-wing Luigi Luzzati and of the leftist liberals, he became minister of agriculture in 1910, and again in 1916–17. After the war, he was minister for the 'freed territories', the formerly Austrian areas annexed in the wake of First World War.

Serpieri, Arrigo (1877–1960): he was a pupil of Ghino Valenti and Vittorio Niccoli, and graduated in 1900 from the University of Milan to become professor at the Scuola Superiore di Agricultura in Milan, and then in Perugia. In 1911, Francesco Saverio Nitti appointed him at the Istituto Forestale of Vallombrosa, eventually to become part of the University of Florence. From 1923 to 1925 was undersecretary of state for agriculture in Mussolini's government. Between 1929 and 1935, he was undersecretary of state for land reclamation. After 1945, he became the chief expert of the conservative Confederazione Generale dell'Agricoltura.

Valenti, Ghino (1852–1921): born in a family of provincial landowners, Valenti collaborated with the Jacini Enquiry on agriculture. In 1892, he became the first Secretary-General of the Association of Italian Agriculturalists (SAI). He taught economics in Modena, Padua, and Siena. Between 1906 and 1911, he directed the Bureau of Agricultural Statistics. After the First World War, he concentrated on issues of trade policy.

Tassinari Giuseppe (1891–1944): he studied with Serpieri in Perugia and Florence. In 1926, he became professor of agricultural economics in the University of Bologna, where he established an accounting office. Among the founders of INEA, he succeeded Serpieri as President of the Institute in 1939. He joined the Fascist party and was elected to parliament in 1929. His election was followed by a rapid a brilliant career in the ranks of the Party and the government: member of the Fascist Gran Consiglio since 1931, Undersecretary of State for Agriculture from 1935 to 1939, Minister of Agriculture between 1939 and 1941. In 1943, following the creation of the Repubblica Sociale Italiana, he became minister of agriculture in German-controlled puppet state and died in 1944.

Organizations

Federazione Italiana dei Consorzi Agrari: the Italian Federation of Agricultural Cooperatives was established in 1892, in Piacenza. Its early leaders included Enea Cavalieri and Giovanni Raineri. The Federation, eventually named Federconsorzi, grouped cooperatives of farmers from all over Italy, and provided them with financial and technical services. Federconsorzi contributed to buying fertilizers and machines for its members. Federconsorzi grew immensely over the decades, including more and more cooperatives. Starting with 1935, the Fascist regime assigned to it new responsibilities, including the task of managing the strategic stocks of wheat. In 1938, the number of cooperatives was reduced to 94, and they took the official denomination of *consorzi provinciali*, marking their full integration into the peripheral administration of the state.

ICS: the Central Statistical Institute was established in 1926 as the primary producer of statistical data. It was attached to the Presidency of the Council of Ministers, which means that its director took his instructions directly from Mussolini. Between 1926 and 1928, the first president of the ICS, Corrado Gini, managed to obtain control over the production of agricultural statistics, after a struggle with Arrigo Serpieri.

IGM: the Istituto Geografico Militare, the army ordnance survey, acquired its current name in 1882. In 1878, the predecessor of IGM, the Istituto Topografico Militare, began a complete survey of the territory of the Italian state for a 1:100,000-scale map. Agricultural economists and statisticians used this map and the 1:50,000 and 1:10,000 partial maps of IGM for the survey of the area under crops.

IIA: the International Institute of Agriculture was established in Rome, in 1905 as the first international organization. The initiative, sponsored by the King of Italy, Vittorio Emanuele III, had been proposed by the American citizen, David Lubin. Lubin wanted to foster the circulation of information on agriculture in the globalizing world, in order to stabilize prices. The supreme organ of the IIA was the general assembly that met every two years and was formed of the representatives of the member states (usually high-ranking officials and ambassadors). Daily decisions were made by the permanent committee with delegates of the member states (primarily the agricultural attachés of the embassies in Rome), the president, elected by the general assembly (usually an Italian), and the secretary-general, with the task of coordinating the work of the various offices. The three branches of the organization were the Bureau of General Statistics, the Bureau of Agricultural Intelligence and Plant Disease, and the Bureau of Economic and Social Research. The Bureau of General Statistics was by far the most important, and published a bulletin containing data on production and trade of agricultural commodities obtained from the statistical bureaux of the member states and from the specialized press. After the First World War, the IIA collaborated with the League of Nations, and in 1930 produced the First Agricultural Census, that recorded all farms (larger than a minimum size) in the participating countries and colonies. The position of the Institute became increasingly difficult with the growth of tensions between Italy and France, Great Britain, and the Soviet Union. After the Second World War, the Institute was absorbed by the UN Food and Agriculture Organization, which preserves the IIA library and archives.

INEA: to coordinate and promote research in agricultural economics, in 1928 Arrigo Serpieri established the National Institute of Agricultural Economics. It took over the task of the Institute of Agricultural Economics and Statistics (IESA), established by Serpieri in 1923, with the exception of the statistics of agricultural output and of livestock. INEA had local branches, named 'provincial observatories' in different Italian cities, including Florence, Bologna, Naples, Milan. In 1929, INEA launched an enquiry into the condition of smallholders.

MAIC: the Ministry of Agriculture, Industry, and Trade was responsible for defining the policies and regulations concerning technical education, trade tariffs, and trade. The ministry also collected and published demographic and economic statistics, thanks to the work of the General Directorate of Statistics. In 1916, the ministry was split into the Ministry of Agriculture and the Ministry of Industry. In 1923, these two ministries were merged again into the Ministry of National Economy. An undersecretary of state was responsible for agriculture. In 1929, the ministry was again split into the Ministry of Industry and the Ministry of Agriculture and Forests.

SAI: the Società degli agricoltori italiani (Association of Italian Agriculturalists) was established in 1895 in order to bring together different groups of agriculturalists. SAI represented the most important lobby of landowners and capitalist tenants in the Italian parliament. Its first president was the southern landowner Giuseppe Devincenzi, a supporter of free trade, and a former member of the free-tradist Society of Viticulturalists. Raffaele Cappelli, a protectionist producer of wheat, succeeded Devincenzi in 1896 and held the post until 1911. The society's moderate stance during the strike crisis around 1910 weakened the standing of its leadership. Between 1911 and 1919, SAI was directed by Edoardo Ottavi and Luigi Rava. Under the leadership of its last president, Giovanni Battista Miliani, SAI merged with the more conservative Confederazione Nazionale Agraria, to form the Confederazione Generale dell'Agricoltura, which supported the Fascist takeover.

SAL: the Società agraria di Lombardia promoted the development of agriculture in Lombardy after 1861. Founded by the landed elites of Milan and surrounding cities (such as Jacini, and Gaetano Cantoni), it published journals that advertised new machines and techniques. It also contributed to the establishment of the itinerant chair. Its president in the early years of the twentieth century was a famous plant physiologist, Vittorio Alpe.

SBV: the Union of Swiss Peasants (Schweizerischer Bauernverband) was established in 1897 amidst the controversies for a new protectionist tariff. The early leadership of the SBV consisted of members of the conservative landed elite, but the organization was extremely ramified (including a great number of local agricultural unions) and had thousands of members, including peasants, especially from central Switzerland (*Mittelland*). In 1901, the Union's secretary, Ernst Laur, established the accounting office of the SBV in Brugg.

SUM: the Società umanitaria di Milano was created in 1893 thanks to the legacy of Prospero Moisè Loria in order to assist the working classes. It included an agriculture office and a labour office, which were responsible for the collection of data on peasants and workers.

1 Three forms of observation

A quotation apocryphally attributed to the former president of the European Commission, Jacques Delors, has him saying: 'We will never fall in love with a rate of growth'. More than 20 years after Delors' speech to the European parliament, when he wondered, with Fernand Braudel, whether 'a European consciousness can be built only on figures', macroeconomic statistics are ubiquitous in the political debate, and the craving for growth in some European countries borders on some form of emphatic and unreciprocated love.[1]

Economic and macroeconomic statistics in particular are not only shaping our conception of the economy, they also figure prominently among the elements of national identity and people's self-perception. But, as Tooze remarked, they 'are of surprisingly recent origin'.[2] Historians of statistics, since the seminal works undertaken at the French INSEE in the 1970s and 1980s, retraced this story with a variety of approaches. A substantial corpus of work investigated the institutional arrangements that gave statistics such a prominent role within the administrative machine of the modern state: this was especially the case with Italian histories of statistics written in the 1990s, for instance, within a wider renewal of attention in the history of the administrative machine of the state. This historiographical approach explored the problematic relationships between statistics as a science and statistics as an instrument of the state, and produced respectable histories of the different national statistical institutes and of their position vis-à-vis competing centres of information and statistics gathering.[3] On a conceptual level, statistics appeared as a part of a wider process of bureaucratic rationalization along Weberian lines, of the construction of a powerful state machine. They were, in Michel Foucault's phrase, 'technologies

1 Jacques Delors, 'Déclaration sur les orientations de la Commission: faite devant le Parlement européen ... Strasbourg, 17 et 18 janvier 1989', Bulletin des Communautés européennes Supplément 1/89 (1989).

2 J. Adam Tooze, *Statistics and the German State, 1900–1945: The Making of Modern Economic Knowledge*, Cambridge Studies in Modern Economic History (Cambridge: Cambridge University Press, 2001)

3 Dora Marucco, *L' amministrazione della statistica nell'Italia unita* (Roma-Bari: Laterza, 1996); Giovanni Favero, *Le misure del regno: Direzione di statistica e municipi nell'Italia liberale*, Ricerche / [Poligrafo] 19 (Padova: Poligrafo, 2001).

of power'. James C. Scott's notion of 'legibility', which played an important role in the conception of this book, fits well into this approach. 'Schemes to improve the human condition', whether they failed or not, relied on the ability of states and other actors to 'see' social reality.[4]

Increasingly, and more optimistically, statistics came to be understood in terms of a new relationship between the state and civil society, a relationship that was made more democratic by counting everyone equally, whether rich or poor, aristocrat or commoner.[5] At the end of the eighteenth century, August Ludwig Schlözer famously said that 'statistics and despotism cannot stand together'. It seemed indeed that statistics provided power with an objective, rather than arbitrary, technology that offered a neutral and trustworthy source of information.

The progressive simplification of the output of statistical investigations was essential to this process. Statistics in the eighteenth century were mostly verbal descriptions interspersed with tables. Quantitative information was indeed collected, most obviously in the census, and production was also counted.[6] But histories of statistics rightly describe a process of increasing quantification, with statistical information evolving from the discursive *statistiques* of Napoleon's time to modern datasets. Comparability and transparency of the information made statistics trustworthy and useful in new ways.[7]

A great part of this growing 'trust in numbers' was due to the 'objective' procedures of statistics. These procedures included both the statistical methodology for the manipulation of figures (averaging, in particular) and the more mundane procedures for the collection of such figures. During the course of the nineteenth century, and with a renewed intensity during the twentieth, these procedures acquired a specifically industrial character, mirrored at first in an advanced division of labour, and then in the mechanization, and eventually digitalization of statistical work.[8] These latter steps lent to the figures produced

4 Institut National de la Statistique et des Études Économiques, ed., *Pour une histoire de la statistique: Matériaux* (Paris: Institut national de la statistique et des études économiques, 1977); Michel Foucault, *Sécurité, territoire, population: cours au Collège de France, 1977–1978,* Hautes études (Paris: Gallimard, 2004); James C. Scott, *Seeing like a state: How certain schemes to improve the human condition have failed,* Yale ISPS series (New Haven: Yale university press, 1998).

5 Theodore M. Porter, *The Rise of Statistical Thinking, 1820–1900,* Princeton paperbacks (Princeton: Princeton University Press, 1986) discusses how in France and Britain, political arithmetick, 'vital for controlling the population', evolved into statistics, a science that 'tended to equalize subjects', p. 23. Gérard Klotz, 'L'Économie saisie par la statistique', *Romantisme* 36.133 (2006), remarks that 'Le chiffre étant supposé éclairer l'opinion, les statistiques sont devenues une composante essentielle de l'exercice des libertés démocratiques', p. 59.

6 See, for instance, Lars Behrisch, *Vermessen, Zählen, Berechnen: Die politische Ordnung des Raums im 18. Jahrhundert,* Historische Politikforschung Bd. 6 (Frankfurt am Main, New York: Campus, 2006), for eighteenth-century statistics of agricultural output.

7 A process of professionalization of the 'field' of Italian statistics that went hand-in-hand with an increasing quantification is described in J. G. Prévost, *Total Science: Statistics in Liberal and Fascist Italy* (Montreal: MQUP, 2009).

8 Tooze, *Statistics and the German State, 1900–1945,* pp. 18f.; Theodore M. Porter, *Trust in Numbers: The Pursuit of Objectivity in Science and Public Life* (Princeton: Princeton University Press, 1996): 'In public

by statistical office the legitimacy of mechanical objectivity. The division of labour, the reliance on instruments, and the manipulation of numbers according to averaging, variance and other mathematical procedures shared by statistics and astronomy (in particular, by what Aubin, Bigg and Sibum called 'sciences of the observatory'), led Theodore Porter to the definition of statistical institutes as 'social observatories'.[9]

By the time the Second World War broke out, economists and technocratic policymakers in the leading countries were mostly relying on the data to be accurately produced and packaged within such observatories. The macroeconomic statistics whose history Tooze describes came to the economists already 'black-boxed' by statisticians, with a clear-cut division of labour between theory and observation.[10] The most crucial of such economic statistics, National Income Accounting, is often used by economists and policymakers alike without awareness of the complex classificatory work behind it, that for pioneers, like Phyllis Deane, had been such a frustrating conceptual challenge.[11] In the *Bildungsromane* written by many historians of statistics, macroeconomic datasets of GDP, inflation, unemployment, trade and financial statistics ready to be manipulated by economists and econometricians, are the protagonists, and shape the whole narrative (with most of the chapters dedicated to the antecedents of their birth, as in Lawrence Stern's *Tristram Shandy*).

The most significant difference between the present book and the majority of the literature mentioned above lies elsewhere, namely in the shift of focus from data to observation. While data clearly are the output of the processes that took place within 'statistical observatories', observation, as Daston and Lunbeck stressed in their *Histories of Scientific Observation*, points to the middle between process and result. Observation is, at the same time, a practice (observing), the informative content (what has been observed), and the record of what has been observed. By shifting to observation, I was able to restore the multiplicity of observatory practices (and of their output) available to (agricultural) economists at the beginning of the twentieth century. The focus on the production of data overlooked the complexity of the work of economists actively engaging in collecting data, often in competition with statistical institutes. Economists were

affairs, reliance on nothing more than seasoned judgement seems undemocratic . . . Ideally, expertise should be mechanized and objectified', p. 7.

9 Lorraine Daston and Peter Galison, *Objectivity* (Cambridge, MA: Zone Books, 2007); David Aubin, Charlotte Bigg and Heinz Otto Sibum, *The heavens on earth: Observatories and astronomy in nineteenth-century science and culture,* Science and cultural theory (Durham: Duke Univ. Press, 2010); Theodore M. Porter, 'The statistical office as a social observatory', *Centaurus* 49 (2007).

10 Harro Maas and Mary S. Morgan, *Observing the Economy: Historical Perspectives,* History of Political Economy (Durham: Duke University Press, 2012).

11 Mary S. Morgan, 'Seeking parts, looking for wholes', in Lorraine Daston and Elizabeth Lunbeck, eds, *Histories of Scientific Observation* (Chicago: University of Chicago Press, 2011), pp. 326–48 and Daniel Speich, 'Travelling with the GDP through early Development Economics' History', Working Papers in The Nature of Evidence: How well do Facts Travel? 33 (Department of Economic History, London School of Economics and Political Science, 2008).

not passive receivers of statistics but active producers of them (as the articles collected in Maas and Morgan convincingly show[12]) and, in observing, they did not confine their investigations to the macroeconomic statistics that came to feed the hungry Keynesian revolution.

Italian agricultural statistics provide a useful case for this enterprise because they share in a double marginality. In the early twentieth century, Italy was 'the smallest of the great powers', with an administrative machine that struggled to live up to models from most advanced nations, but was often inconsequential and ineffective. Historians of statistics and of the public administration have stressed the lack of specialist training among state employees, and the lack of coordination between national and local offices, and between different offices at national level. Of all sectors, agriculture defied the 'objectivization' of statistics: it preserved a diffuse structure of production with a huge number of small producers, whereas industry came to be dominated by trusts, and cartels, and vertically integrated groups (a process whose consequences for statistics have been briefly sketched by Tooze). The case of Italian agricultural statistics enabled me to emphasize the continuities and unsuspected genealogies of the current 'statistical order', because transitions happened more slowly and with 'a hundred indecisions, a hundred visions and revisions', not entirely outside but certainly at the margin of the main narrative.

Observations: enquiries, statistics, surveys

Once we investigate observation as an active process, as a set of practices, we realize that economists were collecting information on a variety of issues and in a variety of formats. These formats differed as much in the scope and content of the information and the way the information was collected (the practice of economists), as in the way the information was presented (in turn, to a varied public). The main characters of this book are three forms of observations, namely enquiries, surveys, and statistics. These three forms were all included in the toolbox of statisticians of the nineteenth century, and were often discussed together, although the status of two of them was disputed. This means that the terminology I use is 'emic': it is the very terminology used by Italian statisticians and social scientists at the end of the nineteenth century and through the first half, at least, of the twentieth century. The statistician Giovanni Battista Salvioni, for instance, distinguished enquiries from statistics and surveys. Although he never ventured into formal definitions, statistics were for Salvioni collections of numerical data on the social and economic situation of a country. Statistics led to 'numerically determined conclusions over the units existing in a given mass'.[13] They were impersonal collections of quantitative data, in principle

12 Harro Maas and Mary S. Morgan, 'The observation and observing in economics', *History of Political Economy* 44 (2012), pp. 1–24.

13 Giovanni B. Salvioni, 'Ai confini della statistica', *Rassegna di scienze sociali e politiche* 217 (1892), p. 38.

covering the whole relevant population. Such data could be subject to statistical elaboration: the computation of averages, variance, and the drawing of graphs. Samples smaller than the whole population would have distorted the results, and made the averages meaningless.

For agricultural economists, agricultural statistics almost invariably meant annual statistics of areas classified by crops and agricultural output. The development of agricultural statistics in Europe and the United States reflects the expansion of national statistical institutes. Certain states of the *ancien régime* already tried to assess the annual production of certain agricultural commodities, especially wheat, by means of expert estimates and farmers' reports. Figures of production and trade of grains had a crucial role in the debate on the liberalization of trade in France and Naples, for instance, as the state was trying to assess the size of the surplus or deficit of foodstuff. The effectiveness of these assessments, though, was sometimes very controversial at the time.[14]

The conquests of Napoleon extended to a number of other countries the administrative practices established by the French revolutionary government, including the collection of data on the sales and prices of foodstuff. This was for instance the case in Italy, and in the Low Countries (including Belgium) during the French occupation.[15] The Napoleonic statistics of agricultural sales and prices relied on local administrators (prefects and mayors), who were also charged with the task of collecting information on the condition of crops, the area under crops, market prices, and quantities sold. During the nineteenth century, most continental European countries, from France to the unified Kingdom of Italy, Austria-Hungary, and the Netherlands, adopted systems that derived from this early French practice.[16] They were based on the participation of local notables and local authorities, especially the municipalities. Over the course of the nineteenth century, the French ministry of agriculture, industry, and trade asked mayors and prefects to assess agricultural output for key crops, referring to a 'normal year'. Every ten years, the ministry was supposed to carry out a comprehensive enquiry fixing the area under crop. In the case of Belgium and Austria, statistics were based also on another innovation that Napoleon spread over continental Europe, and that played a very important role in Italy

14 For the case of agricultural production in France see the already-mentioned Behrisch, *Vermessen, Zählen, Berechnen*. Probably the most famous estimate of France output, during the early revolutionary period, was Lavoisier's, republished by Jean-Claude Perrot: Antoine-Laurent Lavoisier, *De la richesse territoriale du royaume de France*, ed. Jean-Claude Perrot (Paris: Comité des travaux historiques et scientifiques, 1988).

15 For more details on the statistics of market prices and their application in Italy and the Low Countries, Ernest Labrousse, Ruggero Romano and F.-G. Dreyfus, *Le prix du froment en France au temps de la monnaie stable (1726–1913)* (Paris: S.E.V.P.E.N, 1970)

16 In France itself, after the suppression of the Napoleonic Bureau des Statistiques, a new Bureau de Statistique Générale de la France was re-established in 1833, see Klotz, 'L'Économie saisie par la statistique', p. 64. For the Dutch case, see M. Klatzmann, 'La statistique agricole aux Pays-Bas', *Etudes et conjuncture* 10.12 (1955), pp. 1057f.

after the reorganization of the 1900s: the modern *cadastre*, a comprehensive survey of productive land.[17]

Countries that had remained untouched by the expansion of French models of governance, collected agricultural data differently. In the United States, statisticians surveyed the area under crop during the ten-yearly census. This survey served as the basis of yearly assessments of production. Britain relied on the yearly declaration of farmers, who were asked to report the area under crop and the annual yield. In Russia, the system centred around literate respondents to the questionnaires of the local statisticians without much precision on acreage.[18]

During the course of the nineteenth century, the traditional role of agricultural statistics changed. While in the first part of the century, the collection of data, especially in continental Europe, issued essentially out of concerns for the supply of foodstuff, in the later part of the century international trade became the crucial element.[19] Statistics of production acquired an unprecedented role in the decades around the turn of the century. The creation of the International Institute of Agriculture in 1905 stands as a witness to the importance attributed to the data on agricultural production during the so-called 'first globalization'. International organizations and international cooperation played an important role in this period slowly increasing the degree of standardization and the availability of figures concerning agricultural commodities exchanged on the world market.[20]

The enquiries (It. *inchieste*) were designed to investigate social and economic problems but they included also qualitative data and took advantage 'of the knowledge of all those who have the skills and interest to express what they know

17 Michel Augé-Laribé, 'Les statistiques agricoles', *Annales de Géographie* 54.294 (1945) criticized the 'delusional behaviour' of the French government that expected local administrators to actually provide reliable data, p. 84, and explains the importance of the cadastral survey of productive surface, p. 85ff.

18 The most complete study of American statistics is in the first part of Emmanuel Didier, *En quoi consiste l'Amérique? Les statistiques, le new deal et la démocratie,* Série Anthropologie des sciences et des techniques (Paris: Éd. La Découverte, 2009); studies on Russian statistics by Alessandro Stanziani, 'Les statistiques des récoltes en Russie, 1905–1928', *Histoire & Mesure* 7.1 (1992), pp. 73–98; for the role of Russian statisticians in the countryside: Martine Mespoulet, 'Statisticiens des zemstva', *Cahiers du monde russe Russie, Empire russe, Union soviétique, États indépendants* 40.4 (1999), pp. 573–624 and Martine Mespoulet, *Statistique et révolution en Russie un compromis impossible, 1880–1930* (Rennes: Presses Universitaires de Rennes, 2001).

19 Extremely significant, for instance, the case of the subdivision of France into three types of 'departements': self-sufficient, in surplus, in deficit during the last years of Napoleon's empire, see Nicolas Bourguinat, 'Libre-commerce du blé et représentations de l'espace français: Les crises frumentaires au début du XIXe siècle', *Annales. Histoire, Sciences Sociales* 56.1 (2001).

20 In 1926, the International Institute of Agriculture prepared an important collection of figures on agricultural output, trade, and input costs for the World Economic Conference held in Geneva under the auspices of the League of Nations: International Institute of Agriculture, *Agricultural problems in their international aspect* (Rome: Printing office of the International Institute of Agriculture, 1927). The following year, they began preparing International Institute of Agriculture, *The first world agriculture census (1930),* 1–5 (Rome: International Institute of Agriculture, 1939). The American Leon M. Estabrook, who led the project, had previously helped various South American nations setting up their bureaux of agricultural statistics.

about the topic of the enquiry'. The truth, in this case, would emerge from 'the clash of opinions and the comparison of often contradictory witnesses'.[21] These witnesses came as respondents to a questionnaire. Legitimate answers were not impersonal. Instead, they were valuable because of the position of the respondent (geographical position, social status, profession, and so on).[22] Their answers summarized a long (often experiential) acquaintance with the phenomenon under scrutiny or with certain aspects of it. The task of the enquirer was to analyse and recombine these answers in a sufficiently impersonal and consensual report, by weighing them against his or her own direct investigation and by trying to offset the partisanship of the respondents' positions.

Enquiries were often highly publicized sources of information and are characteristic of the later part of the nineteenth century. In countries ruled by parliamentary regimes, British parliamentary enquiries on social and economic issues were influential models.[23] For the rest of Europe, the parliamentary enquiry became the epitome of British liberalism. In Germany, a country with a relatively weak parliament, academic enquiries instead had the most prominent role. The ground-breaking work of Max Sering on internal colonization, and of Max Weber on the peasants of the provinces east of the Elbe were published by the *Verein fuer Sozialpolitik* around the turn of the century. Friederich Dettweiler's often quoted enquiry on the agricultural labour force (1905) was funded by a local society, the *Meklemburgische Patriotische Verein*.[24]

One of the characteristics of the German enquiries was the reliance on farm and family surveys to show the distribution of income and the behaviour of the working classes. Surveys were for Salvioni similar to enquiries, but instead of observing a great number of facts of a given type, they investigated a single instance, often a typical instance, of a kind. There were surveys on families, of farms, of villages, and provinces. At the core of the family and farm surveys, there was a budget: a list of assets and liabilities that characterized the life of the family or the farm. By combining many of such budgets, it became possible to treat surveys statistically (computing averages and variance, and drawing

21 Salvioni, 'Ai confini della statistica', p. 32: '[Le inchieste] si giovano delle cognizioni di tutti coloro i quali hanno capacità ed interesse ad esporre quanto sanno relativamente a quest'oggetto; dall'urto delle opinioni e dal confronto delle deposizioni spesso contradditorie, ma non perciò meno utili, balza fuori la verità' (all translations in the text are mine, when not stated otherwise).

22 The term *position* or *positionality* is borrowed from Amartya Sen, 'Positional Objectivity', *Philosophy & Public Affairs* 22.2 (1993), pp. 126–45.

23 On social concerns in Britain as a driver of investigations, see the essays in Micheal J. Lacey and Mary O. Furner, eds, *The State and Social Investigation in Britain and the United States* (Cambridge: Cambridge University Press, 1993).

24 Max Sering, *Die innere Kolonisation im östlichen Deutschland,* Schriften des Vereins für Socialpolitik (Duncker & Humblot, 1893); Maximilian Weber, *Die Verhältnisse der Landarbeiter im ostelbischen Deutschland (Preussische Provinzen Ost- und Westpreussen, Pommern, Posen, Schlesien, Brandenburg, Grossherzogtümer Mecklenburg, Kreis Herzogtum Lauenburg),* Schriften des Vereins für Socialpolitik (Duncker & Humblot, 1892); Friederich Dettweiler, *Die Handarbeit in der Landwirtschaft* (Jena: Fischer, 1905).

graphs). Farm surveys then became the raw material for aggregate statistics of businesses. The way that surveys recorded the information was impersonal (a budget), but the selection of the individuals to be studied relied on a combination of contingent factors, including experiential and positional knowledge.

Surveys on working class families were, by the beginning of the twentieth century, the basis of sociological and economic enquiries into the income and consumption patterns of the working class, suitable for the aims of right wing reformers such as Le Play and Emil Cheysson, as well as for those of socialists of various orientations.[25] Farm surveys were conceived according to very similar criteria, and the distinction is often blurred by the inextricable connection of farm and family. Farm surveys had a steady fortune in the twentieth century.[26] Their methodological codification is linked to the spread of farm accounting services in the second half of the nineteenth century. The real champion of the importance of farm surveys for the study of agricultural economics was Ernst Laur, who established the accounting office of the Swiss Peasant Union in 1901. Laur's method rapidly attracted the attention of European agricultural economists (the Russian Aleksandr Čajanov, for instance, visited Laur for the first time in 1912), but it was especially after the First World War that they became the tool of choice of agricultural economists. In the second half of the 1920s and during the 1930s, farm surveys were used increasingly for measuring the depth of agricultural depression and evaluating the success of the ensuing policies of relief to farmers. In France, an *Office de comptabilité agricole* was established in Soissons in 1927, soon to be followed by a number of other accounting offices. Italy's INEA began a systematic collection of surveys in the following year. By 1930, the Soviets were collecting farm and family surveys in the thousands. A national farm survey began in the UK in the late 1930s. In the same period, Germany began collecting the *Hofkarte*, a form whereby farmers reported their stock of capital and land, the value of the buildings, and the labour they employed.[27]

25 Maria R. Protasi, 'Tra scienza e riforma sociale: Il pensiero e il metodo d'indagine sociale di F. Le Play e dei suoi continuatori in Italia (1857–1914)', *Studi Storici* 37.3 (1996); Bernard Kalaora and Antoine Savoye, *Les Inventeurs oubliés: Le Play et ses continuateurs aux origines des sciences sociales,* Collection Milieux (Paris: Champ Vallon, 1989); Paul Rabinow, *French Modern: Norms and Forms of the Social Environment* (Chicago: University of Chicago Press, 1995).

26 Farm surveys are a relatively ancient practice. Loic Charles and Christine Théré documented the careful study of farm budgets by the Physiocrats. Aleksandr Chajanov attributed the beginning of 'budget enquiries', how Russians called farm surveys, to Arthur Young. Surveys of peasant and urban families became popular in the nineteenth century, primarily thanks to Frederic LePlay and his pupils

27 For household budgets in late Tsarist and Soviet Russia, see the review in Aleksandr V. Čajanov, *O budžetnikh issledovanjakh* (Moskva: Izdatel'skij Dom Tonču, 2006), pp. 91ff.; for Central Asia, see Beatrice Penati, 'On the Soviet discovery of rural Central Asia. The Karp commission in context', *Monde(s). Histoire, Espaces, Relations* no. 4 (2013), pp. 105–25. While this was going to press, a very interesting study of Hofkarten and farm accounting in Austria by Ernst Langthaler came out: Ernst Langthaler, *Schlachtfelder: Alltägliches Wirtschaften in der nationalsozialistischen Agrargesellschaft 1938–1945* (Wien-Koeln-Weimar: Böhlau Verlag, 2016); par. 2.3 and 2.4 are especially relevant.

The picture differs substantially from that painted in the histories of statistics discussed above. The proud solitude of macroeconomic statistics breaks into a crowded world of methods and investigations. Certainly, agricultural economists collected also macro-data on agricultural production, and these were to enter statistics on national income and wealth during the 1920s.[28] But surveys of families and farm surveys were one of the most important instruments in their toolbox, intermediate between the micro-level of individual businesses and the macro-level of income distribution and economic cycles.

Farm surveys have not attracted the attention of historians of statistics, and have been considered almost exclusively as a source for economic historians rather than as historical phenomena in their own right.[29] In the early decades of the twentieth century, though, a whole economic ontology was built on this form of observation. The economy was understood rather as a combination of individual firms (or farms) and families of consumers than in terms of aggregate values of outputs and inputs. Cyclical oscillations as well as social problems were captured by means of the budgets of families and farms.

Enquiries have had an only slightly better historiographical fortune; somewhat similar to the qualitative surveys of today's sociology, their peculiarity as a form of observation of social and economic facts has not often been recognized, notwithstanding the great deal of attention dedicated to the parliamentary enquiries of the nineteenth century.[30] Only recently, a group coordinated by Nadine Vivier published a volume dedicated to enquiries that can serve as a starting point for interesting methodological comparisons. In many ways, the composite nature of nineteenth- and early twentieth-century enquiries made their specificity particularly elusive.[31] The most celebrated enquiries had the ambiguous nature of an

28 MAIC, *Valutazione della produzione lorda della agricoltura italiana* (Roma: Tip. Luzzatti, 1925), for instance, contains an estimate of the contribution of agriculture to the general income of Italy.

29 For instance, Francesco Galassi and Vera Zamagni, 'L'azienda agraria: un problema storiografico aperto. 1860–1940', in Pier P. D'Attorre and A. D Bernardi, eds, *Studi sull'agricoltura italiana: società rurale e modernizzazione*, Annali (Fondazione Giangiacomo Feltrinelli, 1994), pp. 3–17; Rita Garstenauer, Ulrich Schwarz, and Sophie Tod, 'Alles unter einen Hut bringen: Baeurliche Wirtschaftsstile in zwei Regionen Niederoesterreichs 1945–1980', *Historische Anthropologie* 20.3 (2010), pp. 382–426; Rita Garstenauer, Ernst Langthaler, and Sophie Tod, 'Wachsen, Weichen, Weitermachen: Familienbetriebliche Agrarsysteme in zwei Regionen Niederoesterreich 1945–1985', *Historische Anthropologie* 20.3 (2010), pp. 346–82; the introduction of Roberto Tolaini, *Contadini toscani negli anni Trenta: Monografie di famiglie dell'INEA 1931–1938,* Collana del Centro di documentazione e ricerca sulla storia dell'agricoltura e della società contadina 0002 (Ospedaletto, Pisa: Pacini, 2005); and Paul Brassley et al., 'Accounting for agriculture: The origins of the Farm Management Survey', *Agricultural History Review* 61.1 (2013), pp. 135–53, examine farm surveys as a historical phenomenon.

30 Alberto Caracciolo, *L'inchiesta agraria Jacini* (Torino: Einaudi, 1959); Sandro Rogari and Eugenio Faina, *Mezzogiorno ed emigrazione: L'inchiesta Faina sulle condizioni dei contadini nelle province meridionali e nella Sicilia 1906–1911* (Firenze: Centro editoriale toscano, 2002), for the two major economic and social enquiries concerning Italian agriculture.

31 Nadine Vivier and Corinne Marache, eds, *L'État et les sociétés rurales: Enquêtes agricoles, enquêteurs et enquêtés aux XIXe et XXe siècles* (*Annales du Midi* special issue, 284, 2013). See also the very interesting Oz Frankel, *States of Inquiry: Social Investigations and Print Culture in Nineteenth-Century Britain and the*

administrative hermaphrodite, half-scientific, half-political. Moreover, the materials collected for the enquiries usually included quantitative reports, and tables of figures, alongside maps, statements of witnesses, and many other heterogeneous elements. This vagueness of definitional boundaries notwithstanding, the enquiry was a prolific genre, and the great economic and social enquiries of the nineteenth and twentieth century, like the Jacini and Faina enquiries in Italy, represented an important attempt at keeping together the different dimensions of economic observation and analysis, so that economic analysis could guide the decision makers. The packaging of observations in ways that enabled them to travel from geographical and social peripheries and land on the desks of politicians is the main thread of the chapters dedicated to enquiries below.

Moreover, the macro-data of agricultural output were circularly based on micro-data on farm productivity. The different forms of observation were interwoven methodologically but also practically, relying on similar networks of trust and participation. With respect to the growing 'mechanical objectivity' that permeated statistics in other sectors, agricultural statistics manifested a much higher degree of reliance on 'expert judgement', but also, implicitly, on networks of trust built around agricultural economists. Observation therefore was not a matter for unskilled, rapidly trained data gatherers, as it was increasingly the case with other forms of statistics (an evolution underlined by Thomas Stapelford in the American Bureau of Labour Statistics);[32] it required instead agricultural specialists with connections to the society they observed.

Three generations of agricultural economists

Next to the three above-mentioned forms of observations, another essential character of this book is the observer, the agricultural economist. As I remarked above, agricultural economists were not statisticians, but specialized agricultural economists actively engaging in the observation of Italy's agricultural life. The focus on observation practices and ideals spared the author from making a choice between telling the story of a discipline (agricultural economics) and the story of a broad, extremely heterogeneous professional group, that of graduates in agricultural sciences. I discuss here three generations of agricultural economists, following an 'intergenerational' model exploited by Frank Uekoetter for German agronomists.[33] The first generation, gathered

United States (Baltimore: Johns Hopkins University Press, 2006), which explores the peculiarities of the 'encounter' between enquirers and people, and follows the fate of enquiries after they are printed and sold as books.

32 Thomas A. Stapleford, *The cost of living in America: A political history of economic statistics, 1880–2000* (Cambridge: Cambridge University Press, 2009), ch. 1, provides a very interesting account of the conflict between 'centralization and its discontents' in the American Bureau of Labour Statistics, in the age of T. Roosevelt.

33 Frank Uekötter, *Die Wahrheit ist auf dem Feld: Eine Wissensgeschichte der deutschen Landwirtschaft*, Umwelt und Gesellschaft 1 (Göttingen: Vandenhoeck & Ruprecht, 2010).

around Ghino Valenti and Vittorio Niccoli were directly connected to the great agronomists of the Risorgimento, such as Cantoni and Stefano Jacini. The creation of Bureau of Agrarian Statistics in 1906 was their achievement. The second generation, led by Serpieri and Giuseppe Lorenzoni took part in the enquiries of the early 1900s and promoted the creation of the National Institute of Agricultural Economics (INEA) in 1928. The third generation is that of Serpieri's and Giuseppe Tassinari's pupils who had a leading role in Italy's agricultural economics during the 1930s and after the Second World War. They were educated within the INEA and employed on INEA's studies of agriculture.

Katja Bruisch made a similar attempt in her *Als das Dorf noch Zukunft war*, discussing the role and practices of agricultural experts in late Tsarist and early Soviet Russia. Her approach, which she names collective biography, does justice to the complexity of scientific networks that survived, at least in part, the dramatic political changes of the twentieth century, but it necessarily gives prominence to the political and ideological sides of the action of agricultural experts. Consequently, Bruisch seems inclined to adopt a definition of expertise in terms of social recognition of the expert. She opts primarily, in other words, for an externalist account of the discipline. The study of observation – of the related practices, methodological principles, and institutional framing – sheds light instead on the way scientific expertise is constructed by means of a peculiar legitimizing approach to experience and reality. This book is an attempt at bridging the rift, remarked upon by Bruisch, between disciplinary histories of agricultural economics, and social histories of expert groups. It falls in between externalist and internalist histories of science.[34]

For this reason, I decided to study these three generations of agronomists, rural sociologists, and agricultural economists, looking at the forms of investigation they adopted, since they reflect the evolution of disciplinary concerns, the changing methodological attitudes, the shifting focus, and the continuities of agricultural economics. The model with which I propose to describe their relationship to information and data is that of innovation and adaptation. The International Statistical Institute, the International Institute of Agriculture, the Congresses of Agriculture were only a few of the institutional fora in which exchanges on statistical methods and comparisons of results took place. At the same time, the adoption of these innovations meant adaptation to the peculiarities of the local context, and the idiosyncrasies of agricultural economists. In the process of adaptation, a professional group was forged, which moved between different alliances.

34 Katja Bruisch, *Als das Dorf noch Zukunft war: Agrarismus und Expertise zwischen Zarenreich und Sowjetunion*, Beiträge zur Geschichte Osteuropas 47 (Köln: Böhlau Köln, 2014) refers to Eric J. Engstrom, Viktor Hess, and Ulrike Thoms, 'Figurationen des Experten', in Eric J. Engstrom, Viktor Hess, and Ulrike Thoms, eds, *Figurationen des Experten. Ambivalenzen der wissenschaftlichen Expertise im ausgehenden 18. und frühen 19. Jahrhundert* (Frankfurt a. M.: Peter Lang Verlag, 2004), pp. 8ff.

Alliances were essential to the work of investigators. They enabled agricultural economists to access the personnel resources and computational power of the state and of the agriculturalists' associations and, even more important, they opened the doors of rural houses to them so that they could talk to their inhabitants. Historians have often stressed the particular activism of interest groups during the Giolittian era, and underlined how certain branches of the civil service served then as 'clearing houses' for public and private interests.[35] As the career of Ghino Valenti and Francesco Coletti make sufficiently clear, agricultural economists constituted a crucial link between the civil service and interest groups.[36] They moved through revolving doors between academia, interest groups, and the civil service, and their expertise depended on the information they could collect in all three roles.

The Jacini Enquiry, in the nineteenth century, was still very much the concern of the landed elites. With the new century, the standards of validity of observation became more complicated. The investigation of social facts was entrusted primarily to academics, but the judgement of experts still required some form of validation by stakeholders. The dualism between the commissioners and the provincial committees of agricultural statistics that I describe in Chapter 5 institutionalized this double criterion of validation. For this reason, I refer to the statistics of agricultural output produced in this period 'statistics of stakeholders'.[37]

In 1911, Rome celebrated the fiftieth anniversary of the proclamation of the unified Kingdom of Italy by hosting the Universal Exposition. For the occasion, the *Accademia dei Lincei* (the most important learned society in Italy) published two volumes to document the accomplishments of the half-century since unification, with a wealth of statistical data on all spheres of activity, from legislation to the hydroelectric industry, from meteorology to engineering. Ghino Valenti compiled the section devoted to agriculture, unveiling to non-specialists for the first time the work of the reorganized Bureau of Agricultural Statistics. For this commemorative book, Valenti sketched the line of the development of Italian

35 This definition is in Guido Melis, 'Amministrazione e mediazione degli interessi: le origini delle amministrazioni parallele', in Istituto per la scienza dell'amministrazione pubblica, ed., *L'Amministrazione nella storia moderna*, Archivio (2 vols, Milano: Per i tipi dell'editore Giuffrè, 1985), II, pp. 1434–41.

36 Marco E. Guidi, 'Cooperazione, socialismo ed economia agraria: note su Ghino Valenti', in Marco E. Guidi and Luca Michelini, eds, *Marginalismo e socialismo nell'Italia liberale, 1870–1825*, Annali (Fondazione Giangiacomo Feltrinelli) (Milano: Feltrinelli, 2001), pp. 327–56.

37 Agriculture was not the only case: Marco Teodori and Andrea Zanini, 'Institutions publiques et associations patronales:: le cas de l'Associations italienne des hoteliers (1899–1943)', in Danielle Fraboulet, Clotilde Druelle-Korn and Pierre Vernus, eds, *Les organisations patronales et la sphère publique* (Rennes: Presses Universitaires de Rennes, 2013), pp. 171–82 reconstructs the case of the statistics of tourism; recently Maria Letizia D'Autilia proposed to name 'participative statistics' for the attempt by Giovanni Montemartini to involve employers and the trade unions in the making of the statistics of unemployment, see: Maria L. D'Autilia, 'Statistics. Giovanni Montemartini's ideas and actions', Paper presented at the European Business History Association, Glasgow, 27 August 2010' (unpubl.), http://www.gla.ac.uk/media/media_169409_en.pdf.

agriculture since 1861. His account reveals how the statistics of agricultural output responded to the same need for self-representation that had motivated the enquiries of the nineteenth century, when the elites of the *Risorgimento*, like Stefano Jacini, were creating the first image of the unified country.[38] Fifty years after its political unification, and 30 years after the conclusion of the Jacini Enquiry, Italy appeared as a country of regional contrasts. Easy measures of agricultural success, such as wheat productivity – the most commonly used measure in international comparisons – could not be justified, because of the variety of soils and climates. In the meantime, though, agricultural economists and statisticians had gained a more prominent role, partially replacing the landed elites, of which Jacini was an eminent representative, as the repository of knowledge about agriculture.

The new statistics of output enabled Valenti to measure and quantify the ongoing trends and authoritatively intervene in the debate on future of Italian agriculture. Data made the comparison across regions and with other countries more conclusive and less episodic than in the Jacini Enquiry of 1877–81. The unsteady advance of Italy's production and exports, even in such a celebratory publication, demonstrated that the country had not been able to catch up the other nations of Europe, at least until 1900. In the figures that described the conditions of national agriculture, Valenti found reasons to support a specific path of development for the country's agriculture. Output statistics for one thing confirmed the finding of the early enquiries, in that production greatly differed across the country, and that it was pointless therefore to attempt to satisfy the whole national demand for wheat with internal production. Wheat imports instead had to be offset by an increase in the traditional Italian exports (especially arboreal crops like olive trees, silk, vines, citrus fruits), but also, as production and trade figures showed, in the export of value-added and dairy products. Specialization meant more capital invested. Mechanization and chemical fertilizers would help agriculturalists to catch up with the rest of Europe.[39]

The approach proposed by Valenti clearly reflected the concerns and ambitions of the modernizing agriculturalists who led the associations that lobbied for statistics. The agricultural groups of Lombardy and of the Po plains, the agriculturalists of the biggest cities in northern and central Italy, and the owners of the citrus fruit plantations of Sicily were the most deeply involved in the reorganization of the Bureau of Agricultural Statistics between 1907 and 1910 and were the most reliant on commercial agriculture. Reliable

38 R. Accademia Dei Lincei, ed., *Cinquanta anni di storia italiana,* 3 vols (Roma: Tip. della R. Accademia Dei Lincei, 1911), and in particular, Ghino Valenti, 'L'Italia agricola dal 1861 al 1911', in R. Accademia Dei Lincei, ed., *Cinquanta anni di storia italiana* (3 vols, Roma: Tip. della R. Accademia Dei Lincei, 1911), II, p. 2. In 1911, the monument to Vittorio Emanuele II popularly known as 'the typewriter' was also unveiled. The frieze of the monuments expresses a similar need for self-representation: female figures represent the different statistical compartments of the Kingdom, often displaying attributes based on the most iconic economic activities of the compartment.

39 Valenti, 'L'Italia agricola dal 1861 al 1911', p. 9.

production statistics had a key role in determining the trade and tariff policy of the kingdom.[40] The convergence between the various groups in the period of Giolitti, therefore, should not come as a surprise, as it corresponded to the crucial importance of trade policy in this period.

There was also another essential contribution that statistical figures offered to the politics of the early twentieth century. The differences in production and productivity made apparent by the figures strengthened the rationale for the regional policies of the period. In contrast with the United States, where the government published output statistics in order to stop price speculation, the numbers that came out of Valenti's office and its successor aimed to highlight the condition of agriculture in comparison with that of other countries and between Italian regions.

The meaning of the numbers changed with the war, and even more with the Fascist *battaglia del grano*, in the late 1920s. In this period, food supply became a crucial topic of debate. With the war, statistics focused on the availability of food per capita, and on the mobilization of horsepower for the troops, rather than on commodities destined for foreign markets.[41] After the initial restoration of Italian export trade that followed the war, the monetary revaluation of 1926, and the political will to make the country independent (as far as possible) from wheat imports turned the statistics of production into a crucial political indicators. The numbers recorded in the agricultural *cadastre* of 1929 and the subsequent harvest statistics were now supposed to shed light not on the potential of different products for the balance of trade, but on the quantity of wheat produced and the productivity per hectare. The regime made the productivity per hectare of wheat into a preoccupation, which often entered Mussolini's speeches. Anti-Fascists questioned the reliability of the figures, but it is very difficult to assess whether the figures were significantly wrong and this assessment will not be attempted here.[42]

40 The statistics on foreign trade, probably the most precise series collected by the Italian government was not the work of agricultural experts and remains outside of the scope of this work; they have recently been published online by the Banca d'Italia, see Giovanni Federico et al., *Il commercio estero italiano, 1862–1950*, Collana storica della Banca d'Italia. Statistiche storiche 4 (Roma-Bari: Laterza, 2012): Chambers of commerce, and *comizi* also collected data on prices, at least discontinuously, but the analysis of price and inflation statistics would lead us too far.

41 In Italy, as in other countries, there had been attempts at estimating the nutritional needs of families and the food available for consumption at least since the 1880s. For the war period, see Salvatore Adorno, 'L'Italia agricola e il suo avvenire: Note sul ruolo della Commissione di studi tecnici ed economici della Federconsorzi', in Severina Fontana, ed., *La Federconsorzi tra stato liberale e fascismo*, Biblioteca di cultura moderna 1084 (Roma, Bari: Laterza, 1995), pp. 61–108. During the 1930s, these efforts were stimulated by the autarky policies, see Benedetto Barberi, 'Indagine statistica sulle disponibilità alimentari della popolazione italiana dal 1922 al 1937', *Annali di Statistica* III (serie VII) (1939). On the importance of 'calories' for interwar policy: Nick Cullather, *The hungry world: America's Cold War battle against poverty in Asia* (Cambridge, MA.: Harvard University Press, 2010), ch. 1.

42 Gaetano Salvemini, 'Mussolini's Battle of Wheat', *Political Science Quarterly* 46.1 (1931), pp. 25–40, and the reply of Italian statisticians, Giorgio Mortara, 'Italian Economic Statistics: A Reply to Professor Salvemini', *Political Science Quarterly* 46.4 (1931), pp. 593–95.

Later chapters of this book show how the internal development of the discipline, new institutional arrangements, and social concerns increasingly questioned the equilibrium reached in the Giolittian era between experts and stakeholders. Chapter 6 and 7 show how the collection of farm budgets changed after the Great War, from mere surveys to quantitative accounts, as expert judgement became increasingly problematic. While Serpieri remained convinced of the validity of surveys of typical farms, Giuseppe Tassinari and Giuseppe Medici, although preserving the general accounting framework, felt compelled to multiply the observed farms, and questioned the validity of isolated surveys. The separation between statistics and agricultural economics, with the establishment in the second half of the 1920s of the Central Institute of Statistics and the National Institute of Agricultural Economics, was a manifestation of the crisis of validity.

In the course of the 1920s and '30s, agricultural economists came to be identified primarily with the drawing up of farm budgets. Farm surveys responded to very different requirements and had a different range of functions. They primarily depicted the relationships between different social actors, and were, therefore, particularly important in the early part of the twentieth century, when, with the rise of peasant unrest, agricultural economists were addressing social issues. This is the case with the Faina Enquiry of 1907–09, discussed in Chapter 3. With the post-war slump, the export crisis of 1926–27, and the depression of the early 1930s, farm surveys came to answer a new type of question. They enabled agricultural economists to see the differentiated impact of the crisis on different types of producer. At this point, farm surveys acquired importance for the definition of macroeconomic policies, and their collection attracted more resources, also because the new function required an increase in the number of surveys involved and a standardization in their format (as explained in Chapter 7). Italians were thus among the first to seize the importance of the use of farm surveys following Laur's example, but only after the first world war did they manage to set up a network of accounting offices, and even then they lacked the regularity of farm surveys in countries such as Switzerland, Russia, Britain, and Germany.[43]

Farm budgets were the core method of research in agricultural economics.[44] Thanks to the cost accounting method, agrarian economists – like production engineers in industry – became the standard-bearers of rationalization in agriculture.[45] They claimed for themselves a more explicit leading role in agriculture. As Charles S. Maier suggested, early twentieth century rationalization

43 While the Soviets managed to collect thousands of surveys of peasant families and farms, the results reached in the '30s by the *Osservatorio* in Bologna were significantly smaller.

44 Tolaini, *Contadini toscani negli anni Trenta*, Introduzione; in France, the same identification took place: Denis R. Bergmann, 'Les études d'économie rurale', *Économie rurale* 39–40 (1959), pp. 259–68.

45 See, for instance, Richard K. Fleischman, 'Completing the triangle: Taylorism and the paradigms', *Accounting, Auditing & Accountability Journal* 13.5 (2000), pp. 597–623; and on the rise of cost accounting in modern industry, Peter Miller and Ted O'Leary, 'Accounting and the construction of the governable person', *Accounting, Organizations and Society* 12.3 (1987), pp. 235–65.

plans optimistically assumed that rational management could find solutions that would solve class struggle and benefit labour and capital alike.[46] Although agricultural economists fostered a nuanced sociological analysis, which acknowledged the complexity of the rural class structure and considered class-struggle basically exogenous, they did look for ways of reconciling diverging interests.

The support of agricultural economists (for instance, Serpieri and Tassinari) for Fascism depended on the expectation that, after the suppression of class struggle, the regime would turn the struggle against the lack of capital and of land into the struggle for 'intensification' and 'ruralization'.[47] Day labourers were excluded from the recognized rural classes, while the regime reassured peasants that their industriousness and toil could, eventually, be rewarded with land ownership. This was a form of modernization, achieved through smallholdings and access to landownership, that provided a constant role for agricultural experts and agricultural economists, that of supervising the new landowners.[48]

Alternative modernity

What was the healthy development of Italian agriculture that agricultural economists desired? They dreamed of an agrarian landscape of orderly, spread-out family farms, with larger villages here and there. Family farms, either owned by the farmer or on long-term lease, would form the backbone of Italian agriculture but they would not entirely supplant large capitalist farms. Fascist *ruralismo* and agricultural policies, I suggest, should be understood within the framework of the general 'agrarianism' that appeared in Europe and the United States before the First World War.[49] This was not an ideology

46 On this topic, see among others Charles S. Maier, *In Search of Stability: Explorations in Historical Political Economy,* Cambridge Studies in Modern Political Economies (Cambridge: Cambridge University Press, 1988), ch.1.

47 Maier, ibid., claims: 'The ideology of fascism was a non-zero-sum doctrine that celebrated the national state or the racial people. Most Western political orientations accepted trade-offs and sacrifices as inherent in historical development. They presupposed conflict and faction at home (. . .) Fascism, in contrast, rejected a vision of domestic losers. Instead, it called for subordinating all traditional cleavages at home, especially class conflict, to the maximization of national power and energy', p. 115. In fact, it seems that, in the case of agriculture, the 'enemy' was mostly a natural enemy that had to be subjugated in order to promote abundance, rather than an external enemy (this holds true even in the case of colonial agriculture, since the rhetoric of the regime insisted on the fact that Lybia, in particular, was a desert). The state would then coordinate the forces of the nation according to the plans of the experts.

48 The technocratic element of Fascist policies that targeted smallholdings has been recently stressed in a comparative perspective by Lourenzo Fernández-Prieto, Juan Pan-Montojo and Miguel Cabo, eds, *Agriculture in the age of fascism: Authoritarian technocracy and rural modernization, 1922–1945,* Rural history in Europe 13 (Turnhout: Brepols, 2014).

49 Helga Schultz and Angela Harre, eds, *Bauerngesellschaften auf dem Weg in die Moderne: Agrarismus in Ostmitteleuropa 1880 bis 1960,* Frankfurter Studien zur Wirtschafts- und Sozialgeschichte Ostmitteleuropas (Harrassowitz Verlag, 2010) in the introduction denies that Fascism shared an

of backwardness, an anti-modern utopia, in Italy. 'We can foresee', wrote Cesare Longobardi in 1936:

> that a new type of family business, partly agricultural, partly industrial, will arise, which will form a connecting link between the farm and the factory, a new social cell combining the functions of family life with those of production. Such concerns conserve the individuality of the worker, they utilize all the labour power of the family, take full advantage of the adaptability of electric power, and ensure that due care is taken of the savings invested in equipment.[50]

This was not a reactionary modernism in the sense in which Herf uses the term.[51] This was an alternative modernity, where smallholdings and sharecropping would overcome class struggle and build a viable, autonomous future for agriculture. Smallholders and sharecroppers would ensure that there would be no direct clash between capitalists and wageworkers. It would be a modern system of production that would be resilient and flexible and, thanks to its small size and its use of family labour, able to adapt to changing market conditions. Not two steps back but one step forward toward 'higher social standards', thanks to land reclamation, land consolidation, a new inheritance law, savings banks, and producers' cooperatives that would ensure that smallholders could access new technologies. In this respect, there is relatively little difference between the ideas of agricultural economists before and after the Fascist takeover of 1922.

The consistency of this vision of the future has not been fully recognized. Growth in scale and mistrust of competition were part of the *leit Motiven* of state interventionism, also of Fascist *corporativismo*, as well as fundamental attributes of early twentieth-century modernity. For this reason, many interpreters have considered *ruralismo* a sort of ideological backlash of Fascistprojects of industrial modernity. While the modernizing project of Fascism manifested itself in industry, agriculture was to be preserved as an idyllic *Arcadia* and sacrificed to the development of industry.

Antonio Gramsci was among the first to stress the contrast between agricultural and industrial policies of the regime:

> In Italy there have been the beginnings of a Fordist fanfare: exaltation of big cities, overall planning for the Milan conurbation, and so on; the affirmation that capitalism is only at its beginnings and that it is necessary

agrarian ideology, but this is because the editor overlooks the fact that agrarianism also aimed at a more efficient use of resources (land, capital, and labour) in agriculture.

50 Cesare Longobardi, *Land-reclamation in Italy* (London: King, 1936), p. 5.

51 Jeffrey Herf, *Reactionary modernism: Technology, culture, and politics in Weimar and the Third Reich* (Cambridge: Cambridge University Press, 1984).

> to prepare for it grandiose patterns of development [. . .]. But afterwards came a conversion to ruralism, the disparagement of the cities typical of the Enlightenment, exaltation of the artisanat and of idyllic patriarchalism, reference to craft rights and a struggle against industrial liberty.[52]

Fascist *corporativismo* would not start in Italy the kind of 'technical-economic change' that the United States, Soviet Russia and the most advanced industrialized countries were then experiencing. Following Gramsci, Emilio Sereni had in the 1940s already polemically attacked the rhetoric of Italian agricultural economists, who had shed hypocritical tears for the death of small property ever since unification, while their actions continued to show that they were subservient to the combination of capitalist and feudal exploitation that dominated the Italian countryside.[53] This interpretation is probably the origin of a long-standing tradition in the literature on Italian agricultural economists of the twentieth century, which sees a contrast between modernizing tendencies, embodied by a few supporters of the industrialization of agriculture, often identified with the model of the large capitalist tenant farmers of the Po Valley, and a majority of agricultural economists who, gathering around Serpieri after he moved to Florence, extolled the virtues of more traditional forms of agriculture, praised Tuscan sharecropping, and revelled in local peculiarities.[54]

Although Gramsci denied the existence of Fascist modernizing project, the relationship between Fascism and modernity is notoriously controversial. More recently, postmodernist critics of techno-scientific expertise proposed an interpretation of Fascist agricultural policies, as a whole, in terms of mega- (or meta-)projects and (high-)modernism directed by techno-scientific experts and social engineers. For these historians, genetic manipulation, land reclamation, social engineering, and the demographic and racial policies of the Fascist regime, regardless of their effectiveness, bear the marks of high modernism and techno-scientific supremacy.[55]

These acknowledgments of the modernity of Fascist agricultural policies characteristically underestimate the importance of economic arguments that agricultural economists pushed forward in favour of internal colonization and

52 Antonio Gramsci, *Quaderni del carcere,* 4 vols, Einaudi tascabili. Saggi 835 (Torino: Einaudi, 2001), p. 2147; translation from Antonio Gramsci, *Selections from the Prison Notebooks* (New York: International Publishers, 1971).

53 Emilio Sereni, *Il capitalismo nelle campagne: (1860–1900),* Piccola biblioteca Einaudi (Torino: Einaudi, 1968).

54 Lea D'Antone, 'La modernizzazione dell'agricoltura italiana negli anni Trenta', *Studi Storici* 22.3 (1981), pp. 603–29.

55 Carl Ipsen, *Dictating Demography: The Problem of Population in Fascist Italy,* Cambridge Studies in Population, Economy and Society in Past Time no. 28 (Cambridge: Cambridge University Press, 1996), Tiago Saraiva and M. Norton Wise, '"Autarky/Autarchy: Genetics, Food Production, and the Building of Fascism,"', *Historical Studies in the Natural Sciences* 40.4 (2010); Tiago Saraiva, '"Fascist Labscapes: Geneticists, Wheat, and the Landscapes of Fascism in Italy and Portugal,"', *Historical Studies in the Natural Sciences* 40.4 (2010), and again Fernández-Prieto, Pan-Montojo and Cabo, *Agriculture in the age of fascism.*

(moderate-sized) smallholdings. Moreover, they give excessive importance to the ideological ruptures of the Fascist period, while, as we said, most of the theoretical presuppositions of ruralist policies had accumulated through the repeated agricultural crises and during the Great War. One of the aims of this book is to provide the reader with a reconstruction of the statistical data and their economic interpretations, upon which Italian agrarianism rested.

I would like to qualify the phrase 'Italian agrarianism'. In agriculture, modernity was not necessarily identified with industrial agriculture on large extents of land as it was on Soviet or American farms.[56] Especially in Europe, but also to some degree in the United States (according to agronomists of the New Deal), modernity often took the seemingly conservative form of the promotion of smallholdings. While the first globalization pushed factories to grow in size, and companies united in huge *trusts*, the effect on large estates of the inflow of cheap products from outside the European core was disruptive. Although to manufacturing firms growth and gigantism were inevitable strategies of survival, small agricultural businesses proved unexpectedly more resilient to economic crises, because, to a great extent, they produced for the consumption of the peasant family itself or specialized in products such as cheese or garden vegetables that were not shipped over long distances.

Even some Marxists were forced to admit this. Already at the end of the nineteenth century the German social-democrat Eduard David had explained this phenomenon, which seemingly contradicted Marx's predictions, in these terms: in agriculture, Nature, not the machine, produces, and small farms can thus win the competition against big ones. In agriculture, therefore, the tendency towards concentration of capital would not take place.[57]

Microeconomic observations confirmed the efficiency of relatively small farms for many crops (this issue emerged in particular from Ernst Laur's data on Swiss agriculture), with higher yields per hectare. Lower recourse to external inputs, cheaper labour, a more efficient use of land, determined a larger agricultural surplus and a more resilient farming system especially in times of crisis, like the 1920s and the 1930s.

The slogan that dominated the first decades of the twentieth century was not 'industrialization' but 'internal colonization'. Projects had started before the First World War in many European countries, but the period between 1918 and 1945 saw a spurt in such projects often coupled with land reforms.[58]

56 Scott, *Seeing like a state*, pp. 197ff., describes the transatlantic resonance of the Campbell Farm, for instance.

57 Eduard David, 'Oekonomische Verschiedenheiten zwischen Landwirthschaft und Industrie', *Die neue Zeit Revue des geistigen und öffentlichen Lebens* 2.41 (1895), pp. 449–55. Eduard David was a legal social-democrat and a follower of Bernstein.

58 For the case of Spain: Javier Monclus and José L. Oyon, *Politicas y tecnicas en la ordenacion del espacio rural* (Madrid: I.E.A.L., 1988); for the Netherlands, Liesbeth van de Grift, 'On New Land a New Society: Internal Colonisation in the Netherlands, 1918–1940', *Contemporary European History* 22.4 (2013), pp. 609–26; for a Europe-wide survey of internal colonizations see Jan G. Smit, 'Laendliche

Internal colonization meant the intensive use of land that was previously underexploited either for social reasons (for example because it was part of vast latifundia) or because of natural causes (marshes, distance from population centres, and so on), by creating consolidated plots with their model rural houses.

Even for industry, some economists envisaged a potentially different path of development. Nitti, for instance, claimed that electric power would be mostly advantageous for small and medium businesses, which were too small to benefit from complex coal-powered machines, and the parallel between the kind of efficient small-scale industrial units enabled by electric power and the modern small(er) farms of the future was sometimes drawn explicitly.[59] There was no necessary path of development in terms of size.

Agricultural economists stressed macroeconomic issues as well as microeconomic issues. Both macro- and micro-arguments evoked in favour of their relatively labour-intensive vision of the future of Italian agriculture seemed to justify state intervention, patiently guided by agricultural economists. Ensuring the intergenerational equilibrium in the use of land was a task that could not be left to the forces of the market. The very mix of macro- and micro-approaches reveals how distant the projects of state intervention harboured by Italian agricultural economists were from the ideas of 'Keynesian revolution' that was taking place in the very same years. The survey method was considered a much better guide than aggregate statistics in establishing which kind of farms would be most suitable in the future.

Farm surveys, with their stylized typologies, although methodologically conservative, served their function, giving an empirical foundation to the 'theory of economic place' (*teoria del luogo economico*), since they presented distinct agricultural types. The emphasis on local farming types, which were the results of the slow mutual adaptation of humans and nature, was a durable feature of central European agricultural economics. The form that had been given to the landscape, and the social relationships that had created the agricultural landscapes of Lombardy or Tuscany, were recognized as the embodiment of adaptive knowledge.

This was not an invention of the twentieth century. Already for Carlo Cattaneo, the legislation on canals and the *cadastre* of Maria Theresa, the structure of large tenancy, sericulture and the industry of the cities merged with the natural flows of rivers, geology, and climate into a harmonious whole built by centuries of anonymous farmers and landowners. Cattaneo's masterpiece, *D'alcune istituzioni agrarie dell'Alta Italia applicabili a sollievo dell'Irlanda*[60]

Neusiedlung in Mitteleuropa vom Ende des 19. Jahrhunderts bis zur Gegenwart als nationalpolitisches Instrument: Ziele, zeitgenoessische Stellungnahmen und Ergebnisse', *Erdkunde* 40.3 (1986), especially p. 170. It is important to notice that land reforms usually combined the division of large aristocratic estates and the consolidation of smaller plots. The seminal text for theory of internal colonization is Sering, *Die innere Kolonisation im östlichen Deutschland.*

59 Longobardi, *Land-reclamation in Italy*, p. 3.

60 'Of some agricultural institutions of Upper Italy that could be applied for the relief of Ireland'. On Cattaneo's 'place-based' economics see Martin Thom, '"Liberty and truth" or "the sovereignty of

documents precisely this inextricable connection of nature, human creativity, and history. When, shortly after the catastrophic 'potato famine', in an early example of 'development economics', the British government asked Cattaneo how the best practices of Lombard agriculture could be transferred to Ireland, Cattaneo explained to the British ambassador that Lombard agriculture was closely linked to the complex of Lombardy's social institutions and geographical conditions and concluded that there were no easy lessons from it that could be applied to the island.[61]

In the nineteenth century, the 'moderate' landowners of Tuscany, who gathered in the Accademia dei Georgofili, celebrated Cobden's struggle for a free grain trade, but the manifesto of their system of estate management was Jean Charles Léonard Simonde de Sismondi's *Tableau de l'agriculture toscane*.[62] In this short treatise, Sismondi described the spontaneous and harmonious wisdom that was embodied in Tuscan agriculture: the careful managing of water sources, the participation of sharecroppers in entrepreneurial risks, the integration of vine-growing and fruit gardens and so on – these were all aspects of a living organism that no conscious imitation could reproduce. Sismondi's praise of the social stability engendered by Tuscan sharecropping became a commonplace and passed into Sidney Sonnino's project of agricultural reform around the turn of the century, and even into the scientific debate of the 1920s and 1930s.

Italians were not alone in underlining local variety and local adaptation. The understanding of agriculture as a living organism, the attention to differentiated *agricultural niches*, was a key element of agricultural economics in continental Europe. Whether they fought against or for the intervention of the state in agriculture, agricultural economists insisted on the peculiarities of agriculture, its local and differentiated nature, the fact that it obeyed biological rather than mathematical laws. Two aspects merged in such claims: 1) each agricultural niche was in its own way an organic whole; 2) agriculture, where nature prevailed, differed from industry, where the machine dominated the production process.

The doctrine of economic place was the recognition of the complexity of rural life. Each agricultural niche required different forms of land tenure, of land use, different ratios of land, capital, and labour in order to extract the maximum economic and/or social benefit out of agricultural activities. Agricultural systems, as Serpieri said, differ greatly between agricultural areas. Contracts such as sharecropping could not be deemed universally backward. The contrast between industrialists and ruralists mentioned above, between Serpieri's school and Paolo Albertario's industrial view of agriculture, takes a different meaning once we recognize how

reason": Carlo Cattaneo and the place of politics in the modern world', *Journal of Modern Italian Studies* 6.2 (2001), pp. 178–94; Tiziano Raffaelli, 'The Role of Intelligence, Institutions, and Place in Carlo Cattaneo's Economics', *History of Political Economy* 46.2 (2014), pp. 265–80.

61 Now in Carlo Cattaneo, *Saggi di economia rurale*, ed. Luigi Einaudi (Torino: Einaudi, 1939).

62 Jean Charles L. S Sismondi, *Tableau de l'agriculture toscane* (Genève: Paschaud, 1801).

problematic the notion of modernity was.[63] The solutions envisaged by Albertario were in no way univocally more 'modern' than those proposed by Serpieri. Writing in the 1980s and early 1990s, Italian historians assessed the interwar period with the categories of post-World War Two development. Nowadays we recognize the potential long-term efficiency of low-input agriculture, the importance of resilience and food security, the value of locally differentiated styles of farming, and family farms. Through the reports of the World Bank, and the United Nations, they find their way into the policy recommendations of international meetings.[64] The very notion of development has been so intensely questioned that we can reassess, if not the validity, the internal consistency of early twentieth-century models of agricultural modernization, while still keeping in mind their implications for social and economic struggles.

63 A contrast recently underlined by Simone Misiani, *La Via Dei 'Tecnici': Dalla Rsi Alla Ricostruzione: Il Caso Di Paolo Albertario,* Studi e ricerche storiche (Milano: Franco Angeli, 1998) and Marco Zaganella, *Dal fascismo alla DC: Tassinari, Medici e la bonifica nell'Italia tra gli anni Trenta e Cinquanta,* I fatti e la storia 4 (Siena: Cantagalli, 2010), following D'Antone.

64 Derek Byerlee et al., *World development report 2008: agriculture for development,* World Development Report 30 (Washington, DC: World Bank Group, 2008); Olivier de Schutter, 'Submission to the G20 Development Group Food Security Review' (UN Special Rapporteur on the right to food, 4 April 2014) (unpubl.), http://www.srfood.org/images/stories/pdf/otherdocuments/20140404_UNSR RTF_G20 DWG Food Security Review.pdf.

2 Agrarian landscapes

The period covered in this book was a time of great change for Italy. Needless to say, the forms of observation, the observers, and the observed all changed as did their reciprocal relations. In the political sphere, the 30 years from the beginning of the 1900s to the early 1930s witnessed the end of Italy's parliamentary regime and the rise of Fascism, with the expansion of mass parties and the First World War in between. The economy saw an impetuous spurt of industrialization: agriculture employed 65 per cent of the labour force until 1870, 50.1 per cent in 1905 and 41 per cent in the late 1920s. Agricultural production grew significantly but its share of output, which reached the threshold of 44 per cent of total output before 1870, accounted for only 33 per cent in 1905, and 26 per cent in the late 1920s.[1] Trade specialization also changed: the specialization in agricultural goods that Italy still had at the beginning of the century rapidly gave place to a specialization in manufactured goods of different kind.[2]

As a result, the importance of the landed elites slowly diminished. In the nineteenth century, the landed classes still represented the *universal class*, the nation. The local (landed) elites provided mediation between the state and civil society, and to a certain extent were part of both. For this reason both the political and the cognitive representation of the countryside were entrusted to them. The Jacini Enquiry of 1877 offers a good example of their role. The same was true for the statistics of the nation's agricultural output:

1 Jon S. Cohen and Giovanni Federico, *The growth of the Italian economy, 1820–1960*, New studies in economic and social history (Cambridge, New York: Cambridge University Press, 2001), p. 14, tab 2.5.

2 The export of manufactured products accounted for 28.1% of Italian exports in 1908, and 49.4% on the eve of the Great Depression, Giovanni Federico et al., *Il commercio estero italiano, 1862–1950*, Collana storica della Banca d'Italia. Statistiche storiche 4 (Roma-Bari: Laterza, 2012), p. 22; Giovanni Federico and Nikolaus Wolf, *Comparative Advantages in Italy: A Long-Run Perspective*, Economic History Working Papers 9 (2011), computed the Lafay index (an index which is higher if the ratio of a country's net export of a particular commodity over the total trade for that commodity is higher than the ratio of net export over the country's total trade) for manufactured goods using for this period the new estimates of Banca d'Italia, showing that the index peaked after the Great War and then mildly decreased over the 1930s.

in the nineteenth century these were mainly entrusted to institutions of local notables, the *comizi agrari*.

With the new century, the role of the traditional ruling classes was called into question from below, by the growing social unrest, and from above, by the state itself and the expanding bureaucratic and technical structure. Already the Faina Enquiry of 1906 introduced the intermediation of agricultural experts (It. *tecnici agrari*), as technical delegates. Nevertheless, the decline was slow and not unproblematic.[3] During the first decade of the twentieth century, the landed elites still dominated the relationship between the state and the countryside. The statistics of agricultural output prepared since 1910 by the Ministry of Agriculture, Industry, and Trade (MAIC) thus combined the contribution of traditional elites with that of the administration's technical staff. Historians of the Italian civil service have shown how the governments of the Giolittian era, until the 1910s, generally promoted cooperation between the administration and interest groups, thereby transforming the ministries and, in particular, 'special offices', such as the Bureau of Labour and the Bureau of Agricultural Statistics, into 'reference points' for interest groups.[4]

The decline of the landed elites became more visible when social tensions increased between 1909 and the war. Giolitti's third cabinet, with Francesco Saverio Nitti as Minister of Agriculture, Industry, and Trade, marked a discontinuity, while agricultural experts increasingly saw the state as the source of their legitimacy. From the 1920s, they became more and more a part of the state apparatus, with weaker direct links to the landed elites.[5] The focus of agricultural economics itself inadvertently moved from the management of large properties, as had been the case for the late nineteenth century, to large-scale economic policies that concerned agriculture, like the 'battle for wheat' and the 'total land reclamation' of the Fascist regime.

After unification: Po plains, Tuscan hills, southern latifundia

After unification, the agricultural elite of the former Italian states was widely represented in the two houses of the new parliament. Many of the parliamentarian leaders of the *Risorgimento*, Camillo Benso di Cavour and Bettino

3 The persistence of traditional class structure in the countryside until the First World War has famously been pointed out by the classic Arno J. Mayer, *The persistence of the Old Regime: Europe to the Great War* (Pantheon Books, 1981); historical sociologists interpreted the emergence of mass reactionary movements, like Italian Fascism, to the reaction of shaken but unbroken landed elites to industrial modernity: Barrington Moore, *Social origins of dictatorship and democracy: Lord and peasant in the making of the modern world* (1966; 2nd edn, Boston: Beacon Press, 1993).

4 Guido Melis, 'Amministrazione e mediazione degli interessi: le origini delle amministrazioni parallele,' in Istituto per la scienza dell'amministrazione pubblica, *L'Amministrazione nella storia moderna*, ii, p. 1434; on the *Ufficio del lavoro* see Riccardo Johnson, 'Amministrazione e organizzazione delle informazioni: Il ministero dell'agricoltura e i problemi del lavoro', in Istituto per la scienza dell'amministrazione pubblica, ed., *L'Amministrazione nella storia moderna*, 2.

5 On this shift, see also Manuel Vaquero Pineiro, *Da fattori a periti agrari.: Formazione professionale e modernizzazione dell'agricoltura in Umbria (1884–1929)* (Foligno: Editoriale Umbra, 2011).

Ricasoli, for instance, were the innovative owners of large properties. To a great extent, the most illustrious personalities of the so-called *Destra Storica* were member of the agricultural elite.[6] The right to vote was limited to a tiny minority of taxpayers, and taxes on land rent (*imposta fondiaria*) formed a large share of the total revenue from direct taxation. Therefore, the electoral law sanctioned the pre-eminence of landowners in parliament. In the logic of classical liberalism, they could present themselves, as Sandro Rogari argues, as the 'universal class', the nation itself.[7] More concretely, though, the wealth of this universal class derived from a wide variety of agricultural systems, each prevailing in a different area of the Italian boot. Landowners therefore might have been the universal class of the nation, but, in many ways, they did not form a compact class, sometimes representing virtually diverging economic interests.

> A quarter of a century after the proclamation of the political unification of Italy, we would look in vain – wrote Senator Stefano Jacini in the early 1880s – for a single, objective, agricultural Italy. We find instead a number of agricultural 'Italies'. These many Italies differ from one another not just because they produce different crops, as it will always be, but also because they preserve roughly the same shape, the same physiognomy, the same general attitude that was imprinted and transmitted to each by the political, administrative, and social systems which governed each of them until recently.[8]

The Italian government struggled in order to get a grasp of these many 'agricultural Italies'. Shortly after the unification, in 1866, MAIC instituted, on the French model, the *comizi agrari*, assemblies of farmers and owners, which were meant to give some form of representation and unity to the general interests of agriculturalists, an ambiguous definition that included in principle small peasants and rich absentee latifundists.[9] Among other tasks, the *comizi* were in charge of collecting data on agriculture. French practices explicitly inspired not only the establishment of the *comizi* but also the statistical model, based on the good will of the landowners and mayors that composed the *comizi* rather than a fully-fledged statistical bureaucracy. In the course of the 1870s and 1880s the Ministry printed two series of volumes containing various kinds of data, provided by the *comizii*.[10] The *Relazioni* and the *Notizie*, the name

6 Maria Malatesta, *Le aristocrazie terriere nell'Europa contemporanea,* Quadrante (Roma) (Laterza, 1999) for a comparative and comprehensive discussion of the evolution of European landed elites.

7 Sandro Rogari, *Rappresentanza corporazione conflitto: ceti e figure dell'Italia rurale fra Otto e Novecento,* Politica e storia (Centro editoriale toscano, 1998), p. 138.

8 Stefano Jacini, *I risultati della inchiesta agraria* (1885; 3rd edn, Torino: Einaudi, 1976), p. 77f.

9 Paola Corti, 'I comizi agrari dopo l'Unità (1866–91)', *Ricerche di storia sociale e religiosa* 3 (1973), pp. 247–301.

10 *Relazioni* (MAIC and divisione di agricoltura, *Relazione intorno alle condizioni dell'agricoltura nel quinquennio 1870–1874,* 3 vols (Roma: G. Barbera, 1876–1879)) were intended to precede the regular

given to the two series of reports, contained data on the agricultural output of the different provinces of the kingdom, but special attention was paid to the farming techniques that prevailed in each of them.

Techniques were judged primitive almost everywhere, but especially in the south: wooden ploughs were extremely common, animal power was insufficient, fertilizers virtually unknown. Italian rhetoric had always insisted on the natural fertility and blessed climate of the country, which made it a true *alma parens frugum*. The realization of the extent of the gap between Italy and other Western European countries came as a public shock. Italy, as Jacini commented, discovered herself poor and backward. With the usual exceptions: the *marcite* of the Po Valley, the citrus gardens of Sicily, and the specialized vegetable gardens of Campania Felix, most of the land seemed underexploited and underpopulated.

Agriculture was interpreted according to what the historian Piero Bevilaqua called the 'emulative model'.[11] Landowners of Lombardy and Piedmont praised high farming, and were fascinated by England's large estates. Jacini, a representative of the class of landowners that formed the backbone of the moderate party, saw the capital-intensive and highly specialized agriculture of the Po Valley as the culmination of the evolutionary chain. Southern latifundia represented, instead, the remnants of 'medieval agriculture', and of the 'dark ages', while the mixed cropping practised in most of central Italy was a less-than-optimal way of farming.

Yet Tuscan sharecropping and mixed cropping represented the most important alternative put forward in the last decades of the nineteenth century (and beyond) to the cultural domination of Lombard high farming. Supporters of *mezzadria*, like the landlords Sidney Sonnino and Leopoldo Franchetti, essentially claimed that it ensured social peace, if maybe sometimes it was less effective than Lombard farming, and that it prevented short-sighted exploitation of land, as happened frequently instead in the south. The debate about the forms of land tenure (on the *contratti agrarii*) became a constant of Italian political life in the last decades of the nineteenth century, and establishing the most appropriate form of land tenure for southern Italy was one of the objectives of the Faina Enquiry discussed in Chapter 3.

Who was right in this dispute, who was wrong, and whether the characterization of regional differences according to the evolutionary model actually captured regional differences, is not essential for the argument developed in this book. Historians have long accepted the substance of Jacini's point

collection of data and their periodical publication in *Notizie* (MAIC and Direzione Generale di agricoltura, *Notizie e studi sulla agricoltura* (Roma: Tip. eredi Botta, 1876–98)).

11 Piero Bevilacqua, 'La "storia economica" e l'economia', in Pierluigi Ciocca and Gianni Toniolo, eds, Storia economica d'Italia (2 vols, Roma/Bari: Laterza, 2004), I, pp. 159–69, quot. in Bernardino Farolfi and Massimo Fornasari, 'Agricoltura e sviluppo economico: il caso italiano (secoli XVIII–XX)', in Canali et al., eds, *L'agricoltura e gli economisti agrari in Italia dall'Ottocento al Novecento*, pp. 16f.

of view and the implicit evolutionary model. They pointed accusingly at feudal remnants as well as at *mezzadria* as fundamental causes of the alleged backwardness of Italian agriculture. Opinions are now more varied. The economic rationale of the southern *latifondo* is now generally recognized by economic as well as social historians. In the 1990s, Galassi and Cohen rehabilitated Tuscan sharecropping, stressing its effectiveness as a reaction to the market and climatic conditions of central Italy. In general, historians consider land tenure a less significant explanatory variable.[12]

The whole issue of regional disparities has been reassessed by recent historiography. Vittorio Daniele and Paolo Malanima claimed that differences in the trend of real wages from 1700 to 1860 were non-significant, and that a real economic divergence began with the acceleration of growth in the 1890s.[13] Giovanni Federico's estimates underline the fact that productivity of labour and per capita output, by the end of the nineteenth century, were higher in the south than in the north, and question the real extent of the backwardness. He nevertheless concludes that the total factor productivity was lower in the south.[14] Regardless of the reliability of modern estimates of regional differences, the issue remains that modern scholars tend to minimize differences between the north and the south, although earlier observers considered them to be very significant, even shortly after unification.

The reason for this disagreement lies in the indicators of development chosen. Early observers of economics focused on land productivity. The supply of land was a given, and Italy was not even particularly well endowed with it. The supply of capital and labour on the other hand was vast and expandable. Therefore, agricultural progress consisted in the most intensive use of land, the humanization of the agricultural landscape, with investments and labour flowing onto the land to increase output. The vast extensions of southern latifundia, with their working population concentrated in unhealthy rural towns, with few or no trees, seemed a waste and the product of mismanagement by a class of bankrupt aristocratic landowners. A sound agricultural policy seemed to entail the breaking down of the supposedly barren estates of the south into

12 Marta Petrusewicz, Latifondo: economia morale e vita materiale in una periferia dell'Ottocento, Saggi Marsilio (Venezia: Marsilio, 1989); Francesco L. Galassi and Jon S. Cohen, 'The Economics of Tenancy in Early Twentieth-Century Southern Italy', Economic History Review 47.3 (1994), p. 585 on latifundia; Jon S. Cohen and Francesco L. Galassi, 'Sharecropping and productivity: "feudal residues" in Italian agriculture, 1911', *Economic History Review* 43.4 (1990), pp. 646–56, on Tuscan sharecropping; but see also a revisionist account of latifundia on the socially inefficient effects of the concentration of landownership on the labour market: Pablo Martinelli, *Latifundia Revisited*: Market Power, Land Inequality and Efficiency in Interwar Italian Agriculture (2012), Working Paper 020.

13 Vittorio Daniele and Paolo Malanima, 'Il prodotto delle regioni e il divario Nord-Sud in Italia (1861–2004)', *Rivista di politica economica* 97, 3 and 4 (2007), pp. 267–316.

14 Giovanni Federico, 'Ma l'agricoltura meridionale era davvero arretrata?', Rivista di politica economica 97, 3 and 4 (2007), pp. 317–40.

smaller farms, and the construction of rural houses for the new smallholders.[15] This kind of project came to be known as *internal colonization*.

A geography of agricultural economics: Milan, Bologna, Florence, Naples

In the nineteenth century, the landowners (and the wealthiest tenants), who dominated parliament and the *comizi*, also held an unchallenged intellectual and scientific hegemony over the discourse on agriculture. Raffaello Antinori, Stefano Jacini, and Cosimo Ridolfi were at the same time landowners and celebrated writers on agricultural matters. The schools of agriculture, the agricultural societies, and the agricultural academies that studied the conditions of agricultural areas relied on the monetary and intellectual contributions of landlords.[16]

Agricultural expertise naturally focused on technical issues, with natural sciences as its core. In the curriculum of the two best-studied agricultural schools around mid-century, cultivation methods had a prominent role. For Gaetano Cantoni who directed the courses first in Corte Palasio and eventually in Milan, agricultural expertise should be based on a good mix of the science of agriculture (in itself a combination of plant physiology, pedology, zoology, and chemistry) with accounting.[17] His own research consisted mostly of studies of crop disease and growth conditions. The students would become farmers or estate administrators. The case of Meleto, a farming school opened in Tuscany by Cosimo Ridolfi, was similar.

Cantoni and Ridolfi had an enduring influence on the institutions of higher education that developed in Milan and Pisa following unification. In Milan, Cantoni became director of the Scuola Superiore d'Agricoltura, which was affiliated to the local Museum of Natural History and the Istituto Tecnico Superiore (a school for engineers).[18] Ridolfi's *sezione di agricoltura* at the University of Pisa, where the last grand duke of Tuscany offered him a position, was one of the few institutes in the country that offered agricultural education within a university.

The system of higher education in agriculture in the last decades of the nineteenth century was modelled on the Scuole Superiori d'Agricoltura that existed in Milan and Naples, the agricultural sections of the Universities of

15 See for instance, Ilario Zannoni, 'La colonizzazione interna', L'Italia Economica 2 (1908), pp. 50–6.

16 Rossano Pazzagli, Il sapere dell'agricoltura: Istruzione, cultura, economia nell'Italia dell'Ottocento, Temi di storia 120 (Milano: Franco Angeli, 2008), in particular, pp. 45–8, discusses the case of Ridolfi; see also Giuliana Biagioli and Rossano Pazzagli, eds, *Agricoltura come manifattura: Istruzione agraria, professionalizzazione e sviluppo agricolo nell'*Ottocento (Firenze: Leo S. Olschki, 2004).

17 Gaetano Cantoni, *Trattato completo teorico-pratico di agricoltura del dott. Gaetano Cantoni, professore d'agronomia al R. Museo Industriale Italiano in Torino,* I (2nd edn, Milano: Vallardi, 1866).

18 Gaetano Cantoni, *L'agricoltura in Italia: Dieci anni di sperienze agrarie eseguite presso la R. Scuola Superiore di Agricoltura di Milano dal direttore Prof. Gaetano Cantoni,* Ars et labor (1885; Milano: Lampi di Stampa, repr., 2010), 'Introduction' to the anastatic reprint edited by Tommaso Maggiore.

Pisa and Padua, and the Forestry school that was established in Vallombrosa near Florence. In the schools of agriculture, teaching concentrated on issues related to the botany and zoology of useful plants, chemistry, hydrology, rural architecture, husbandry and hygiene for farm animals, the study of crop rotation, and so on. Courses on farm management, the choice of techniques, and the technologies available completed the curriculum with notions of the art of agriculture. Courses in *economia agraria*, that is land valuation and accounting, finished with the fundamental notions of agricultural industry.[19]

The vast majority of the students, once they had completed their degrees, went on to manage their own farms or the estates of a large landowner. Very few would stay in academia.[20] Agricultural economics was not an autonomous subject of teaching in these schools. Economic theory was left to theoretical economists, either of the so-called classical school, or of marginalist convictions. For Piero Cuppari, who had been Ridolfi's pupil and who taught agricultural economics in the 1860s, agricultural economics was mainly a technique for managing the farm. Although he conducted research on farming families, there was no macro-policy drive behind his research.[21]

The practical, profit-oriented character of this training was underlined by the affiliation of agricultural schools to the Ministry of Agriculture, Industry, and Commerce (MAIC) whose mission was to promote economic activity, rather than science.[22]

Institutions of higher learning were not alone in the effort of fostering agricultural modernization. The landowners, especially in the northern and central regions of Italy, had established a number of agricultural societies. The Società Agraria di Lombardia in Milan, the Associazione Agraria Friulana in Udine, the Florentine Società di Orticoltura and Accademia dei Georgofili, the Subalpina in Turin, the Società Agraria in Bologna and many others gathered the most relevant representatives of the landed elites and the agricultural

19 The distinction between the science, art, and industry of agriculture is made in Cantoni, *Trattato completo teorico-pratico di agricoltura del dott. Gaetano Cantoni*.

20 On the professional outcomes available to agricultural technicians see Lea D'Antone, 'L'intelligenza dell'agricoltura: Istruzione superiore, profili intellettuali e identità professionale', in Piero Bevilacqua, ed., *Storia dell'agricoltura italiana in età contemporanea: Mercati e istituzioni* (Venezia: Marsilio, 1990), pp. 391–426; and Carlo Fumian, 'Gli agronomi da ceto a mestiere', ibid., pp. 345–89.

21 For instance, Pietro Cuppari, 'Spese e proventi di una famiglia colonica', *Giornale agrario toscano* 3 (1860), and id., 'Studi di economia rurale italiana. Territorio Bolognese (Tipo di pianura)', *Giornale agrario toscano* 11 (1864), discussed in Alberto Gabba, '"Lo studio di un'azienda rurale", in una lettera di Pietro Cuppari a Francesco Brioschi', *Aestimum* 39 (2000). These are examples of what Giancarlo Di Sandro defined 'the economy of agronomists', Giancarlo Di Sandro, *Gli economisti agrari italiani tra Otto e Novecento,* Collana di economia applicata 6 (Bologna: Clueb, 1995), and id., 'Il pensiero economico-agrario in Italia (1800–1980)', in Massimo Canali et al., eds, *L'agricoltura e gli economisti agrari in Italia dall'Ottocento al Novecento* (Milano: Franco Angeli, 2011), p. 198f.

22 The Sezione Agraria in Pisa, which was part of the faculty of Natural Science at the local university, was an exception.

experts of each area.[23] They disseminated best practice, and hosted discussions on general topics, such as trade, land tenure, and farming techniques. They also bought machines for demonstrations and organized prize competitions. The members of these societies represented the classical liberalism of the *Destra storica*, and supported the free-trade policies that benefited wine-producers, citrus-growers, and silk exporters: all fundamental components of the Italian balance of trade.[24]

In 1876, with a sudden reversal of the political majority, the *Destra storica* ceded power to the so-called 'Historical Left'. The government of the Left, which, under the guidance of Agostino Depretis and Francesco Crispi, was in power almost without interruption from 1876 until 1896, weakened the position of landowners. The electoral reforms of the 1870s and the industrial development of the country jointly reduced the importance of agriculturalists in parliament, while their traditionally free-trade stance was challenged by the inflow of cheap grains from the Americas.[25] To this sudden inflow was attributed responsibility for the crisis that hit the agricultural sector. The impact of the late 1870s, as well as the extent of the agricultural crisis, have been debated.[26] Revised estimates of agricultural output have recently shown the crisis to have been less deep and general than previously assumed, but this reassessment does not modify the fact that landed elites were very vocal about the crisis. The Jacini Enquiry, at the beginning of the 1880s, was intended to sooth anxieties of agriculturalists concerning their social status and the crisis of the whole sector.

Agriculturalists tried to counteract their relative political weakness, and in 1884 some of them established, with the help of MAIC, the Society of Viticulturalists (*Società dei Viticultori*). Faithful to the principle of free trade, presided over by such a fervent free-trader as Giuseppe Devincenzi, the Society still could not prevent the new protectionist tariffs of 1887 or the ensuing trade war with France, which basically closed to Italian wine-producers their main export market.[27] The new tariff has traditionally been seen as a victory of the

23 Thanks to a well-preserved archive, the Società Agraria di Lombardia is probably the best-known of them: Maria Malatesta, *I signori della terra: l'organizzazione degli interessi agrari padani (1860–1914)*, Democrazia, stato e società industriale (Milano: Franco Angeli, 1989), and Società Agraria di Lombardia, *La Società agraria di Lombardia: la storia e l'anima* (Milano: Società Agraria di Lombardia, 1998).

24 In 1862, raw silk accounted for 35.8% of Italian exports, Federico et al., *Il commercio estero italiano, 1862–1950*, p. 21.

25 Voters rose from 2% of the population in 1880 to 6.9% in 1886; Paolo Farneti, *Sistema politico e società civile: saggi di teoria e ricerca politica*, Pubblicazioni dell'Istituto di scienze politiche dell'Università di Torino (Giappichelli, 1971), pp. 194ff. and Rogari, *Rappresentanza corporazione conflitto: ceti e figure dell'Italia rurale fra Otto e Novecento*, pp. 76f.

26 Cohen and Federico, *The growth of the Italian economy, 1820–1960*, p. 39; the economist Rodolfo Benini believed that the main cause of the crisis had been the introduction of convertibility of liras to gold in 1881, Rodolfo Benini, 'Sei anni di protezionismo o dodici anni di sgoverno?', *Giornale degli economisti* 10 (1895).

27 Rogari, *Rappresentanza corporazione conflitto: ceti e figure dell'Italia rurale fra Otto e Novecento*, pp. 43–54.

industrialists over a front of the most advanced export-oriented agriculturalists (citrus fruits, silk, wine, cheese), while the rise of customs duties on wheat favoured and protected the relatively backward wheat producers.[28] The truth was that the variety of agricultural landscapes and patterns of landownership of the new country determined a multiplicity of diverging interests among the agricultural elite.

In 1894, a group of agriculturalists tried to form an 'agrarian party' in parliament with the explicit intention of pushing Italy toward even greater protectionism, and therefore threatening the balance of Crispi's governmental majority. This initiative was taken by Carlo Compans, Ludovico Fusco and Edoardo Ottavi, among others, and supported by the organizational ability of Tito Poggi. Its failure coincided with the parliamentary debate on wheat duties of June 1894. The 'agrarian party' proposed to exchange a reduction of the excise on salt (a tax that was particularly hated by the people) for an increase in the duty. But Fusco's group collapsed in the face of a compact governmental majority.[29] After 1894, Fusco and his followers reluctantly converged into the Società degli agricoltori italiani (SAI) which Crispi's supporters had created to counter Fusco's manoeuvres. This organization, while offering some sort of representation to landowners and capitalist tenants, posed no threat to the cabinet.[30]

The first Secretary of SAI, charged with mostly technical and organizational tasks, was Ghino Valenti, soon succeeded by Francesco Coletti. SAI attracted not only individual members, but also comizi and associations from all over Italy.[31] After the turn of the century, in particular, its political line resulted from a compromise between its more progressive members and administrators (Valenti, his successor Coletti, the SAI's second president Marquis Raffaele Cappelli, Ottavi, Giovanni Battista Miliani, and Giovanni Raineri) and a large number of agriculturalists, who expected the SAI to assert more firmly the interests of landowners and large tenants against industrialists and farm workers.

Nevertheless, the association was weak and divided, when compared to the articulated organizations of the German *Bund der Landwirte* (established in 1893 by the protectionist German agriculturalists) and the *Schweizerischer*

28 This view and the stress on the political exchange between the heavy industry of the north and owners of latifundia in the south is usually attributed (for instance by Rosario Romeo, *Risorgimento e capitalismo,* Economica Laterza (1959; 2nd edn, Laterza, 1998) to Antonio Gramsci and Emilio Sereni (Emilio Sereni, *Il capitalismo nelle campagne (1860–1900),* Piccola biblioteca Einaudi (1947; Einaudi edn, 1968) and its origin is ultimately ascribed to Gaetano Salvemini. For a review of the positions on economic and trade policies of the 1870s and 1880s, see Giovanni Federico, 'Italy, 1860–1940: A Little-Known Success Story', *Economic History Review* 49.4 (1996), pp. 764–86. For a reassessment of the importance of the tariffs of 1878 and 1887 and the respective weight of protection on agriculture and industry, see the persuasive Giovanni Federico and Antonio Tena, 'Was Italy a protectionist country?', *European Review of Economic History* 2 (1998), p. 84.

29 Rogari, *Rappresentanza corporazione conflitto: ceti e figure dell'Italia rurale fra Otto e Novecento*, pp. 89ff.

30 Ibid., pp. 75–100. Among the founders of SAI, there was Nicola Miraglia, a top official at MAIC.

31 For a discussion of SAI's membership: ibid., pp. 109ff.

Bauernverband (established in 1897 by outraged Swiss agriculturalists) and failed to involve medium and small farmers.[32] The few enquiries made by Coletti among SAI's members prove how difficult it was for the association even to mobilize its members. Notwithstanding the scientific personality of Coletti and Valenti, in contrast with its vociferous German or Swiss counterparts, SAI was technically and politically dependent on the government. The leadership of the SAI inaugurated, therefore, a line of 'friendly cooperation' (as Sandro Rogari calls it) with successive governments. Around the turn of the century, the 'moderate' leadership converged on Giovanni Giolitti, the leader who dominated the first decade of the twentieth century, pursuing modernization and social stability.

The Giolittian boom

Economic historians generally agree that, with the second half of the 1890s, the Italian economy as a whole began growing faster.[33] Technological and managerial progress, alongside new opportunities in foreign trade, seem to have driven growth. Gianni Toniolo argues that: 'the reawakening of Italian agriculture in the years before the Great War was, in effect, characterized by a series of technical and organizational innovations of great importance'.[34] He summarized the policies of the Giolittian period as the combination of 'custom duties, agrarian credit, technical assistance, vocational eduction, and land reclamation'.[35]

Landed elites were active in establishing savings banks and farmers' cooperatives (*consorzi agrari*) for the collective purchase of industrial products such as fertilizers and machines. In 1892, in Piacenza, *consorzi* from different areas of the Po Valley united in the Federazione Italiana dei Consorzi Agrari. Initially directed by Giovanni Raineri and Enea Cavalieri, the Federazione grew constantly over the years as more and more cooperatives joined.[36]

32 The German Bund der Landwirte had around 250,000 members in 1902, according to Joseph Kürschners, *Handbuch der Presse: Für Schriftsteller, Redaktionen, Verleger, überhaupt für alle, die mit der Presse in Beziehung stehen* (Berlin: Hillger, 1902), while SAI in its heyday never exceeded 4,000. For a comparison, see Alberto M. Banti, 'Organizzazioni di agrari in Prussia e nella Valle Padana. 1880–1914', *Annali dell'Istituto Alcide Cervi* 14–15 (1993), who stresses that only the local agrarian associations adopted a strategy equivalent to that of the BdL.

33 Giovanni Federico, 'Le nuove stime della produzione agricola italiana, 1860–1910: primi risultati e implicazioni', *Rivista di storia economica* 3 (2003), pp. 359–82, estimates an higher rate of growth of agricultural production, and TFP for the 1880s and therefore downplays the difference between the 'Giolittian boom' and the previous years, but allows in any case for a significant acceleration of growth.

34 Gianni Toniolo, *An economic history of liberal Italy, 1850–1918* (London, New York: Routledge, 1990), p. 29.

35 Ibid., p 104.

36 On the birth of Federconsorzi, see Severina Fontana, ed., *La Federconsorzi tra stato liberale e fascismo*, Biblioteca di cultura moderna 1084 (Roma, Bari: Laterza, 1995). See also Zeffiro Ciuffoletti,

From the 1890s onwards, moreover, the municipal and provincial administrations – which, thanks to the electoral system, the landlords controlled – began creating and financing itinerant chairs of agriculture (together with *comizi agari* and agricultural societies). The itinerant chair, or *cattedra ambulante di agricoltura*, was a kind of extension office, intended to provide technical assistance to farmers in a variety of disciplines ranging from crop rotation to cattle-breeding and sericulture. The first significant one was probably established in Rovigo by Tito Poggi in 1890, and others were created during that decade, especially in Lombardy, Venetia, and Emilia.[37]

The *cattedre* played a fundamental role both in the transformation of Italian agriculture and in the self-perception of agricultural experts in the 20 years preceding the First World War.[38] As it will be explained in chapters 4 and 5, they also freed the Ministry of Agriculture from the necessity of relying on municipalities and prefects for the collection of statistical data. Each *cattedra* was staffed with a permanent director, with the title of Professor, and a varying number of assistants, usually young graduates from the Scuole Superiori. They were usually funded by agricultural societies, provincial administrations, savings banks, and other local institutions. Until 1907, there was no general rule for the composition of funding or the institutional framing of *cattedre*. They were created and nurtured by different constellations of local forces whose centre was occupied by 'enlightened' landowners, but they also received special contributions from the central state as a reward for the services they rendered (for instance, to the statistical office).[39]

For a variety of reasons, there was a great number of *cattedre* in northern Italy, while they were almost absent from the south, where the budget of local government was usually heavily strained and the associations of civil society weaker. In 1904, after Prime Minister Giuseppe Zanardelli's journey through Basilicata, the central government decided to foster economic growth in the most destitute areas of the south by establishing *cattedre* there, fully funded by MAIC.[40]

'Dirigenti e ideologie del movimento cooperativo', in Giulio Sapelli, ed. *Il movimento cooperativo in Italia: Storia e problemi* (Torino: Einaudi, 1981), p. 111.

37 Although some regional cases were made the object of interesting studies (see f.i. Miriam Olmi's contribution in Sergio Zaninelli, ed., *Le conoscenze agrarie e la loro diffusione in Italia nell'Ottocento* (Torino: G. Giappichelli, 1990), and Osvaldo Failla and Giampiero Fumi, eds, *Gli agronomi in Lombardia: dalle cattedre ambulanti ad oggi* (Milano: Franco Angeli, 2006)), the only accounts of the history of cattedre in the whole country remains Mario Zucchini, *Le cattedre ambulanti di agricoltura* (Roma: G. Volpe, 1970) and the interesting account by Enrico Fileni, 'Cattedra ambulante di agricoltura', in *Enciclopedia Italiana* (1931), http://www.treccani.it/enciclopedia/cattedra-ambulante-di-agricoltura_(Enciclopedia-Italiana)/.

38 In 1907, parliament regulated the legal status of *cattedre* with the Law no. 513 of 13 July 1907.

39 The schools and *cattedre* absorbed a very large share of the (small) total expenditure of MAIC; see Giuseppe Orlando, *Storia della politica agraria in Italia dal 1848 a oggi*, Storia e società (Roma-Bari: Laterza, 1984).

40 Paola Corti, *Inchiesta Zanardelli sulla Basicicata,* Piccola biblioteca Einaudi (Torino: Einaudi, 1976).

The essential activity of the *cattedre*, according to the reports I have seen, consisted of lectures on topics such as fertilizers, machines, the prevention of plant and animal disease, hygiene, and farm management. Besides lectures, professors and their assistants gave individualized consultations, often visiting the farms that requested help. In some cases, the *cattedra* contributed to the establishment of cooperatives. Fertilizers, which have been credited with much of the increase in production of the Giolittian era, were one of the most important issues extension officers addressed, but the activity of the *cattedre* did not concentrate solely on the yields of wheat.[41]

In general, since owners of large estates had independent access to information, the target of the extension officers was small and medium-sized farmers, and the goal was to make them competitive in the marketplace. They fostered a general intensification of labour and land use, promoting wine, silk, dairy production, according to the climate and historical vocation of each area. But there was no uniform recipe, not even for the size of farms. 'It is not true', claimed Serpieri in 1908:

> that the evolution of modern agriculture displays a uniform trend toward large companies, as it happens in manufacture; it is true instead that according to a number of factors [. . .], large or small farms can be more convenient, and they will therefore continue coexisting also in the future.[42]

Therefore, rather than the 'emulative model' described by Bevilacqua, *cattedre* pursued a variety of local models, ideally bringing to perfection what farmers already tended to do.[43]

Although quantitative data are not available, anecdotal evidence seems to suggest that the effectiveness of the *cattedra* varied greatly according to external conditions. While in Milan, for instance, the activities of the *cattedra* could count on the support of the Società Agraria di Lombardia and on the Società's collection of demonstration machines, in Calabria, the *cattedre* established by the Zanardelli's government complained that due to the lack of roads they rarely had the opportunity of meeting the same farmer twice in a year. Their activity was confined to the distribution of seeds and fertilizers.

41 Cattedra di Agricoltura per la Provincia di Milano, *Annuario della cattedra di agricoltura per la provincia di Milano, anno* 1908/9 (1908) (Milano: Tipografia agraria, 1909); Cattedra di Agricoltura per la Provincia di Milano, Annuario della cattedra *di agricoltura per la provincia di Milano, anno 1902–1903* 5 (Milano: Tipografia agraria, 1904); MAIC- Ispettorato del bonificamento agrario e della colonizzazione, *Attività delle Regie cattedre ambulanti di agricoltura della Basilicata e Calabria durante il 1908* (Roma: Bertero, 1910).

42 Arrigo Serpieri, 'La fase presente dell'agricoltura italiana', *L'Italia Economica* 2 (1908), p. 43.

43 An anonymous director of a *cattedra*, for instance, gave a decidedly bottom-up interpretation of his teaching: 'What else should we teach within our *cattedre*, if not the best of what we have learned (from the farmers)?', quot. in Ernesto Marenghi, *Lezioni di contabilità agraria* (Milano: Libreria editrice Politecnica, 1922).

Even the southern extension officiers who were relatively successful in establishing contact with farmers, such as Oddo Romani in Potenza, acknowledged that it was difficult for them to lecture (69 classes were given in 1908 in Potenza compared to the 167 given by the *cattedra* of Milan in the same year), and that classes were only possible 'where the environment was more favourable and allowed a more abundant *use of words*'.[44]

Nowadays, most economic historians maintain that the gap between agriculture in northern and southern Italy increased during the years that preceded the Great War. The central government tried to balance the increasingly evident economic and social disparities with different kinds of measure. The creation of *cattedre* in Basilicata, Calabria, and Sardinia was part of a set of special provisions for the poorest areas of the country. In Sardinia a special office was set up to deal with the economic problems of the island. New measures were proposed in order to promote internal colonization, including a law that offered credit for the creation of smallholdings on Sicilian latifundia.[45] But the intervention of the state in the economy was on the increase throughout the country. More funds went to the itinerant chairs (in 1910, they received 391,100 Lire from MAIC, 530,390 Lire from the provincial administration, and 446,090 Lire from municipalities). The Ministry also financed experimental stations, schools of agriculture and similar organizations that promoted the development of agriculture,[46] and established land reclamation authorities and consortia for the fight against the phylloxera plague. The historian Giuseppe Orlando characterized the combination of these initiatives as *politica produttivista* and attributed to it the rapid growth of TFP and output of the period. Overall, the *politica produttivista* probably contributed to increasing the divide between the northern and southern provinces. The uneven distribution and effectiveness of *cattedre*, for instance, widened the gap, and so did reclamation authorities, which were very successful in the lower Po Valley, but had very little result in the south due to lack of capital and investors.

Giolitti's long cabinet and the alliance with agriculturalists, 1906–09

Giovanni Giolitti's so-called 'long cabinet' (1906–09) was probably the high point in his political career. After the first nationwide general strike of 1904, his conciliatory policy rallied the votes of the Catholics and all sorts of moderates. He became 'indispensable': the only politician who could save Italy from the violent escalation of repression and revolution that socialists and right wing

44 MAIC–Ispettorato del bonificamento agrario e della colonizzazione, *Attività delle Regie cattedre ambulanti di agricoltura della Basilicata e Calabria durante il 1908*, p. 9 (my emphasis).

45 R. Decreto 9 dicembre 1909, n.773 and R. D. 9 agosto 1910, n. 738.

46 Carlo Desideri, *L'amministrazione dell'Agricoltura (1910–1980)*, Paperback/Officina 9 (Roma: Officina, 1981), p. 16.

reactionaries would have ignited.[47] Supported by a vast parliamentary majority including the left liberals (but not yet Francesco Saverio Nitti's radicals, as would be the case in Giolitti's 1911 cabinet alliance), Giolitti presided over an unprecedented economic expansion.

Public opinion was not altogether convinced by Giolitti's propagandized 'neutrality' in economic conflicts. For many a member of the old landed and industrial elites in particular, the government had 'surrendered to the mob', and ceased to protect the citizen's freedoms.[48]

The hostility toward the government in powerful conservative circles eventually strengthened after 1909, and led a vast agrarian grouping to rally under the banner of first the Nationalist party and eventually Fascism. For the moment, though, the cabinet proceeded at full steam. To underline the confidence of the civil service and the growing importance of the administration, the Ministry of Agriculture Industry and Trade (MAIC) decided to move out of its old building (which had become too small) and begin the construction of a new building in Via XX Settembre, in front of the Ministry of War and not far from the imposing façade of the Ministry of Finance. Francesco Cocco-Ortu, the Minister, a leftist liberal lawyer from Cagliari, celebrated the laying of the foundation stone in front of King Vittorio Emanuele III on 8 June 1908.

The Ministry that Cocco-Ortu headed had survived thanks to a coalition of manifest and opaque interests and the vehement criticisms of supporters of free trade and *laissez-faire* policies and had enlarged its tasks immensely. An official report stated:

> the field of action of the Ministry embraces all the phenomena of economic activity, it follows the progress of social legislation, it studies and regulates all new institutional forms that the increase in traffic, the spirit of prudence and association are continuously creating, it promotes and encourages private initiatives whenever they strive for the economic progress of the country, it directs the rational and practical preparation of all those productive forces that have been meaningfully called the armies of agriculture, industry, and trade.[49]

47 Carlo Mozzarelli and Stefano Nespor saw the key of Giolittis' success 'in putting aside, in many ways, the politicial value of social conflicts and in reducing struggle to a matter of good administration' ('quella multiforme rimozione delle valenze politiche dei conflitti sociali e nella loro riduzione a tentativo di soluzione in termini di buon governo amministrativo'), Carlo Mozzarelli and Stefano Nespor, 'Amministrazione e mediazione degli interessi: le Camere di Commercio', in Istituto per la scienza dell'amministrazione pubblica, ed., *L'Amministrazione nella storia moderna*, p. 1674.

48 See for instance the positions of capitalist tenants recalled in Anthony L. Cardoza, *Agrarian elites and Italian fascism: the Province of Bologna, 1901–1926* (Princeton University Press, 1982) and Antonio Roveri, *Le origini del fascismo a Ferrara, 1918–1921,* I Fatti e le idee, saggi e biografie (Feltrinelli, 1974).

49 MAIC, *L'azione del Ministero nell'ultimo triennio* (Roma: Tip. G. Civelli, 1909).

The Ministry was a sort of Logistics Corps of the 'armies of agriculture, industry, and trade'. Although Giolitti did not support the hard line against day labourers and small tenants that the many local associations invoked, in particular in northern Italy, the activism of MAIC compensated for this by addressing some of the new demands of agriculturalists and their associations. In the early twentieth century, their demands significantly differed from those of the previous decades. The interests of the landed elites were now connected with a great number of initiatives that depended on MAIC for legal recognition and/or financing.[50] In exchange for the activism of MAIC, Giolitti and Cocco-Ortu gained the support of a parliamentary group of agriculturalists and the leadership of SAI. The cabinet realized in some ways a sort of magical equilibrium in its relationships with the agricultural elites. Owners of large properties such as Marquis Raffele Cappelli, leader of SAI between 1896 and 1911, or Giovanni Battista Miliani, embodied the group of agriculturalists that was close to Giolitti's cabinet.

Miliani, for instance, was among the founding members of the National Agricultural Committee in 1908.[51] This was a group formed by MPs and agricultural experts as a study group for legislative activities that concerned agriculture. Together with Miliani, many other significant personalities sat on the committee: Giovanni Raineri, and Edoardo Ottavi (future president of the SAI), among others. The group was not simply the expression of the interests of landowners. It had a clear conciliatory stance, against class struggle, but in favour of social change (so much so that even such a reformist socialist as Giuseppe Canepa joined it).[52] The leading members of the group, like Miliani, were close to the majority in the cabinet.[53]

The cooperation between Giolitti's cabinet and the representatives of the most important groups of agriculturalists in parliament were particularly strong in the field of trade policies. After the introduction of the protectionist tariff of 1887, the world of trade had changed significantly. Bilateral trade agreements acquired

50 This nexus of interests corresponds to what Mozzarelli and Nespor describe for urban interests around the Chambers of Commerce: the law of 1910 put electoral lists under the control of the government, while it allocated to the chambers public tasks and public funding, Cesare Mozzarelli and Stefano Nespor, 'Amministrazione e mediazione degli interessi'.

51 *Bollettino dell'associazione delle Cattedre Ambulanti di Agricoltura*, anno 2, maggio–giugno 1910; Sandro Rogari, 'La Società degli agricoltori italiani', in Pier P. D'Attorre and A. D Bernardi, eds, *Studi sull'agricoltura italiana: società rurale e modernizzazione*, Annali (Fondazione Giangiacomo Feltrinelli, 1994), pp. 139–56; id., *Proprietà fondiaria e modernizzazione: La Società degli Agricoltori Italiani 1895–1920*, La società moderna e contemporanea Analisi e contributi 40 (Milano: Franco Angeli, 1994); Fontana, *La Federconsorzi tra stato liberale e fascismo*, p. 45.

52 Ibid., p. 52; Rogari, *Proprietà fondiaria e modernizzazione*.

53 The behaviour of Raineri when he eventually ascended to ministerial responsibilities (1910), the stance that the SAI adopted on the question of the strikes of 1910 derived from this political position, see ibid. and Luigi Musella, *Proprietà e politica agraria in Italia, 1861–1914*, Storia 23 (Napoli: Guida, 1984).

a central position in international trade.[54] Statistics were particularly important in trade policy. The negotiation of preferential tariffs required a certain knowledge of national agricultural output and involved a high degree of lobbying from producers. MAIC thus also provided the ordnance for the army of producers. Statistics, from demography to meteorology, from justice to education, from the trade balance, to output, and credit, had always been the ministry's main task. The cooperation of Giolitti's cabinet with the main associations of agriculturalists enabled the overall reorganization of the Bureau of Agricultural Statistics at MAIC. The Bureau, under the guidance of Ghino Valenti, produced statistics that responded to the multiple needs of agriculturalists.

Within the environment of the Bureau, associations of agriculturalists interacted with the ministry's bureaucracy. Agricultural economists and agricultural experts were at the crossing of all these groups, possessing the competence needed by officials and agriculturalists alike. Locally, associations were in contact with agricultural experts in the itinerant chairs, or in the *comizi agrari*, or hired them to write in the specialized press. The *Scuole superiori di agricoltura* were also well integrated in the network of landowners and the exchange between associations and professors of agricultural sciences was constant wherever the two coexisted (the cases of Milan and Bologna are particularly significant). The central administration hired experts, like Ghino Valenti, or required the assistance of experts who worked for the associations. This was the period when the 'revolving doors' between academia, interest groups and the public administration worked most smoothly.

Agriculturalists against Giolitti and Nitti 1909–22

The labourers' strikes of 1907–08 and 1909–10, which were particularly harsh for the capitalist tenants of Romagna and Emilia, moved significant groups of agriculturalists towards the right and against the government. Already in 1901 and 1904, when repeated waves of strikes had hit the large tenants and landowners of northern Italy, some agrarian associations had proposed to form, beside the SAI, an agrarian league (*Unione agraria italiana*) with the task of defending the interests of landowners and tenants against day labourers.[55] The SAI's leadership decided not to support this initiative. Associations of agriculturalists of the lower Po Valley thus remained isolated at national level, while the SAI re-stated, at least in principle, its mission: representing the interests of 'agriculture as a whole', including day labourers and sharecroppers. Despite

54 The change in policy was soon followed by a growing inclination by even some economic theorists of the marginalist school like Enrico Barone and Maffeo Pantaleoni to accept some degree of protectionism, Fabrizio Bientinesi, *La parziale eccezione: Costi comparati e teorie del commercio internazionale in Italia dalla metà dell'Ottocento alla Seconda Guerra mondiale*, Biblioteca storica degli economisti italiani 242 (Milano: Franco Angeli, 2011), pp. 87–97.

55 Pier Paolo D'Attorre, *Novecento padano: l'universo rurale e la 'grande trasformazione'*, Saggi: Storia e scienze sociali (Donzelli, 1998), p. 13.

this, the society increasingly confined itself to the encouragement of scientific studies.[56] Coletti's enquiry on strikes, mentioned above, mirrored this orientation of the SAI's leadership.

The contradictions between SAI's inclusive (and pro-Giolitti) attitude and the will of the capitalist tenants exploded in 1908–09. In 1909, an alliance of capitalist tenants and some landowners from the Po Valley and the Adriatic coast launched in Bologna a new organization with nationwide ambitions, the National Agricultural Confederation (*Confederazione nazionale agraria* or CNA). Its leadership stressed the differences between CNA and 'neutral and apolitical organizations of agriculturalists such as SAI or the National Agricultural Committee'. They accused the SAI and the Committee of Miliani and Raineri of 'addressing merely technical problems'.[57]

The political project of CNA, in any case, failed. At the elections of 1909, only a few members of the association were elected, and once the wave of strikes died away, local sections of the CNA, outside Romagna and Emilia, were dissolved.[58] After two short-lived cabinets without Giolitti (under Sonnino and Luzzati), the wavering parliamentary alternative to Giolitti finally dissolved in 1911 and the old prime minister was able to form his fourth cabinet. Giolitti's new cabinet (March 1911–March 1914) was supported by a broad coalition. It included the radical Francesco Saverio Nitti (who became Minister of Agriculture, Industry, and Trade) and the nationalists. Its policies were correspondingly ambiguous: it approved an electoral reform that granted universal male suffrage but it also declared war on Turkey in order to make conquests in the Mediterranean.

In these years, the *Federazione Italiana dei Consorzi Agrari*, under the leadership of Raineri, supported the Premier's efforts to preserve social peace and political stability. They asked, therefore, Giuseppe Tassinari to collect data on the distribution of agricultural income.[59] The aim was to find a 'scientific' solution to the struggle between labourers and entrepreneurs: how much could wages grow without eating the just profit of farmers, and discouraging investment? From this point on, as we see in Chapter 7, analyses of farm budgets were identified as the main source of empirical evidence on issues of distribution. Knowledgeable agricultural experts were supposed to be able to technically determine the middle ground between competing claims.[60]

56 Rogari, *Proprietà fondiaria e modernizzazione*, pp. 138f.

57 D'Attorre, *Novecento padano: l'universo rurale e la 'grande trasformazione'*, pp. 15f.

58 On the reasons of a supposedly 'delayed formation, at national level, of an employer's organization of agriculturalists', see ibid., p. 9; the *Bund der Landwirte* was the recurring model of those who wanted a more assertive organization, Severina Fontana, 'Les associations agraires et industrielles en Italie entre la fin du XIXe siècle et le début du XXe siècle', *Histoire, économie et société* 16.2 (1997) and Banti, 'Organizzazioni di agrari in Prussia e nella Valle Padana. 1880–1914'.

59 'Introduction' to Giuseppe Tassinari, *Saggio intorno alla distribuzione del reddito nell'agricoltura italiana* (Piacenza: Federazione italiana dei consorzi agrari, 1926).

60 In 1911, Serpieri was also asked to give a scientific opinion on contracts of sharecropping in the dispute between landowners, sharecroppers and day labourers over the use of threshing machines: Rogari, *Rappresentanza corporazione conflitto: ceti e figure dell'Italia rurale fra Otto e Novecento*, p. 167.

The war amplified their technocratic role, just as it did with engineers and economists in the industrial sector. As Salvatore Adorno has shown, agricultural experts were included in the study groups that directed the war economy at central level, while the war effort entrusted itinerant chairs of agriculture with tasks relating to the food and horsepower supply of troops and civilians.[61]

The war nevertheless also marked the end of the political stability of Giolitti's era. In the elections of 1919, parliament filled with members of the Socialist and Popular Party (the Catholic centre), elected for the first time with male universal suffrage. Economically, the disruption of international trade, the loss of migrants' remittances, the growing trade and budget deficits, the huge foreign debt accumulated, and a rampant inflation shook the pre-war order.[62]

In the countryside, during the last years of the war, inflation disposed landowners to sell their lands to their tenants or to speculators who would then parcel them out and sell smaller plots. Peasants, on the other hand, benefited from the high price of foodstuffs, and low real interest rates, and were willing to buy. The market was not the only channel for peasants to access the land. The ruling classes had been generous with their promises in 1917 when the front collapsed and peasant-soldiers had to be persuaded to fight. The promises included the distribution of 'unexploited land' to veterans, but left undetermined what counted as unexploited land. In the year 1919–20, the so-called *biennio rosso*, the socialist revolution ('like in Russia') seemed to be a real and imminent possibility. This led to a wave of occupations of land by agricultural workers and small peasants. 'Communist riots' – recalled Serpieri in 1930 – had forced 'weak' landowners to sell.[63] Giovanni Lorenzoni wrote retrospectively 'that peasants took advantage of panicking landowners under the threatened or actual pressure of communist upheaval'.[64]

61 Salvatore Adorno, 'L'Italia agricola e il suo avvenire: Note sul ruolo della Commissione di studi tecnici ed economici della Federconsorzi', in Severina Fontana, ed., *La Federconsorzi tra stato liberale e fascismo,* Biblioteca di cultura moderna 1084 (Roma, Bari: Laterza, 1995), pp. 61–108. The war marked, nevertheless, new and more consistent advances for manufacturers. The Ministry of Agriculture, Industry, and Trade was split in 1916 into the Ministry of Agriculture on one side and the much more powerful Ministry of Industry on the other. The war economy fostered contacts between representatives of heavy industry and the government that had no equivalent in agriculture; see Lucio Villari, *Il capitalismo italiano del Novecento* (Laterza, 1975) for some examples of the inclusion of representatives of heavy industry in 'planning' experiments.

62 For a classic presentation of the political and economic situation, see Charles S. Maier, *Recasting bourgeois Europe: Stabilization in France, Germany, and Italy in the decade after World War I* (Princeton, N.J.: Princeton University Press, 1975).

63 Arrigo Serpieri, *La guerra e le classi rurali italiane,* Carnegie endowment for international peace. Division of economics and history. Storia economica e sociale della guerra mondiale. Serie italiana (Bari: G. Laterza & figli, 1930); he believed that those who sold their land under the threat of socialism were 'weak', and the whole process had been a sort of natural selection of the strongest landowners.

64 Giovanni Lorenzoni, *Introduzione e guida ad un'inchiesta sulla piccola proprietà coltivatrice postbellica in Italia,* Studi e monografie / Istituto Nazionale di Economia Agraria 5 (Roma: Treves Dell' Ali, 1929), p. 3.

The issue of the occupations was addressed within the broader framework of the fight against *latifondo* and of internal colonization by different draft laws presented by the Catholics and by the socialists.[65] Finally, the minister of agriculture, Angelo Mauri, brought to parliament a draft on internal colonization, which, among other things legalized some occupations, and severely curtailed the property rights of negligent owners, in the name of 'social utility'.[66] The land had a 'social, but not socialist' nature, commented the southern leftist Raffaele Cotugno, and 'the owner's right to land depends on the owner's ability to make it productive'. The dismemberment of latifundia would bring more employment but also more output.[67]

The common assumption behind these law proposals was that there was a lot of land left barren by the negligence of landowners and that a change in land tenure, and additional labour, would suffice to unleash the land's economic potential. The final compromise, reached before the Fascists came to power, referred case-by-case decisions on productive and unproductive land to commissions that were formed of representatives of landowners and peasants, crucially assisted by agricultural experts to determine land use and land tenure.[68] Scientific management would attain higher levels of productivity *and* employment.

The reaction of landowners was particularly violent. Fascist violence was employed to repress workers' protests and the connections intensified between the local leaders of the Fascist movement and the agriculturalists of Emilia, Romagna, and Tuscany.[69] The Fascist party also became a refuge for 'moderate' leaders of agricultural organizations, who had previously supported Giolitti. In the end, a manifest sign of the swing to the right of Giolitti's social bloc, SAI, under the presidency of Miliani, merged with CNA and dissolved into the Fascist Confederation of Agriculture. When the old Miliani died, in 1937, the president of the Italian Senate, the Fascist Federzoni, commemorated him as 'the purest fascist'.[70]

65 Serpieri, *La guerra e le classi rurali italiane*, pp. 181–2, remembered with execration the socialist proposal presented on 17 Dec. 1921 by Canevari and Piemonte,'in order to begin the process of socializing the land', while the Catholic Partito Popolare supported the participation of farm workers to the profits (*cointeressenza*).

66 The socialist Emilio Canevari and the conservative Attilio Fontana struggled over the limitation of social utility. Fontana wanted to introduce the clause 'in order to attain a higher productivity', and stressed the importance of the technical point of view; Canevari countered that the law had first of all 'social aims', Camera dei Deputati, *Atti del Parlamento del Regno d'Italia: Legislatura XXVI, Sessione 1, 2a Tornata del 23 giugno 1922* (Roma, 1922), pp. 6756ff.

67 Ibid., 6762f.

68 This is a clear example of what Maier, *Recasting bourgeois Europe*, called corporatism (pp. 580ff.)

69 Alongside the already-mentioned Cardoza, *Agrarian elites and Italian fascism: the Province of Bologna, 1901–1926*; and Roveri, *Le origini del fascismo a Ferrara, 1918–1921*, see Marco Palla, 'I fascisti toscani' in *Storia d'Italia. Le regioni dall'Unità a oggi, La Toscana*, Giorgio Mori, ed, (Torino: Einaudi, 1986), pp. 456–528.

70 'Miliani, Giambattista', in *I Senatori d'Italia: A cura dell'Archivio Storico del Senato della Repubblica*, http://notes9.senato.it/Web/senregno.NSF/1dbf7f5088956bebc125703d004d5ffb/074d5fa43da04f204125646f005d8415?OpenDocument.

The bureaucratization of the countryside under Fascism

The Fascist regime, as Paolo D'Attorre underlines, rewarded the support of landowners with a tough policy against unions of daily workers and sharecroppers.[71] When Mussolini came to power at the end of 1922, the government intervened to repress illegal seizures of land, abolished the local agricultural commissions in charge of examining claims of landowners and workers, forbade strikes, and restored order in the countryside against all threats to private property.[72]

In 1925, when the economic interventionist, Giuseppe Volpi di Misurata, became Finance Minister, the government began focusing on the stabilization of the exchange rate and the balance of trade.[73] Volpi adopted a combination of strong deflationary measures and the return to the gold standard, suspended during the war.[74] These measures weakened the competitiveness of Italian products on world markets. In parallel, the government tried to reduce imports, reintroducing the import duty on wheat, which had been lifted during the war period. These policies favoured *rentiers*, creditors, and other categories that had fixed incomes. Oligopolies also benefited from the new policies, at the expense of industrial exports. Revaluation and deflation hit farmers who had recently purchased their land, taking advantage of low real interest rates, very badly. Dario Preti sees protectionism, together with the reduction of agricultural workers's wages, as a consistent attempt at transferring surpluses from agriculture to industry, without recourse to foreign capital.[75]

The rationale behind Volpi's policies, though, was not only the restoration of bourgeois order. In the decade 1919–29, the trade deficit of Italy equalled on average 6.8 per cent of GDP.[76] During the economic boom of the Giolittian period, imports had been financed by remittances from migrants, but migration flows had significantly reduced in the interwar period, and the debt inherited from the war also weighed very heavily.[77] Prices of agricultural products and of

71 Tables from ICS on agricultural workers' wages in Pier P. D'Attorre, *Novecento padano: l'universo rurale e la 'grande trasformazione'*, pp. 126f.

72 The minister of agriculture in the first Mussolini government, De Capitani D'Arzago, immediately shut down the local commissions that were supposed to mediate struggles between workers and employers/landowners; on strikes of Tuscan sharecroppers, in English, see: Desmond Gill, 'Tuscan sharecropping in United Italy: The myth of class collaboration destroyed', *Journal of Peasant Studies* 10, 2–3 (1983), p. 160ff.

73 Charles S. Maier, *In Search of Stability: Explorations in Historical Political Economy*, Cambridge Studies in Modern Political Economies (Cambridge: Cambridge University Press, 1988), p. 83.

74 Very enlightening article on the political economy (American meaning) of inflation, ibid., pp. 187–224.

75 Domenico Preti, 'Per una storia agraria e del malessere agrario nell'Italia fascista: la battaglia del grano', in Massimo Legnani et al., eds, *Le campagne emiliane in periodo fascista: Materiali e ricerche sulla battaglia del grano* (Bologna: Clueb, 1982), especially p. 31.

76 Federico et al., *Il commercio estero italiano, 1862–1950*, p. 8.

77 In the period 1911–13, with a balance of trade negative by 5% of the GDP, the balance of payments on current account showed no deficit, Toniolo, *An economic history of liberal Italy, 1850–1918*, p. 19.

traditional Italian exports in particular dropped once with the post-war slump of 1919–21, and again after 1926, anticipating the Great Depression.[78] Farmers lamented especially the increase in relative prices of inputs, including farm machinery, fuel, and imported fertilizers, rather than simply complaining about the low prices of agricultural commodities.

The decision taken in 1925 to launch the so-called 'battle for wheat' was perfectly consistent with the stabilization of the balance of trade. The regime thought that self-sufficiency in food production, together with the expansion of the hydroelectric and chemical industries, would help to shelter the country from the risks of an adverse balance of trade.[79] The increase in the output of wheat was considerable. It was partially obtained by means of an increase in acreage, but also new high-yield hybrid cultivars contributed to the result.[80] This measure has often been criticized because it took land away from high-value crops, extending the cultivation of wheat to land unfit for it, but it is unclear whether valuable crops would have found responsive export markets. Studies show that the prices of export products, such as wine, olive oil and rice declined more steeply after the beginning of the agricultural crisis than the prices of products for domestic consumption, wheat in particular.[81]

The 'battle for grain' was just one aspect of the 'ruralist' ideology that put the countryside and its traditional values at the core of the nation.[82] The preservation of a healthy rural population, 'i forti rurali' praised by Mussolini, against the corruption of the cities was a key slogan for the regime, in line with agrarianist movements elsewhere in Europe and in the US.[83] A healthy peasantry consisted of peasant families with enough land to make a decent living. Internal colonization still had a great appeal for the regime. In 1924, when

78 Giovanni Federico, 'Not Guilty? Agriculture in the 1920s and the Great Depression', *Journal of Economic History* 65.04 (2005), pp. 949–76, minimizes the contribution of the agrarian crisis to the general depression, but his interpretation is not necessarily convincing because his data do show a deterioration in the conditions of agriculturalists.

79 Domenico Preti, 'Per una storia agraria e del malessere agrario nell'Italia fascista: la battaglia del grano', p. 30, within the interpretative framework that sees fascism as 'industrialist'.

80 The outstanding foreign debt of Italy, which had grown by 750 million dollars in the period 1924–30, grew indeed by only 50 million dollars in the period 1931–37 (Charles H. Feinstein, Peter Temin and Gianni Toniolo, *The world economy between the world wars* (New York: Oxford University Press, 2008), p. 83), but the Great Depression, the drop in American and British investments, and the economic sanctions of the League of Nations, had probably a more significant effect.

81 Alexander Nützenadel, 'Economic Crisis and Agriculture in Fascist Italy, 1927–1935. Some New Considerations', *Rivista di Storia Economica* 18.3 (2001) p. 290.

82 On the background of fascist *ruralismo* see: Rogari, *Rappresentanza corporazione conflitto: ceti e figure dell'Italia rurale fra Otto e Novecento*; a very readable analysis of a specific form of propaganda (stamps) in Federico Zeri, *I francobolli italiani: grafica e ideologia dalle origini al 1948* (Il melangolo, 1993).

83 Helga Schultz and Angela Harre, eds, *Bauerngesellschaften auf dem Weg in die Moderne: Agrarismus in Ostmitteleuropa 1880 bis 1960,* Frankfurter Studien zur Wirtschafts- und Sozialgeschichte Ostmitteleuropas (Harrassowitz Verlag, 2010), for Europe and Jess Gilbert and S. M. Brown, 'Alternative Land Reform Proposals in the 1930s: The Nashville Agrarians and the Southern Tenant Farmers' Union', *Agricultural History* 55 (1981) for the US.

Serpieri was undersecretary for agriculture in the recently created Ministry of National Economy, the government reformed the law on land reclamation.

The Act of 18 May 1924, No. 753, introduced the 'land-conversion areas' where reclamation had a markedly public interest, made landowners pay for the reclamation works and threatened them with confiscation of their properties if they did not. Land reclamation, moreover, would ensure the availability of land for peasants and former soldiers. Serpieri, the real author of the act, believed that, as far as land reclamation was concerned, 'the machinery of private production, left to its own resources, works very imperfectly'.[84] He resumed the ideal of transforming the land from 'a gift of nature' into 'a constructive work of man' within the new Fascist framework.

In some ways, the Act of 1924 resembled the projects of 1922 deprived of their progressive content, but the regime seemed to ensure greater capacity for the coordination of private and public resources, and an environment of national concordance where agricultural experts would be able to overcome the opposition of conflicting vested interests. The claims of workers would be kept in check.

The government expanded and deepened its reclamation policies with the so-called *Legge Mussolini* of 1928, the beginning of total land reclamation (*bonifica integrale*). A huge sum (4.3 billion Liras) was allotted by the government to land reclamation, while an additional 2.7 billion was expected from the landowners over a period of 14 years (up to 1942).[85] Extensive works were undertaken in an effort to reclaim marshy areas, especially in Latium and in the south. The reclamation of the Pontine marshes, in particular, became the showcase of the regime's agricultural policies, with thousands of settlers moving in from different parts of the country to occupy new polder farms.[86]

Again, the effects of these measures are ambiguous. Many economic historians argue that the 'ruralist' ideology was a propaganda cover for policies that greatly depressed the economic vitality of the countryside, and that the regime transferred to peasants and day labourers the effects of the agricultural crisis of the 1920s.[87] According to the data collected in the 1920s, smallholders, especially

84 Arrigo Serpieri, *La politica agraria in Italia e i recenti provvedimenti legislativi* (Piacenza: Federazione italiana dei consorzi agrari, 1925), quot. in Cesare Longobardi, *Land-reclamation in Italy* (London: King, 1936), p. 59.

85 Ibid., p. 64.

86 The technoscientific aspect of fascist demographic policies has been stressed by Carl Ipsen, *Dictating Demography: The Problem of Population in fascist Italy*, Cambridge Studies in Population, Economy and Society in Past Time 28 (Cambridge: Cambridge University Press, 1996); see also Federico Caprotti, 'Internal colonisation, hegemony and coercion: Investigating migration to Southern Lazio, Italy, in the 1930s', *Geoforum* 39.2 (2008).

87 This interpretation largely prevails in Italian historiography, see for instance Massimo Legnani, 'Battaglia del grano e istituzionalizzazione del regime reazionario di massa nelle campagne', in Legnani et al., eds, *Le campagne emiliane in periodo fascista: Materiali e ricerche sulla battaglia del grano*, pp. 15–26, and many of the studies collected in D'Attorre and Bernardi, eds, *Studi sull'agricoltura italiana: società rurale e modernizzazione*.

those who had acquired their land after the First World War, remained strangled by the combination of falling prices and deflationary policies.

One concrete effect of these policies, though, was the progressive expansion of state activity in the countryside. Within the framework of the *economia corporativa*, the decentralized approach that agriculturalists had always favoured[88] was replaced by a much more directive attitude on the part of the state. Interventionism required a new institutional setting and accelerated the transformation of the institutions that landowners and large tenants had established and controlled since the late nineteenth century into branches of the central government.

The first necessity was the systematic collection of data to steer the agricultural transformation. Serpieri, in 1923, had established the Istituto di Economia e Statistica Agraria (IESA), which took over the tasks of the Bureau of Agricultural Statistics of the former MAIC. In 1926, Mussolini established the Central Institute of Statistics (ICS) that was intended to concentrate the production of statistics, including the statistics of agricultural output, until then assigned to the IESA. At the local level, the Provincial Councils of National Economy replaced the obsolete *comizi agrari* for the collection of economic data:

> the spirit of this law is that the Provincial Councils of National Economy will beam into the provinces the directives that the government intend to give the national economy, while at the same time they will inform the centre about the conditions and needs of the local economy of the province.[89]

Although the nature of such organs was never fully clarified, their establishment was an attempt at extending centralized control onto the peripheries.[90] Deprived of its statistical division, the IESA gave way to the National Institute of Agricultural Economics (INEA). INEA became the centre of all scientific debates relevant for agricultural policies, and the focus of the technocratic ambitions of agricultural economists.[91] Agricultural experts had indeed an

88 See Ghino Valenti, *Per la riforma della pubblica amministrazione: studi* (Unitas: Milano, 1919), but also D'Attorre, 'Novecento padano: l'universo rurale e la 'grande trasformazione', who stresses the importance of decentralization in the program of the short-lived Partito Agrario Nazionale, p. 53.

89 R. Balzanini, W. Cesarini Sforza, and G. Chiarelli, *L'organizzazione sindacale e corporativa* in *Trattato di diritto corporativo*, a cura di G. Chiarelle, Giuffré, Milano, 1940, p. 795, quot. in Carlo Mozzarelli and Stefano Nespor, 'Amministrazione e mediazione degli interessi: le Camere di Commercio', in Istituto per la scienza dell'amministrazione pubblica, ed., *L'Amministrazione nella storia moderna*, p. 1648. The Councils were created with the RD 30 XII 1923 n 3229. They would be succeeded by the Consigli Provinciali dell'Economia Corporativa.

90 Maria Letizia D'Autilia, *L'amministrazione della statistica nell'Italia fascista: Il caso dell'agricoltura* (Roma: Gangemi, 1992) recalls the constrast between the Ministry of Corporazioni and ICS over the Councils.

91 Paola Magnarelli, *L'agricoltura italiana fra politica e cultura*, Studi e ricerche di scienze sociali (Edizioni di Comunità, 1981); INEA was also the battlefield of countless power struggles, on which, see

important role in the new course, as state initiatives required their technical skills.[92] Their tasks extended not only to the grand projects of the total land reclamation policy, but also to the micromanagement of agriculture.

During the 1930s, price controls were extended to rice and wheat by the systematic purchase of excess production. Farmers' cooperatives (*consorzi agrari*) adhering to the Federazione Italiana dei Consorzi Agrari, in principle private organizations, became public organs, and purchased wheat on behalf of the state.[93] The itinerant chairs were first entirely nationalized and then in 1935 renamed the 'Provincial inspectorate of agriculture'.

In this way, according to the historian Paolo D'Attorre, Fascism introduced at the core of the social relationship in the countryside a 'third element' next to labourers and 'padroni': the state and its bureaucracy:

> While in the 1920s, in many areas of the Po Valley, the centre of social relations is still 'the lord of the land', who directly mediates between the rural masses and the state, thanks to his organizations, since the 1930s this connection is increasingly assured by the apparatuses of state that are autonomous from the class of landowners.[94]

Marco Zaganella, *Dal fascismo alla DC: Tassinari, Medici e la bonifica nell'Italia tra gli anni Trenta e Cinquanta*, I fatti e la storia 4 (Siena: Cantagalli, 2010).

92 See Mauro Stampacchia, *Ruralizzare l'Italia! Agricoltura e bonifiche tra Mussolini e Serpieri, 1928–1943*, Franco Angeli Storia 274 (Milano: Franco Angeli, 2000) on Serpieri's role in the *Bonifica Integrale*. The already mentioned Zaganella, *Dal fascismo alla DC* insists on the divergence between a more liberal group of agricultural economists, headed by Serpieri, and more technocratic one, headed by Serpieri's pupil and rival Giuseppe Tassinari, and closer to the position of Paolo Albertario (a very interesting biography of Albertario exists, Simone Misiani, *La Via Dei 'Tecnici': Dalla Rsi Alla Ricostruzione: Il Caso Di Paolo Albertario*, Studi e ricerche storiche (Milano: Franco Angeli, 1998)); agricultural economists were not the only group of agricultural experts to figure prominently during Fascism: Tiago Saraiva, 'Fascist Labscapes: Geneticists, Wheat, and the Landscapes of Fascism in Italy and Portugal', *Historical Studies in the Natural Sciences* 40.4 (2010); Tiago Saraiva and M. Norton Wise, 'Autarky/Autarchy: Genetics, Food Production, and the Building of Fascism', *Historical Studies in the Natural Sciences* 40.4 (2010) discuss biologists.

93 On the system of *ammassi*, a few indications in Donatella Strangio, 'The Policy of Stockpiling Grain and its Costs to the Italian State after World War II', *Rivista di storia economica*, 3 (2012), pp. 453–86.

94 D'Attorre, *Novecento padano: l'universo rurale e la 'grande trasformazione'*, p. 153.

3 Packaging agricultural variety[1]

In 1875, three wealthy students of the University of Pisa, Enea Cavalieri, Leopoldo Franchetti, and Sidney Sonnino, set up to solve one of the most pressing problems of the young Italian state: what was wrong with the peasantry in the south? They decided travel to Sicily and look for themselves. During their four months journey through the island, the three interviewed hundreds of people. They carried with them a panoply of revolvers and rifles to defend themselves from the brigands and they slept in cots with legs that were specially isolated from insects.[2] It was a sort of hunting party, but hunting for facts, facts that would demonstrate the superiority of Tuscan sharecropping over southern latifundia, and prove how advantageous the introduction of sharecropping in Sicily and the continental Mezzogiorno could be.

Two years later, the Italian parliament decided to investigate into the conditions of the agricultural classes.[3] Their decision to do so was the result of growing concern and frustration. Concern for the first appearence of the 'social question' in the countryside, and frustration with the inability of the new state to catch up with the most advanced European states. Parliament felt that data were insufficient, that the reports that the government received from the *comizi agrari* were not answering the pressing questions of the political debates: is Italy rich or poor? Are we better off than we were before unification? What are the reasons for peasant unrest? In 1878, a special commission of twelve members was elected under the leadership of Senator Stefano Jacini. Commission members travelled and interviewed. They requested the help of local authorities and officials, and of all citizens of good and trustworthy faith, sent questionnaires asking them to describe the conditions of agriculture (output, system of land tenure, conditions of the working classes, technology) in their area. In 1884, the results of the investigation were presented to parliament and the public in

1 Part of this chapter is based on Federico D'Onofrio, 'Making variety simple: agricultural economists in Southern Italy, 1907–1909', *History of Political Economy* 44.5 (2012).

2 Leopoldo Franchetti and Sydney Sonnino, *La Sicilia nel 1876* (2nd edn, Firenze: Vallecchi, 1926), 'Prefazione' by E. Cavalieri.

3 Alberto Caracciolo, *L'inchiesta agraria Jacini* (Torino: Einaudi, 1959), p. 27.

a long report by Jacini, while a series of volumes containing the data collected was published.

What the investigations undertaken by the students and by parliament had in common was their format. They were both enquiries. In the nineteenth and twentieth centuries, from the celebrated British parliamentary enquiries to the German enquiries of the *Verein für Sozial Politik*, enquiries played an essential role in influencing public opinion, parliaments, or cabinets. In this chapter, I try to single out the essential features of an enquiry, as a format distinct from quantitative statistics and farm surveys. By discussing the Faina Enquiry of 1907, I explore the strategies adopted to make observations valid and relevant following the decline of the 'universal class' which dominated the enquiries of the nineteenth century.

Definitions

> [The modern state] rarely approaches a great change in policy or a reform of the administration, if their necessity is not proven by the demand of the public, which reveals at the same time how the reforms have to be carried out. And among the most important means available to the modern state in order to find out the political and social conditions and the measures to be taken, according to the general expectations, to tackle them, there is the public enquiry.[4]

When Carlo Francesco Ferraris introduced in this way the conception of enquiry, Jacini and his enquiring commission were still collecting the data for their monumental work. Ferraris' definition shows that while enquiries and statistics had not been sharply distinguished in the early nineteenth century, by the second half of the century, enquiries had assumed a clearly defined specificity.[5]

Ferraris' words make apparent the characteristics of enquiries. First, they were punctual investigations of pressing social, economic, and political questions.

4 Carlo Francesco Ferraris, *Saggi di economia, statistica e scienza dell'amministrazione* (Torino-Roma: E. Loescher, 1880), p. 98.

5 For the celebrated French Napoleonic Statistics: Marie Noelle Bourguet, *Déchiffrer la France: la statistique départementale à l'époque napoléonienne*, Ordres sociaux (Editions des archives contemporaines, 1988); for the Statistics ordered by Murat in Naples: Renata de Lorenzo, 'Strategie del territoria e indagini statistiche nel Mezzogiorno fra Settecento e Ottocento', in Renata de Lorenzo, ed., *L'organizzazione dello Stato al tramonto dell'Antico Regime*, Collana di storia (Morano editore, 1990), pp. 129–85; a discussion of eighteenth- and early nineteenth-century statistics/enquiries in Italy: Francesca Sofia, *Una scienza per l'amministrazione*, Quaderni di Clio (Carucci, 1988), in particular the chapter on Galanti's *Descrizione del le due Sicilie*, which was an enquiry as here defined. For example, the papers presented at a session introduced by Nadine Vivier at the 2010 Rural History Conference held in Brighton offered cross-national comparisons but avoided comparisons between different ways of observing and collecting information, see also Nadine Vivier and Corinne Marache, eds, *L'État et les sociétés rurales: Enquêtes agricoles, enquêteurs et enquêtés aux XIXe et XXe siècles* (*Annales du Midi* special issue, 284, 2013).

Their aim was to influence the deliberative process.[6] They were therefore essentially political acts. Second, Ferraris specified that they collected two kinds of information. They collected factual data on social and economic conditions, but documented the 'demands of the public' as well.

Enquiries combined two parts, referred to as 'objective' and 'subjective'. The objective part of an enquiry consisted of the impartial ascertaining of facts.[7] However distant their methods were from the 'mechanical objectivity' of statistics, in the objective part, observers were asked to be impartial. But there was a subjective part too. This part paved the way for a political synthesis that was not supposed to be impartial. Jacini's final report, for instance, moved between facts and requests, between 'objectively' ascertained facts, and 'subjective' demands of agriculturalists, so that the result was a hybrid of political involvement and scientific distance.

This hybrid nature reveals the administrative roots of this form of investigation. Methodologically, it suited rather well the principles and concerns of the *scienza dell'amministrazione* (science of administration), a school of thought in juridical and economic matters that had dominated the teaching of economics, finance and statistics in Italian universities since the late 1870s. The *scienza dell'amministrazione* considered social, juridical, and economic facts as inseparable, and claimed that the analysis of social phenomena should treat them together. The main representatives of the school, Angelo Messedaglia and Ferraris himself, were under the influence of German methods in the social sciences, and German doctrines of state socialism and protectionism. The *Scuola lombardo-veneta* of Messedaglia and Ferraris claimed that the state should 'moderate the social machine' and harmonize the conflicting classes on the basis of a thorough understanding of economic and social dynamics.[8]

There were two essential methods of enquiry: questionnaires and field surveys. Social scientists of the late nineteenth and early twentieth centuries therefore distinguished direct (survey) from indirect (questionnaire) enquiries. The Italian parliamentary enquiries of the 1870s combined both direct and indirect methods, but other enquiries were made by means of mailed questionnaires alone. Questionnaires were addressed to institutions (for instance, foreign or local statistical offices) but also to individuals. This variety was justified by the

6 In 1933, the *Enciclopedia Italiana* offered this definition: 'È termine che in senso tecnico si applica alle indagini straordinarie di carattere transitorio ordinate dall'autorità competente a un organo appositamente creato o designato per ottenere (mediante persone perite, con la visita di luoghi, con l'esame di documenti, con l'interrogazione d'individui che possono dare notizie) un complesso di approfondite conoscenze intorno a una cosa o a un fatto speciale, per cui le fonti normali d'informazione risultino insufficienti o non idonee'.

7 Stefano Jacini, *I risultati dell'inchiesta agraria* (1885; 3rd edn, Torino: Einaudi, 1976).

8 Nicola Miraglia, quot. by Cesare Mozzarelli and Stefano Nespor, *Giuristi e scienze sociali nell'Italia liberale: il dibattito sulla scienza dell'amministrazione e l'organizzazione dello stato*, Saggi Marsilio (Venezia: Marsilio, 1981), p. 67; see also pp. 51ff; for Austrian enquiries in nineteenth-century Lombardy see again Paolo Tedeschi, 'Notes sur les enquêtes agraires en Lombardie au XIXe siècle', in Vivier and Marache, eds, *L'État et les sociétés rurales*, pp. 525–41.

low rate of return expected (not everybody answered) and by the desire to gather as many sources, and listen to as many (possibly conflicting) sides as possible. The weight of state authority increased the number of questionnaires answered in the case of parliamentary and governmental enquiries, but it did not necessarily increase their accuracy. A cooperative attitude of the respondents towards the enquirers and towards the subject matter of the enquiry was, therefore, essential. For this reason, for instance, Jacini's Commission offered prizes to those who contributed reports written according to the questionnaire.[9]

There was a trade-off between quantity and quality of informants and available answers, because good observers were a precious rarity. While quantitative statistics struggled for impersonality, the answers to the enquiries' questionnaires were valued according to the quality of the informants. The quality, or position, of informants was a matter of political loyalty and knowledge of facts, good will (sincere or simulated) towards the enquiring institutions and familiarity with the topics investigated. The agronomist Oreste Bordiga, a voluntary contributor to the Jacini Enquiry, stated: 'if sometimes I drew from these data some peculiar assessments, I always tried to be in these assessments precise and impartial. Truth above all, this is the maxim that inspired me'.[10]

A good informant had to be honest and knowledgeable: 'the quality of information, the image of the existing situation, depend entirely on the attitudes the honesty, and the objectivity of local experts'.[11] As Paolo Tedeschi observes, in many cases 'the answers of single person are reported, whose opinion becomes the final result of the enquiry for the area entrusted to him'.[12] Obviously, the choice of the people involved in the enquiries was of great importance.

This explains the crucial importance attributed to field surveys. Field surveys (and I will not investigate here the 'prehistory' of this administrative practice[13])

9 In the case of the Jacini Enquiry in the 1870s, a network of trustworthy officials and friends was essential to the enquiry. Jacini commented that the enquiry owed so much to the cooperation of 'so many people outside the enquiring commission [. . .] that we can very well say that [. . .] is not the product of twelve men, but hoards all the knowledge and experience that contemporary Italy can offer on the essential problems of agriculture', Jacini, *I risultati dell'inchiesta agraria. Relazione pubblicata negli Atti della Giunta per la Inchiesta agraria.* We know for instance that in the area of Forlì, the commissioner Marquis Luigi Tanari referred first to the head of the local corps of civil engineers. He in turn asked the local librarians to indicate any young people who might be interested in taking part in competitions for the best monographs The committee even offered prizes to encourage well-meaning citizens to contribute reports, but with an uncertain degree of success, Carla Catolfi, *L'inchiesta Jacini in Romagna: I materiali inediti del Riminese* (Rimini: Maggioli, 1990), p. 20.

10 Oreste Bordiga, *L'agricoltura e gli agricoltori del Novarese, memoria distinta col premio massimo di lire 500 dall'Onorevole giunta parlamentare per la Inchiesta agraria* (Novara: Tipografia della Rivista di contabilità, 1882).

11 Paolo Tedeschi, 'Notes sur les enquêtes agraires en Lombardie au XIXe siècle'.

12 Ibid.

13 From the *missi dominici* to the Royal visitors of the Spanish Monarchy (for Naples see Mireille Peytavin, 'Le calendrier de l'administrateur: Périodisation de la domination espagnole en Italie suivant les visites générales', *Mélanges de l'Ecole française de Rome. Italie et Méditerranée* 106.1 (1994)), and the visitations of Catholic bishops after the Council of Trent, to the *commissario* of the Italian

allowed the critical assessment of facts and reports. The statistician Francesco Colletti warned that 'ordinarily, enquiries conducted by means of mail, according to scientific rigour, should be integrated, at least in some parts, with direct surveys and face-to-face interviews'.[14] By inspecting places, often during long and wearisome journeys, investigators could check the answers of informants against their own impressions, and they could reach informants otherwise inaccessible to them, like illiterate peasants. Visits and inspections established new channels of communication between those who observed and those who were part of the phenomena observed.

Both questionnaires and field survey, though, pose similar epistemological problems. If the combination of direct and indirect methods offered some guarantee to the enquirer, who could guarantee the good faith of the enquirer in the teeth of public opinion? Carlo Francesco Ferraris argued that the guarantee lay precisely in public nature of the enquiry,[15] but was this realistic? It seems that at least the good faith, a notorious bourgeois virtue,[16] of the members of the commission of enquiry was guaranteed only by their well-meant dedication to the general good. The striking epistemological naivety of this conception of objectivity seems to rest essentially on the concept of *positionality*, in particular on the fact that members of enquiring commission and the public belonged to the same universal class.

By the time of Giolitti, good faith had become more controversial, and positionality seemed a less promising foundation for the validity of the enquiry. The Faina Enquiry reverted to a more explicit role for experts in order to guarantee the indisputability of the objective part.

Indisputability, remoteness, trust, and packaging

Some 30 years after the mother of all Italian agricultural enquiries, the Jacini Enquiry of the 1870s, parliament decreed a second controversial enquiry on agriculture. Almost 40 years after unification, the debate on the economic gap between different areas of the peninsula had only grown more intense, maybe – as economic historians hold nowadays – because the gap had actually grown wider.

The enquiry into the conditions of the peasants in the southern provinces and Sicily, commonly known as the Faina Enquiry, began in 1906 and ended in

administration, the central powers always tried to get a grasp on the peripheries by means of visitors, inspectors, and so on.

14 Francesco Coletti, 'I contratti agrari e il contratto di lavoro agricolo in Italia: Inchiesta intorno ai disegni di legge presentati alla Camera dai Ministri competenti il 26 novembre 1902. Relazione del prof. dott. Francesco Coletti, Segretario generale della Società degli agricoltori italiani', *Bollettino quindicinale della Società degli Agricoltori Italiani* VIII, 4–5–6, 30 aprile 1903 (1903), p. 94.

15 Ferraris, *Saggi di economia, statistica e scienza dell'amministrazione*, p. 104.

16 See Deirdre N. McCloskey, *The Bourgeois Virtues: Ethics for an Age of Commerce* (Chicago: University of Chicago Press, 2010), pp. 297ff, for an interesting discussion of the Marxist dictum that good faith is a bourgeois virtue.

1909. It represents a significant episode in the history of Italian agricultural economics: Coletti, Ernesto Marenghi, Giovanni Lorenzoni, a whole generation of agricultural economists and statisticians contributed to the work of the commission of enquiry. They had to overcome three intermingling classes of problem, named here as the problems of indisputability, remoteness, and packaging.

First, let us consider indisputability. Ideally, facts had to be so far beyond dispute that they could determine the outcome of the deliberation. How could facts be put above the disputes of politicians and parties? The Italian parliament relied on specialists in data gathering in order to provide a solid foundation for its work: statisticians and experts in agricultural economy collected the information. Because of their disciplinary training they were not only more skilful at collecting information than – say – state officials, but they were expected to be more 'independent' of political interests. Hence, they could summarize the opinions of a variety of social actors, making the facts that they collected less disputable in the eyes of the public.

Agricultural economists acted as experts in different ways, first, as experts called upon by politicians in parliament; second, as members of a national and international scientific community distinct from the hyper-local perspective of peasants and landlords in the south; finally, as experts in agriculture and in techniques for collecting and handling information. I do not want to stress here the penetration of a foreign and hostile expert rationality in the life of laymen, as Judith Pallot does with the case of the 'rationalization' of land holding in Russia under Stolypin's reform.[17] My desire instead is to show how agricultural economists were asked to act as a communication channel between different elements of Italian society, and hence their work depended on the trust they gained. Beyond the 'postmodern' critiques on modernist attempts to create legible spaces for the purpose of domination, I want to show how information was exchanged in the actual field-work of an enquiry, with local agents contributing to shape the representation of their own life through the investigators' expertise.

Second, let us consider remoteness. For facts on southern peasants to reach the studies of the educated public, they had to travel a long distance through barriers of language, class, and geography.[18] This implied that enquirers had to travel the other way round into the southern provinces. If not as romantic as the journey of Cavalieri, Franchetti and Sonnino, travelling through southern Italy could still be an uncomfortable experience in the early 1900s. Giuseppe Zanardelli on his visit to Basilicata as prime minister had to travel on an ox-cart.[19] The writings of agricultural economists who took part in the

17 Judith Pallot, 'Imagining the rational landscape in late imperial Russia', *Journal of Historical Geography* 26.2 (2000), pp. 273–91.

18 On travelling facts, see the 'Introduction' to Peter Howlett and Mary S. Morgan, eds, *How Well Do Facts Travel? The Dissemination of Reliable Knowledge* (Cambridge: Cambridge University Press, 2010).

19 On Zanardelli's enquiry on Basilicata see the introduction to Paola Corti, *Inchiesta Zanardelli sulla Basicicata,* Piccola biblioteca Einaudi (Einaudi, 1976), and on the iconic ox-cart, the dispatches of news agency Stefani, in Mario Dilio, *Il viaggio di Zanardelli in Basilicata* (Bari: Adriatica Editrice, 1970).

Faina Enquiry reveal how remote the Mezzogiorno's peasants appeared to the educated elite. Most reports transmit the same feeling that Carlo Levi described in *Cristo si è fermato a Eboli.*[20] Investigators were overwhelmed by local specificities, by different and competing visions of society, or faced the hostility of groups and regions that, for different reasons, refused to cooperate with them.

This is what I call the problem of remoteness. The task of agricultural economists who engaged in the Faina Enquiry was to translate locally embedded knowledge into a framework that could be understood elsewhere, to sever its ties with a specific configuration of politics, geography, and routines in order to mobilize it for nationwide political and scientific debates.[21] At the same time, for this process to be successful, they had to engage local interests in the enquiry; they had to mediate between the distant ruling classes represented in parliament and the needs, hopes and aspirations of the provincial population.

Third, let us consider packaging. The issues of mobilization and representation lead us to the problem of 'packaging facts'.[22] How did they make the evidence they collected significant for the political debate? Only the facts that could be easily produced and easily read were politically relevant, for neither parliament nor the public opinion generally had time to examine an endless list of particular observations. Statistics (a large, comprehensible collection of observations) by means of averaging and graphs seemed to offer early twentieth-century positivists a good synthetic representation of facts.[23] Enquiries, notwithstanding their *ad hoc* nature, could turn out impossible to use in the political debate. Already before the conclusion of the Jacini Enquiry, for instance, Carlo Francesco Ferraris had warned that its results might not really contribute to the decision-making process. 'Even after a huge mass of information has been collected, with an extraordinary effort, will the legislator be able to give a new start to our agriculture, to change the distribution of population, to transform large estates in small properties or viceversa?' Ferraris rhetorically asked, and answered: 'It would be childish to think that, since the results of the enquiry will age before we have even minimally benefited from them'. Such a disproportionate 'collection of incongruous peculiarities' would be totally useless.[24] But statistics, on the other hand, were slow to emerge, and facts aged quickly. Moreover, they required permanent institutions and statistical observatories were expensive.

20 Carlo Levi, *Christ stopped at Eboli: The story of a year* (New York: Farrar, Straus and Giroux, 2006).

21 On mobilization, see Bruno Latour, *Science in action: How to follow scientists and engineers through society* (Cambridge, MA: Harvard University Press, 1987), pp. 223–8.

22 I take this definition from Howlett and Morgan, *How Well Do Facts Travel? The Dissemination of Reliable Knowledge.*

23 On the importance of Quételet's average: Theodore M. Porter, *The Rise of Statistical Thinking, 1820–1900,* Princeton paperbacks (Princeton: Princeton University Press, 1986).

24 Ferraris, *Saggi di economia, statistica e scienza dell'amministrazione*, pp. 102f; Also Ghino Valenti, who was a collaborator of Jacini, shared this opinion, Ghino Valenti, *Per l'ordinamento della statistica agraria in Italia: Relazione a S. E. Il comm. Cocco Ortu, Ministro di agricoltura, industria e commercio* (Roma: Tip. Nazionale di G. Bertero e C, 1907), p. 6.

What to do, then, with the mass of information collected through questionnaires and inspections? The facts that the enquirers collected concerned the peasants' way of life: their income, their labour participation, their patterns of consumption, their health, their propensity to crime, and their political associations. All these factors varied greatly across southern Italy and were heavily affected by local contexts. In order to detach such local and varied facts from their context and enable them to reach public opinion nationwide, they had to be recast into a package that preserved variety and specificity but that could also be handled far away from the places and the people described. Types were the available format in which to crystallize varieties.[25] If an individual case was not isolated but typical, it acquired the necessary strength to illustrate and support 'general observations'.[26] Surveys of types, in Coletti's words were 'the synthesis and the index' of the prevailing conditions of the area and he claimed that the budget they contained 'will be for us, on one side the confirmation (*riconferma*) of the observations made generally over a mass of cases, and on the other side a specification of those very observations'.

In the tradition of agricultural economics, farm types were classes of farm that were similar in some geographical, dimensional, technological and juridical features, such as the extensive farm of Basilicata, or the Tuscan *podere*. Types presupposed structural differences imposed by natural (climate, altitude, soil) or social (contracts, labour conditions, technologies) constraints, not a continuum of variation. The concept had many intellectual roots and a plurality of empirical application in farm valuations, tax surveys, farm management, and so on.[27] In order to study types, observers should select typical farms, working farms that were representative instances of the type. In this way, it was possible for agricultural economists, by studying a single farm, carefully selected to be typical, to study a whole class of farm for which no statistics were available. As a result, the use of types made differences easy to handle, not only for the investigators but also for the public and the politicians.

The experts who collaborated to the Faina Enquiry addressed all these issues in a surprisingly conscious and brilliant way. The solutions devised in 1906 represented important methodological achievements for Italian agricultural experts, setting standards that survived for more than 30 years.

25 Alain Desrosières, *Pour une sociologie historique de la quantification: L'argument statistique I* (Paris: Presses de l'Ecole des Mines, 2008).

26 J.A. Mendelsohn, 'The World on a Page: Making a General Observation in the Eighteenth Century', in Lorraine Daston and Elizabeth Lunbeck, eds, *Histories of Scientific Observation* (Chicago: University of Chicago Press, 2011), pp. 396–420.

27 It suffices to look at Joosep Nõu, *Studies in the development of agricultural economics in Europe*, Lantbrukshögskolans annaler, vol. 33 no. 1 (Uppsala, 1967), chs 5, 6, and 8 on Thaer, Thünen and the Swiss school of agricultural economics in particular, to see how deeply rooted was the idea of structural differences among types of farms in agricultural economics.

The Faina Enquiry

On 13 July 1906, after long discussions in the two houses of parliament, the Senate finally passed a new law containing 'Provisions for the southern provinces, Sicily and Sardinia'.[28] The law contained a series of tax reductions to stimulate the (fundamentally agricultural) economy of the decaying Mezzogiorno, together with a list of public works that were to be funded. The most controversial measure introduced by this law, was a complete revolution in land tenancy contracts. The law aimed to extend to the south the Tuscan sharecropping system (30 years after Sonnino's journey through Sicily), replacing the huge variety of tenancy and lease contracts that were in use in southern Italy. A vast coalition of interests opposed this idea, and although the law was approved, the application of the part that concerned tenancy was suspended, pending the results of a parliamentary enquiry that was summoned, immediately afterwards, by a second law voted in the Senate on 19 July.[29]

The enquiring commission was 'to enquire into the conditions of peasants, their relations with landlords, and especially into the nature of the land tenancy contracts (It. *patti agrari*) in the southern provinces and in Sicily'.[30] In fact, some commissioners wanted to turn the enquiry into a narrow discussion of contracts, while others expected an all-encompassing investigation into the conditions of peasants, the state of agriculture, the reasons for peasant discontent, emigration, and so on. The convergence of right-wing opponents of the law (who wanted to gain time by means of a long enquiry) and left-wingers (who hoped to direct the attention of the public to the poverty of the southern peasants) finally extended the commission's mandate and the object of the enquiry.

The model for the enquiry that began in 1906, as with Jacini's enquiry on agriculture and Ellena's investigation into industrial potential in the 1870s, were the British parliamentary enquiries: alongside a large mass of statistical data collected in various ways, a pre-eminent place was reserved for the declarations of various representatives of different sections of society, such as workers, landowners and so on, who testified before the parliamentary commission their views and opinions on the current problems.[31]

28 Legge 15 luglio 1906, n. 383.

29 On the political manoeuvres that led to the laws of 1906, see: Antonio Prampolini, *Agricoltura e società rurale nel Mezzogiorno agli inizi del '900: L'inchiesta parlamentare sulle condizioni dei contadini nelle provincie meridionali e nella Sicilia*, La societa' italiana moderna e contemporanea 7 (Milano: Franco Angeli, 1981); Sandro Rogari and Eugenio Faina, *Mezzogiorno ed emigrazione: L'inchiesta Faina sulle condizioni dei contadini nelle province meridionali e nella Sicilia 1906–1911* (Firenze: Centro editoriale toscano, 2002).

30 The commission had 18 commissioners, 9 members of the lower house of the Italian parliament, the Chamber of Deputies, and 9 senators; law quot. ibid., p. 27.

31 On the Jacini Enquiry see Caracciolo, *L'inchiesta agraria Jacini*; on the industrial enquiry, see Guido Baglioni, *L'ideologia della borghesia industriale nell'Italia liberale* (Torino: Einaudi, 1977); for the British

Testimonies in general show two dimensions: on the one side, they allowed enquiring commissions to listen to the wishes, expectations, and specific needs of certain areas, remote from the country's political centres; on the other, commissions listened to a vast range of classes and people, thus letting the country express its social and geographical diversity (or at least, trying to do that).

When the commissioners first gathered in the winter of 1906–07, after electing their president, Senator Count Eugenio Faina, they decided to split the workload in two: 'the preliminary collection of material, that is documentable data, should be undertaken by special technical delegates (hereafter, TDs); the parliamentary commission should for their part reserve for themselves, beside the task of supervision, and so on, only the political work, that is the survey of the mood of the population, and the *desiderata* in so far as they address the State, of the different agricultural classes in the territories touched by the enquiry'.[32]

The commission's activities were thus divided into 'political' and 'technical'. For each of the six regions of Sicily and the Mezzogiorno,[33] a sub-commission formed of three commissioners fulfilled the 'political' task, while one of the seven TDs collected the 'documentable data'. This represented a clear, institutional division between the objective and subjective parts of the enquiry. Politicians should synthesize the demands of the population and eventually translate them into proposals; 'technicians' should provide neutral and objective information that could offer the politicians grounds for their synthesis. This was considered all the more important because the data already available in official publications were regarded as old and unreliable, and statistics did not provide sufficient evidence for argument.[34]

The technical delegates

Francesco Coletti was chosen as the Commission's secretary-general, tasked with writing the programme and questionnaires for the enquiry.[35] Since Coletti was professor of statistics and demography at the University of Sassari, his appointment shows that statistics were awarded pride of place among the

influence on the 1906 enquiry, see Francesco Coletti, *Programma questionario dell'inchiesta per i delegati tecnici* (Roma: Bertero, 1906), pp. 36–52.

32 ACS, Giunta parlamentare d'inchiesta sulle condizioni dei contadini nelle provincie meridionali e nella Sicilia (hereafter: Giunta), b. 5, f. 6, Verbali della Giunta plenaria, Verbale 2, 2 febbraio 1907. On Faina and his family: Fabio Facchini, *La famiglia Faina: tre secoli di storia* (Todi: Publimedia, 2000).

33 The current administrative Italian regions did not yet exist as such, but *compartimenti* existed as statistical units; see: Silvana Patriarca, *Numbers and nationhood: Writing statistics in nineteenth-century Italy*, Cambridge studies in Italian history and culture (Cambridge: Cambridge University Press, 1996) who discusses the statistical treatment of regional differentiation.

34 This point was raised by Francesco Saverio Nitti in the Committee's meetings; for a recent assessment of the available data on agriculture, see Giovanni Federico, 'Per una valutazione critica delle statistiche della produzione agricola italiana dopo l'Unità (1860–1913)', *Società e Storia* (1982), pp. 87–130, and its bibliography.

35 ACS, Giunta, b.5, f.5, *Adunanze dell'ufficio di presidenza*, Verbale 2, 24 gennaio 1907.

'techniques' that could provide objective and incontestable data. But Coletti was hardly an arid technician, without political connections. First of all, he was known to most of the commissioners as the former Secretary-General of the Società degli Agricoltori Italiani. As many of the commissioners were also members of the SAI, they probably expected Coletti to understand the point of view of landowners (who strongly opposed the law on tenancy contracts), and also to be sensitive to the problems of agriculture in general. Moreover Coletti was close to the leader of radical (left-wing) opposition, Francesco Saverio Nitti, who was also a member of the commission of enquiry: Coletti had collaborated on agricultural problems with Nitti's celebrated journal, *La Riforma Sociale*.[36] Coletti's objectivity thus resulted from three elements: a methodology of investigation, a good knowledge of agriculture, and a political stance in between the different groups that formed the Commission.

Coletti and Faina, then, hired the TDs. Unfortunately it is not clear how the seven TDs were selected, but they had some characteristics in common. They were almost all scholars of economics or agricultural economics (with the exception of the rural sociologist Lorenzoni and the lawyer Enrico Presutti). Oreste Bordiga was by then already an established professor at the Scuola Superiore di Agricoltura (SSA) of Portici, teaching Agricultural Economics, Accounting and Land Valuation.[37] Also Ernesto Marenghi, a graduate of the SSA of Milan, held the chair of Agricultural Economics, Accounting, and Land Valuation in Perugia.[38] Eugenio Azimonti, after graduating from the SSA of Milan, had moved to Basilicata (in the far South) as the director of the Cattedra ambulante di agricoltura in Potenza.[39] Cesare Jarach was a graduate in economics whose main achievement had been an empirical study of the financial sheets of Italian joint stock companies; after the enquiry he became Faina's personal secretary at the International Institute for Agriculture.[40] Giovanni Lorenzoni was a sociologist, educated in Austria and Germany (his main book had been dedicated to the cooperative movement in Germany); as head of the Labour Office at the Società

36 Paola Magnarelli, 'Francesco Coletti' in *Dizionario Biografico degli Italiani* 26 (1982), http://www.treccani.it/enciclopedia/francesco-coletti.

37 Luigi Musella, 'Oreste Bordiga e l'agricoltura meridionale, 1884–1914', in Pier P. D'Attorre and A. D Bernardi, eds, *Studi sull'agricoltura italiana: società rurale e modernizzazione*, Annali (Fondazione Giangiacomo Feltrinelli, 1994), pp. 123–38.

38 For Marenghi's biography: Alberto Gabba, 'L'opera di Ernesto Marenghi', in CESET, ed., *Aspetti evolutivi della scienza estimativa: Seminario in onore di Ernesto Marenghi* (Firenze: Florence University Press, 1995), pp. 5–14.

39 For Azimonti: Luigi Musella, 'Il Mezzogiorno agrario di Eugenio Azimonti', in Severina Fontana, ed., *La Federconsorzi tra stato liberale e fascismo*, Biblioteca di cultura moderna 1084 (Roma, Bari: Laterza, 1995), pp. 108–29.

40 Francesco Forte, 'Cesare Jarach e Achille Necco', in Roberto Marchionatti and Giandomenica Becchio, eds, *La scuola di economia di Torino: Da Cognetti de Martiis a Einaudi* (Torino: Leo S. Olschki, 2005), pp. 149–63. Jarach was the personal secretary of Faina at the IIA between 1909 and 1911.

Umanitaria di Milano he had directed the SUM's social enquiries.[41] Coletti and Faina entrusted the technical enquiries to these men. Their work consisted of a rapid preliminary examination of the sources already available in Rome, the collection of information on the ground, on the basis of the programme that Coletti had elaborated, and the writing of a synthetic report.[42] The dichotomy between the elaboration of data and collection of information is mirrored by the competences required for both TDs and the secretary-general: familiarity with the methodologies of enquiries and knowledge of agriculture (method and content).

The enquiry's programme was 'to investigate in particular the relationships between land labourers and landowners'. Hence, 'it was necessary to examine both terms of this relationship, and reveal, together with the condition of workers, that of the proprietors, or, more precisely that of property, that is, that of agriculture, which is the concrete expression of property'.[43] The condition of peasants was deemed inseparable from that of landownership and from the health of agriculture, as a whole. The first two parts of the enquiry's programme focused, therefore, on 'land and agriculture' and 'patterns of landownership', while the remaining five parts were devoted to the peasants. Part III investigated the different classes of smallholders and peasants according to tenancy and labour contracts. It inquired into the budget of peasant families, their income, wages, the distribution of revenues according to the different patterns of land tenancy and employment. Part IV concerned the standard of living, including the health and moral conditions of peasant life, as well as their demographic consequences. While part III discussed income, part IV investigated expenditures and consumption. Parts V and VI examined the peasant within a wider range of relationships: part V investigated credit and charity; part VI the political grouping of peasants. Part VII was dedicated to emigration, probably the most powerful factor for change in southern societies. Part VIII was to summarize the previous parts and explicate the relations between them.[44]

This being the enquiry programme, the TDs had to proceed to fulfil it by their own direct field surveys (It. *rilievi*), and by means of questionnaires sent to individuals and institutions. Documents (for instance, contracts) formed a third source of information. Matters of landownership (part II), for instance, were to be discussed in terms of total product, net income, and the rent of

41 The essays in Vitantonio Gioia and Stefano Spalletti, eds, *Etica ed economia: La vita, le opere e il pensiero di Giovanni Lorenzoni,* Università (Soveria Mannelli (Catanzaro): Rubbettino, 2005) for an account of Lorenzoni's life; on SUM: Ivano Granata, *In difesa della terra: l'Ufficio agrario della Società Umanitaria, 1905–1923* (Milano: Franco Angeli, 2003); Lorenzoni gave an account of his enquiries for SUM in Giovanni Lorenzoni, *Le inchieste statistiche dell'ufficio del lavoro* (Milano: Ufficio del lavoro, 1903). Lorenzoni was Secretary-General of the IIA from 27 Jan. 1912 to 31 Jan. 1917, Giacinto Cottini-Agostinelli, *L'Istituto Internazionale di Agricoltura: l'affermazione integrale delle sue attività* (Terni: Alterocca, 1933).

42 ACS, Giunta, b.5, f.5, *Adunanze dell'ufficio di presidenza,*Verbale 2, 24 gennaio 1907.

43 Coletti, *Programma questionario dell'inchiesta per i delegati tecnici*, p. 56.

44 Ibid., pp. 56ff.

agricultural estates. These data could be obtained either through direct surveys and estimates of the fundamental parameters of individual estates (these were called 'farm surveys' and formed a type of direct enquiry), or by requiring information from somebody knowledgeable and willing to answer, for instance an official of the Inland Revenue (indirect enquiry). Moreover, part III was to be based on a variety of sources: TDs should collect contracts and describe the most common for each area; they should also note family budgets and farm accounts, for which a direct survey of several families was integrated using the answers of local informants. The combination of multiple sources was a characteristic of enquiries.

Coletti held that the enquiry would have been altogether unnecessary, if a full census of farms had been available, as in Belgium. But there were neither the time nor the resources to conduct a full census. TDs should hence limit themselves, in their direct enquiries, 'to the survey of typical instances of the various phenomena'. Coletti stated that 'it (was) necessary to concentrate on the various categories or degrees that are typical for a given phenomenon, and within these categories or degrees, it (was) necessary to single out and survey an average case'.[45] The observation of typical instances (It. *tipico*) was regarded by Italian social investigators as the only legitimate alternative to a complete survey of the population which alone deserved the name of 'statistics'.[46]

The typical farm

Coletti placed the typical at the point where two ways of investigating social phenomena crossed. The typical was, first, the final result of surveys and elaborations: Adolphe Quételet's average man was constructed by combining the average dimensions of human organs in a single individual and could be treated as the 'type' of a nation.[47] Thus, in Coletti's view, 'statistics survey statistical units. On their basis, they construct the datum. Out of a mass or series of data, statistics extract what is typical'.[48] According to the method of surveys popularized by Frederic Le Play, instead, the identification of typical cases preceded the collection of information. It was based on 'prudent and careful inspection, together with the information provided by experienced and knowledgeable men, of those whom Frederic Le Play called "social authorities"'.[49] The latter's reliability derived from their lifelong exchange with the people observed and their good will in serving the cause of social peace.

45 Ibid., p. 60.

46 For the conception of the 'inductive method' that prevailed in Italy, see Alberto Baffigi, *Cultura statistica e cultura politica: L'Italia nei primi decenni unitari*, Quaderni dell'Ufficio Ricerche Storiche / Banca d'Italia 15 (Roma, 2007).

47 Porter, *The Rise of Statistical Thinking, 1820–1900*, pp. 52f.

48 Coletti, *Programma questionario dell'inchiesta per i delegati tecnici*, p. 61.

49 Ibid..

Coletti believed that these two methods were not incompatible and placed his faith in the conciliation of Le Playan surveys and Quételetian statistics (based on a complete census) produced by Emile Cheysson. For Cheysson, while 'the role of the survey was to describe a subject (individual, family, workshop, commune, or nation); the role of statistics was to insure scientifically the subject's typicality'.[50] As Alain Desrosières points out, Quételet's stress on the stable and essential nature of averages enabled Cheysson to assume that an individual who is close to the average in some significant features, could stand for his group in all aspects. In this way, the survey study fleshed out with details the generality of the enquiry, expanding in depth what the enquiry depicted in extension.[51]

Typical objects allowed generalization and satisfactorily represented a complex phenomenon. As Desrosières put it, 'they depicted the characters of the story to be told'; they built the collective actors of the social drama.[52] But they had to display such characters in their completeness, in their purest form (even when socially pathological). So for instance, Coletti recommended studying 'complete' families with children of different ages, rather than families without children.[53]

In practice, this meant a two-step procedure, faithfully mirrored in Coletti's instructions. Statistical information was required for a preliminary identification of types. In an area where most farms grew wheat extensively and a minority had orange and lemon orchards, for instance, at least two types could be identified beforehand on the basis of even rough figures of production. The TDs were compelled to begin their investigation in Rome by plunging into all the published sources available, to familiarize themselves with such general data. The next step was to choose the individual cases to encapsulate such types. This was considered to depend on a network of 'experienced and knowledgeable individuals' who lived in the area. Coletti suggested that the TDs should 'mobilize' such forces so that they could select the right family budget to choose, the right farm on which to study crop rotation, whose revenues to analyse, the right peasant house of which to take a picture, and so on.[54] This second step could not be strictly planned in advance. Only when they were on the spot, and in the presence of variable and unforeseeable local conditions, could the TDs select their typical cases. It was a combination of experience and skill that would allow them to decide what to include and what to leave out of the picture.

50 Paul Rabinow, *French Modern: Norms and Forms of the Social Environment* (Chicago: University of Chicago Press, 1995), p. 174.

51 Alain Desrosières, 'La partie pour le tout: comment généraliser? La prehistoire de la contrainte de représentativité', *Statistique et analyse des données* 13.2 (1988), p. 96.

52 Ibid., p. 96.

53 Francesco Coletti, *Come si compilano le monografie di famiglia: Estratto dallo Cheysson e Focillon* (Roma: Bertero, 1906), p. 124.

54 Ibid., *passim* and Coletti, *Programma questionario dell'inchiesta per i delegati tecnici*, p. 61.

Unfortunately, the field notebooks that enquirers usually took with them in their journeys have not survived.[55] We can get an idea of the social authorities to whom the TDs might have turned for help in selecting 'typical' instances from the interviews conducted by some of the sub-commissions during their journeys.[56] As noted above, however, sub-commissions had a different, 'political' task and acted differently from the TDs. Sub-commissions interviewed the authorities in charge of the different aspects of the life of the countryside, a sort of Foucaultian bio-power of notables. Medical doctors reported on health and hygienic conditions; judges, police officers, and state prosecutors on criminal statistics and crime determinants; notaries on trends in the land market; Inland Revenue officers (notably the surveyors working for the Land Register, *ufficio del catasto*) were asked for information on land rent and prices. Mayors presented schematic reports on their municipalities, touching on their demography, the municipality's balance sheet, schooling conditions, patterns of ownership, land and labour prices, peasant housing, health and hygiene, and emigration. A crowd of different economic characters, sometimes invited by the Commissioners, sometimes testifying spontaneously, also had their opinions recorded in the sub-commissions' proceedings: peasants, landowners, administrators of large estates, industrialists, craftsmen, and so on (even some women!) Village notables, though, dominated the interviews of the sub-commissions.

Something more specific on the work of the TDs can be deduced from their own reports. Let us examine Eugenio Azimonti's report on Basilicata. Of the three sources of information that Coletti distinguished (questionnaires, documents, and field trips), the questionnaires were addressed to more or less the same types of person as those interviewed by the sub-commission. Only about a third of the questionnaires sent out were completed and returned. As for the documents, Azimonti found no material concerning the managing of agricultural businesses: 'nowhere could be found a systematic and orderly record of the facts about the administration of farms and estates'. If it existed, it was not made available to him. In the case of farm accounting, as for other topics, direct survey remained the only available source of information and Azimonti engaged in extensive surveys.[57]

Unlike other TDs, Marenghi in Calabria, Jarach in Abruzzi, or Lorenzoni in Sicily, who were unfamiliar and foreign to the region they studied, Azimonti knew part of Basilicata very well, since he had for some years been the director

55 For notebooks: Giovanni Lorenzoni, *Introduzione e guida ad un'inchiesta sulla piccola proprietà coltivatrice postbellica in Italia,* Studi e monografie / Istituto Nazionale di Economia Agraria 5 (Roma: Treves Dell'Ali, 1929).

56 Those collected for Abruzzo and Molise, Sicily, Campania, and Apulia are preserved in the ACS, Giunta parlamentare, various boxes.

57 Eugenio Azimonti, *Basilicata: Relazione del delegato tecnico,* Atti della giunta parlmentare di inchiesta sulle condizioni dei contadini nelle province meridionali e in Sicilia 5.1 (Roma: Bertero, 1909), p. xiv.

of the *cattedra ambulante* in Potenza (one of the region's main towns), a itinerant chair that had been established after Sanjust's report. Azimonti thus personally knew a number of farmers, peasants, and landowners who could help. From an agricultural point of view, also, he knew his district very well.

Along with Azimonti, who declared he could not separate the work he did for the enquiry from what he did for the *cattedra*, so closely related were they, the directors and staff of the *cattedre* were well placed to cooperate with the enquiry. They had graduated from Schools of Agriculture, just as most of the TDs of the Faina Enquiry had done. To them, their job appeared to be the dissemination of advanced techniques (which circulated in the world of science, experiments, and academia) into often neglected corners of the country:

> The professor of the *cattedra ambulante* accomplishes a pioneering task, wherever the word of science, for a number of recent or remote reasons, has not yet penetrated, there he is the pioneer of agriculture. He prepares the environment, he looks – as a friend and a counsellor – after the farmer and he suggests things to him that he would otherwise never know.[58]

But the 'word of science' would have been meaningless without the work done to adapt it to local contingencies and local practices. In this way, the *cattedre* acquired over time an essential knowledge of the territory that they operated in, of its farmers and their habits, while preserving the ability to interact with the nationwide community of agricultural experts.

In general, therefore, TDs began the research of the 'typical' from suggestions given them by directors of *cattedre*. In the small region of Basilicata, which had four *cattedre,* Azimonti often travelled with his colleagues and – in their districts – he relied on his colleagues' recommendations when choosing the farms to study; they introduced him to peculiar traditions, put him in touch with relevant private individuals and vouched for him to generally diffident farmers. Without the mix of general notions of agricultural economics and local, contextual, knowledge that the *cattedre* represented, it would have been impossible for the TDs, who were often completely foreign to the territory and equipped only with scanty statistics, to identify within a reasonable timespan the typical families, typical farms, and typical villages for their surveys.

Observation: a farm survey

Let us embark on the examination of one of the commission's reports, to clarify two points: first the amount of sensitive information that farmers had to agree to disclose; second, the importance of accounting as the general framework of observation.

58 Ugo Patrizi, 'La discussione del bilancio di agricoltura', *Bollettino dell'Associazione delle cattedre ambulanti di agricoltura* 2.6 (1910), p. 1.

To illustrate the conditions of agricultural business in Basilicata, Azimonti presented in his report a series of monographs, each one on a farm representative of a prevailing type. The typology considered geographic factors, farm size, and combinations of enterprises. It thus relied on data that could be extracted from published and widely available sources (such as maps, reports, and harvest statistics for the prevailing crops) or that were macroscopically evident in the landscape as well as in the everyday life of markets and people. As we said, the choice of the actual farms to be observed depended, instead, on personal acquaintance.

One of the farms described represented the type of extensive cereal farm joined with husbandry in the eastern zone of Basilicata. Clearly, this typology combines geographical elements with very broad characteristics relating to production and production patterns. I discuss this monograph in detail because it shows the sensitivity of the information that the investigation required (and which could never have been attained without active collaboration from the farmer) and the way that the monograph was structured. In a farm monograph, the TD's ability to obtain information from the farmer preceded the framing of the farmer's information into basic categories of agricultural economics: the farm budget made the fundamental economic and technical features of the farm explicit.

The farm, owned by D. R., was composed of various plots totalling approximately 889 hectares. Azimonti records its climatic conditions, soil, distance from market and roads available. For each crop, Azimonti gives the acreage and rotation; for livestock, the number of each species and the area dedicated to grazing. The livestock's most common diseases are reported. The account of D. R'.s farm also included the tools and machines that constituted the so-called dead stock. Fertilizers (or rather the lack of them) completed the picture. All this was the farm's inventory. It must be noted that machines, livestock diseases, species of herd, and different rotations were all much more familiar entities to the readers of the enquiry than they are to us now. What readers wanted to learn from the enquiry was the peculiar combination of such elements that constituted a typical farm of Basilicata.

The farm consisted not only of its inventory, but also of its workers. Azimonti discusses the budget (income and expenditure) of each category of workers, including the farm manager, D. R. himself. Considerations of management led to the core of the farm monograph: the farm's cash flows, which Azimonti had to compute himself with the help of the owner and of an assistant to the local *cattedra* since 'there exist(ed) no bookkeeping whatsoever, Mr D. R. being almost illiterate'.[59]

Azimonti starts with the gross production of crops and livestock, the only data available concerning the year 1905–06, when Azimonti himself recorded the returns. For crops, after subtracting the products consumed within the farm, Azimonti computes 644 hundred kilograms of durum wheat, 132 hundred kg of

59 Azimonti, *Basilicata: Relazione del delegato tecnico*, p. 311.

soft wheat, and approximately 200 hundred kg of lesser crops (beans, and so on). The yield of husbandry is computed more easily, by the number of lambs sold (180 at 1.10 Lire per kg), and wool (785 kg, at 265 Lire per hundred kg), dairy products (cheese and ricotta, around 700 kg), kids (around 60 kids at 1.20 Lire per kg), old sheep (100 at 25 Lire the pair), and so on.

Once the gross product is known (note that the computation of the value of the gross product requires knowledge of prices), Azimonti lists all the deductions that have to be subtracted from the gross product value in order to obtain the rent, this being the remuneration of the services of the land. Among such deductions are: expenses for labour, including the manager's wages (note that this is a theoretical value, since in this case the owner coincides with the manager); returns on capital, that is the remuneration of the services provided by livestock, dead stock (machines, seeds, fodder, manure) and circulating capital, as if they had been borrowed by the entrepreneur; amortization; taxes on rent (It. *imposta fondiaria)*. In particular, the calculation of returns on capital (It. *beneficio industriale*) involved first a valuation of all forms of stock (live and dead stock), to the value of 57,175 Lire). On this value an interest was imposed of 5 per cent, resulting in a subtraction of 2858.75 Lire from the rent.[60] On the circulating capital, represented mainly by cash payments for labour and amounting to 10,000 Lire, Azimonti estimates an interest of 6 per cent. The total deduction for remuneration of capital and stocks is thus 2858.75 + 600 Lire.

In a good year, such as 1905–06, D.R'.s revenues amount to 34,459.00 Lire, while his expenses (including the remuneration of capital) reach 29,826.00 Lire. What remains to D.R. amounts to 4,633.00 Lire. By simply applying the equations of land valuation, imposing a standard interest rate of 4.50 per cent, the returns on the value of land capital (approx. 90,000 Lire) would be 4,050 Lire, that is, the rent, which is what D.R. earns for owning the land. There are hence 583 Lire that D.R. earns: his profit as an entrepreneur.

Obviously, in the tradition of agricultural studies familiar to the TDs, in the analogy with German *landwirtschaftliche Betriebslehre*, agriculture consisted of farms. Farms were fully described by their inventory and by 'the proportions of the single constitutive parts and their reciprocal interrelations'.[61] These proportions were expressed in terms of the distribution of the farm gross product among the economic factors of production and were supposed to be relatively stable across regions and productive specialization, thus establishing patterns or types.[62] Vittorio Niccoli, who taught agricultural economics to both Marenghi and Azimonti in Milan, published very influential sketches of such regional

60 This 5% rate was the interest rate that the entrepreneur would probably have paid if he had borrowed the stock.

61 Pietro Cuppari, *Manuale dell'agricoltore* (Firenze: Barbera, 1869), 'Introduzione'.

62 Factors of production were called *cooperatori* in the language of the manuals of agricultural economics: land, labour, capital, entrepreneurship, and so on.

farm types.[63] Farm types thus acquired a substantial stability as entities that could be studied and observed.

Thanks to the concept of the typical farm, then, Azimonti's account of an individual farm acquired a wider significance, and was taken to summarize local patterns of production, for instance the interdependence of shepherding and extensive cultivation of cereals. Such surveys served, for instance, as the basis for Nitti's and Azimonti's own claim that latifundia functioned as complex productive units and could not be easily broken into smaller parts, a conclusion with strong political implications.[64]

Observations of such significance rested on the fragile dynamics of trust: enquirers had to trust the local and contextual knowledge of their local guides (and, in the case of Azimonti's farm survey, other agrarian economists working for the *cattedre*); the farmer had to trust the enquirer (and also the enquirer's local guides) in order to disclose information that was so sensitive and could so easily be concealed. The same held for farm and family surveys: who would have let a foreigner enter the house to compute the value of the furniture without trust? And trust was only one aspect of the interaction between enquirers and 'enquirees'. Peasants and farmers who decided to collaborate with enquirers were actually those who desired to be interviewed: they were eager to communicate. As Coletti puts it: 'the enquirer needs to select a family *willing to be observed*' (my emphasis). The motives, obviously, could vary greatly: the pleasure of showing off one's own achievements,[65] or the need for help. Arrigo Serpieri, for instance, who in very same years carried out an enquiry into peasants in the area of Milan, reports that, as soon as peasant women heard that somebody was investigating their housing conditions, they would rush to invite him to visit their dwellings, and to show him their state of disrepair. They hoped that their landowner would build them new houses.[66] Many citizens requested an audience from the sub-commissions in order to express their grievances. At some point, the commission even feared that mayors might hide

63 Vittorio Niccoli, *Economia rurale, estimo e computisteria agraria* (Torino: UTET, 1898); Niccoli 's handbook for agricultural engineers, Vittorio Niccoli, *Prontuario dell'agricoltore: Manuale di agricoltura, economia, estimo e costruzioni rurali* (Torino: UTET, 1897), ran into innumerable editions. It also contained directions for describing farms and exemplifies how the study of individual cases of farms as types was clearly part of the standard training of agricultural engineers, agronomists and agricultural economists. Nõu, *Studies in the development of agricultural economics in Europe*, Ch. 4, traces the origins of this way of investigation to Arthur Young and after him to Albrecht Thaer. The categories used in the calculations derive entirely from the Italian tradition of land valuation.

64 Eugenio Azimonti, *Il Mezzogiorno agrario quale è: relazioni e scritti* (Bari: G. Laterza & figli, 1919). The significance of such conclusions will emerge with particular strength after the Great War, when many suggested that landless peasants could settle in small farms on expropriated latifundia.

65 Coletti, *Programma questionario dell'inchiesta per i delegati tecnici*, quot. in Arrigo Serpieri, *Guida a ricerche di economia agraria*, Studi e monografie / Istituto Nazionale di Economia Agraria 1 (Roma: Treves Dell'Ali, 1929), p. 125.

66 Arrigo Serpieri, *Il contratto agrario e le condizioni dei contadini nell'Alto milanese* (Milano: Editore l'Ufficio agrario della Società Umanitaria, 1910).

the arrival of the commissioners from the population to prevent complaints being made to them. This fear should make clear the value of the enquiry as political representation, in a class-ridden society as Italy. Commissioners tried in apparent good faith to listen to those who otherwise had no voice, but it was not easy.

While Theodore Porter stresses the political conservatism that influenced Le Play's method of monographic inquiries and his dependence on 'social authorities',[67] I would rather highlight here the necessary interactions between local and foreign, between observed and observer inherent in this type of observation. Both social and geographical remoteness required guides and translators before TDs could overcome it, and the literate, Italian-speaking, university-educated locals – when willing to cooperate – constituted the most obvious starting point of observation, just such as Neapolitan aristocrats had guided their European guests making the *Grand Tour* into the exotic Kingdom.[68] As Azimonti writes: 'Out of necessity, due to the illiteracy that is dominant among peasants, we were forced to ask the *galantuomini* for intelligence on the life of the peasants',[69] thus stressing the divide caused by literacy. But were the *galantuomini* faithful interpreters of the peasants? Rarely. The TDs found their best supporters, instead, in the assistants and directors of the *cattedre ambulanti* and in the teachers of the schools of agriculture scattered about the south.

The *cattedre* were able to translate the 'word of science' into propaganda for the peasants,[70] but they were also able – at least in principle – to transform the tacit world of local agricultural practices into a language that could be understood by the general community of experts: accounting sheets, respective proportions of fertilizers, yearly rotations and so on.[71] Not to mention the translation – *stricto sensu* – from local dialects into Italian. In the end, though, the decision to answer the TDs questionnaire was the farmer's own.

Observations such as those combined in a farm survey contained a great deal of communication and translations, as I show; a mechanism similar to Bruno Latour's mobilization, but bidirectional, as the observed, to a certain extent, actively pursued their own representation.[72] In the case of southern

67 Theodore M. Porter, 'The engineer and the sage: Le Play's quest for social renewal and the reconstruction of observation', *History of Observation in Economics Working Paper Series* 2 (2009).

68 Augusto Placanica, 'La capitale, il passato il paesaggio: I viaggiatori come "fonte" della storia meridionale', *Meridiana* 1 (1987).

69 Azimonti, *Basilicata: Relazione del delegato tecnico*, p. xv.

70 'Peasants need to see, or they won't trust' is a common statement in the answers of *cattedre* directors to the enquiring commission.

71 H.M. Collins and R. Evans, 'The Third Wave of Science Studies: Studies of Expertise and Experience', *Social Studies of Science* 32.2 (2002).

72 Latour, *Science in action*. Investigation of agriculture has often been seen in terms of 'quantification' and 'mapping', with statistics making the countryside 'appropriable' for the State (unidirectional): for instance, James C. Scott stresses the top-down character of *cadastres* in continental Europe and South East Asia (James C. Scott, *Seeing like a state: How certain schemes to improve the human condition*

Italy, in fact, for the mobilization to take place, the distant periphery had to have an interest in providing information to the 'centre of calculation', otherwise data could be misreported or simply hidden.[73] Consequently, the effectiveness of both direct and indirect enquiry varied greatly according to the interest shown by the observed populations, not simply by the *galantuomini*, but by farmers in general.

Marenghi, for instance, regretted that in Calabria 'the enquiry would have had more complete results, had public and private offices showed . . . more collaboration' 'private individuals did not welcome the enquiry'.[74] Azimonti complained that in Basilicata the collaboration of private individuals 'was, altogether, very deficient and – so to say – offered unwillingly', 'the civilized strata (*ceto civile*) seemed not to acknowledge the practical utility of the enquiry and of collaborating with it'.[75] In contrast, Lorenzoni praised the welcome offered by the Sicilian villages that he visited, and in particular the collaboration of peasants 'full of trust and – so to say – of gratitude for the interest shown in them'. And he could not 'recall without emotion the long evening meetings [. . .] when they described their conditions [. . .] in an orderly way, without impatience or exaggeration'. It was together with such peasants or with equally participative landowners that Lorenzoni visited cooperatives and estates.[76]

Communication, the typical and statistics

It might seem that the two aspects of observation that emerged from the discussion of the Faina Enquiry, i. e., the role of the 'typical', with all the fuzziness of its definition, and the importance of communication, are limited to enquiries and remained at the edges of statistics. It was not so, as we can see in more detail in the next chapter: the most seemingly objective numerical

have failed, Yale ISPS series (New Haven:Yale university press, 1998), p. 44f.) In fact, a closer look at the way *cadastres* were actually made shows that local communities participated in the making of maps and the attribution of values; the landowners interviewed by the Faina Enquiry, for instance, almost invariably invoked the completion of the *catasto terreni* that they expected would lower the land tax to a more reasonable level.

73 Emmanuel Didier, *En quoi consiste l'Amérique? Les statistiques, le new deal et la démocratie,* Série Anthropologie des sciences et des techniques (Paris: Éd. La Découverte, 2009) stresses the importance of reliable information for American farmers against speculators, but see also, Marcel Boumans on deception: M. Boumans, 'Observations in a Hostile Environment: Morgenstern on the Accuracy of Economic Observations', *History of Political Economy* 44, Supplement 1 (2012).

74 Ernesto Marenghi, *Calabria: Relazione del delegato tecnico,* Atti della giunta parlmentare di inchiesta sulle condizioni dei contadini nelle province meridionali e in Sicilia (Roma: Bertero, 1909), p. xxvii.

75 Azimonti, *Basilicata: Relazione del delegato tecnico,* p. xvi.

76 Giovanni Lorenzoni, *Sicilia: Relazione del delegato tecnico,* Atti della giunta parlmentare di inchiesta sulle condizioni dei contadini nelle province meridionali e in Sicilia (Roma: Bertero, 1911), 'Introduzione', *passim.*

statistics relied on the same elements.[77] Also computations of agricultural output depended on typical farms.[78]

In fact, there was no clear-cut opposition between the subjectivity of the methods of enquiry and the indisputability of the resulting facts. The description of types was a reasonable way for politics and science to summarize variety. It was the expertise of TDs in combining consistently the answers to questionnaires (indirect enquiry) and their own investigations and travel impressions (direct enquiry) enabled politicians to discuss the needs of the south, by detailing for them the characteristics of each farm and family type.

Questionnaires were answered, with different degrees of precision, by a variety of individuals dominated by diverging concerns, and talking about different experiences and places. They had to be merged into a unique text: 'once the questionnaires were collected' – writes Lorenzoni:

> we had to think how to summarize them: by municipalities first and by district afterwards. Neither of the two was an easy job. The questionnaires coming from the same municipality but from different individuals frequently diverged from one another. And the difference was not only merely formal or quantitative, but sometimes, although rarely, substantial. How to select?[79]

It was a direct knowledge of places, direct observation of circumstances and surveys of typical instances of social phenomena (direct enquiry) that guided the selection of questionnaires and the judgement on their reliability.

Statisticians thought that, in principle, the observation of a whole region – of all the farms, families, villages – could be acquired only through a continuous and comprehensive census, through statistics, but, since statistics were not at hand, the TDs of the Faina Enquiry travelled through almost a *terra incognita* of social phenomena. Only the observation of a few 'typical' points (and not random samples) made generalization possible, on the basis of 'typicality', at a reasonable cost. The choice of typical instances out of necessity preceded the observation of them and was thus confided to the expert's *coup d'oeil*. Although it depended on a complex interaction between different kinds of expertise: local and academic, tacit and explicit, methodological and agricultural; and different interests: the farmers' and the enquirers', the final decision fell entirely on the shoulders of the TDs.

The characteristics that in principle fitted the TDs to make the right observations and to giving to such observations their best synthesis were two: their

77 I define here 'objective', and conversely 'subjective', following Theodore M. Porter, *Trust in Numbers: The Pursuit of Objectivity in Science and Public Life* (Princeton: Princeton University Press, 1996), as 'knowledge based completely on explicit rules'.

78 See Chapter 4 below.

79 Lorenzoni, *Sicilia: Relazione del delegato tecnico*, p. xxv.

university training (decontextualized knowledge, so to say), and their ability to translate such university training into local contexts. These characteristics they shared with their fellow graduates from agricultural schools, who worked in the *cattedre ambulanti*. They all belonged to the same group – that of agricultural experts – whose task was translating the expertise of local agriculturalists and farmers about contracts, techniques, technologies, and human factors, into the language of economic theory (capital, labour, rent) and vice versa. By so doing, the community of agricultural experts gave stability and substance to agricultural types (types of farm, types of peasant family) which the government and parliament could legislate about (or at least, talk about) and which agricultural experts themselves could study in further investigations (as in the case of the statistics of harvest).

Statisticians summarized masses of quantitative data by means of mathematical averaging and a study of the distribution. Enquiries – remarked the already-mentioned Salvioni – required a different approach. Something of statistics – 'a statistical quid' – still characterized them, but they collected a different kind of evidence. Surveys of types were the way to make this evidence significant. They were not only a heuristic device, but also a narrative device. For Coletti, they were 'an episode in the warp of an historical narration'. Types were the protagonists of the narrative that the enquiry told. In 1908, Arrigo Serpieri, wrote that surveys 'were no less necessary than statistics, in order to give colour and life to statistical figures, and manifest phenomena that find no expression in the rigid language of numbers'.[80] Serpieri remained faithful to this conception well into the 1920s and 1930s, as his *Guida a ricerche di economia agraria* and the scientific activity of INEA under his direction sufficiently proves.

80 Arrigo Serpieri, 'La fase presente dell'agricoltura italiana', *L'Italia Economica* 2 (1908), p. 42.

4 Measuring stocks, conjecturing flows

The previous chapters introduced a threefold distinction between general observations, which summarized the questionnaires of enquiries; types, which were described by monographs; and statistical series. At the end of the nineteenth century, statistics were characterized by their quantitative nature and by the large number of observations on which they were based. The population census was the most impressive achievement of this science. Statistics of agricultural production, however, were extremely problematic, at least in Italy. Luigi Bodio, for many years director of the General Directorate of Statistics, recalled: 'When superficial commentators wanted to ridicule statistics, they invariably mentioned the agricultural statistics'.[1] Among agricultural statistics, statistics of crop production were the most important. Because of their importance, they were simply called 'agricultural statistics' (*statistica agraria*), without further qualification.

There was a great difference between the collection of crop statistics and the holding of enquiries. If the enquiry was intended, at least in theory, as the precursor of 'a great legislative reform', it should not investigate – argued Ferraris – 'the kind of plant production'. This data should be collected 'with endless patience and care'; they contributed towards the 'great system of information which, for the modern state, is statistics'.[2] The fundamental difference, for Ferraris as for Salvioni was in the regularity of the collection of statistical data, as opposed to the punctual and *ad hoc* nature of enquiries.

In any case, enquiries required statistics. We have seen already that, at the time of the Faina Enquiry, researchers acknowledged the lack of satisfactory statistics on agricultural production. They lacked the repeated and comprehensive series of data on agricultural output they required for a general framework for the surveys of farms and families. Monographs could provide the colour, but there was no canvas.

1 Luigi Bodio, quot. in Roberto Tolaini, *Contadini toscani negli anni Trenta: Monografie di famiglie dell'I-NEA 1931–1938,* Collana del Centro di documentazione e ricerca sulla storia dell'agricoltura e della società contadina 0002 (Ospedaletto, Pisa: Pacini, 2005), p. 2.

2 Carlo Francesco Ferraris, *Saggi di economia, statistica e scienza dell'amministrazione* (Torino-Roma: E. Loescher, 1880), p. 101.

To provide the necessary data, researchers needed – in addition to enquiries – specifically dedicated structures. In short, they required statistical observatories. This chapter explains what it meant to observe agricultural output. It describes the making of the *catasto agrario* (agricultural *cadastre*, or land survey). It goes at great length into the details of the process of coding, with the painstaking process of categorizing reality, and shows how statistical coding depended to a great extent on knowledge of the typical. The next chapter describes the alliances between agricultural experts and social groups that made possible a network of observatories and observers.

Agricultural statistics were considered among the most difficult statistics of production. Alfredo De Polzer, in the manual of statistics that Corrado Gini edited in the 1940s, acknowledged that 'from the point of view of statistical techniques, agricultural economy possesses very peculiar features that hinder the survey and make the interpretation of results difficult'. According to De Polzer, such elements are, among others:

> the variety of crops cultivated, the division of productive processes among a large number of businesses of different size, the asynchrony of harvesting periods both of different products and of the same product across different regions of the same country, or also the variability of products due to the effect of meteorological and cosmic [sic] factors.[3]

Since directly measuring production was impossible owing to the sheer number of farms that operated in the country, and since direct reports from producers themselves (such as are elicited by a census of population) would have been unreliable, statisticians were left with conjectural statistics, as they called them.[4] An example from another economic sector, industry, should clarify here what they meant by conjecture. In order to compile the statistics of wool yarn production, the statistician Luigi Bodio adopted the following method. He knew the number of spinning mills of each type (although his figures were more precise for the big steam mills than for the small house mills). He then contacted the wool industrialist Alessandro Rossi and asked him for an estimate of the daily production of mills of each type. By multiplying the number of mills of each type by their daily production, Bodio achieved an estimate of the production of wool yarn that

3 Alfredo de Polzer, *Statistiche agrarie* (Milano: Giuffrè, 1942), p. 5.

4 Ghino Valenti, *Per l'Ordinamento della Statistica agraria in Italia: Relazione a S. E. Il comm. Cocco Ortu, Ministro di agricoltura, industria e commercio* (Roma: Tip. Nazionale di G. Bertero e C, 1907), p. 26. To us it seems that sampling could have probably suited better the demand for production data. A sample of thousands of farms is now used by ISTAT, the Italian Bureau of Statistics, for similar purposes. When random sampling methods were first presented at the International Statistical Institute, by Anders N. Kiaer in 1895, Italian statisticians, together with many of their colleagues, generally rejected the legitimacy of the method, see Jean-Guy Prévost and Jean Pierre Beaud, *Statistics, Public Debate and the State, 1800–1945: A Social, Political and Intellectual History of Numbers* (London: Pickering & Chatto Publishers, 2012), p. 155.

the mills could yield.[5] This estimate was a conjecture: it rested on a number of unverified assumptions. Moreover the coefficients were not observed directly by the statistician but suggested by an expert informant. Conjecture enabled Bodio to move logically from stocks (of spinning mills) to flows (of production).

The basis for estimating crop production, the equivalent of spinning mills in the example above, was the most observable and macroscopic of all data: the area under crop. This formed the stock of the nation's productive land. From different kinds of informant, statisticians were then able to obtain rough coefficients of production per unit of area and hence estimate the yearly flow of production. This way of solving the problem was far from peculiar to Italy. On the contrary, Italians devised their system after a careful examination of international best practice.[6] Counting stocks was clearly very advantageous for statisticians. It was possible (at least in principle) to make a complete census of the area under crop in a certain country.

In the case of Italy, the adoption of conjectural statistics was made easier by the operations undertaken in 1886 by the Ministry of Finance for the making of the Italian *cadastre* (*catasto terreni*, hereafter CT) in order to collect the land tax. The CT offered Italian statisticians the model for a different national land survey, this time only intended for statistical purposes and with no relationship with the land tax, the *catasto agrario* (hereafter CA). This included a census of the entire stock of agricultural land divided by crop. The unfortunate similarity of the two names can, and in fact did, give rise to misunderstandings, but the CT and the CA were very different surveys. Instead of the rent of parcels, the CA recorded the extent of areas under different crops and the product per unit of area of a reference year. As Nallo Mazzocchi Alamanni put it when he took over the task of directing the revision of the CA in 1929, the CA was to annual statistics what a still image is to a movie.[7] The figures recorded in the CA served as a base year, while annual statistics were computed using the variation of areas and yields with respect to the base year.

In the first of the following sections, I sketch a short history of Italian agricultural statistics before the crucial date of 1907. In this year, the Ministry of Agriculture, Industry, and Trade (MAIC) ordered a complete renovation of the statistics of agricultural production. The responsibility for this radical reorganization of the Bureau of Agricultural Statistics fell on Ghino Valenti. In the second section, I examine the options that Valenti took into consideration; I discuss in the third section the relationship between the CT and the CA, and in the fourth and fifth sections the experiments that led to the establishment of the CA (sixth section).

5 Giovanni Favero, 'Business Attitudes Toward Statistical Investigation in Late Nineteenth Century Italy: A Wool Industrialist from Reticence to Influence', *Enterprise and Society* 12.2 (2011).

6 Valenti discusses the proceedings of two congresses of the ISI held in St. Petersburg in 1899, and Budapest in 1903.

7 Istituto centrale di statistica, *Catasto agrario 1929* (Roma, 1929–39), 'Premessa', by N. Mazzocchi Alamanni, i, p. 1.

Agrarian statistics before 1907

'Since the very first stages of existence of the Ministry of Agriculture, Industry, and Trade' – so Guido Cavaglieri wrote to the Society of Italian Agriculturalists (SAI) in 1900 – 'the Government was aware of the need to achieve an overview of the real conditions of Italian agriculture; they believed that it was first of all necessary to investigate what area was dedicated to each crop, and what was the ordinary yield that was to be expected from them'.[8] Since national unification in 1861, different systems had been tried. The estimates published in the first *Annuario statistico* by Cesare Correnti and Pietro Maestri were very rough approximations.[9] The Second War of Independence had just finished and the south of Italy was still ravaged by the *briganti*. In 1866, the *comizi agrari* were asked by the government to provide a yearly report on the conditions of agriculture. But the *comizi* were very unevenly spread over the territory of Italy and their reports therefore were unfit to form the basis of comprehensive national statistics. In the 1870s, the chambers of commerce and the *comizi* contributed to *Relazione intorno alle condizioni dell'agricoltura in Italia*, four volumes that contained, province by province, details of the areas under crop, the average production per hectare and the total production of 13 crops.[10] The assessment of average production and of the areas under crop that were contained in the *Relazione* became the basis of yearly statistics.

After 1876, MAIC entrusted the compilation of the provincial statistics of agriculture to the prefects (*prefetti*). Following the French model, the prefects represented the central government in the 69 provinces of the Kingdom. They were also in charge of agricultural statistics.[11] The prefects cabled the data to the Bureau of Agricultural Statistics established by the Directorate of Agriculture at MAIC. In turn, the prefects relied on the data provided by municipalities, chambers of commerce, and *comizi*. The system closely replicated the nineteenth-century French system of agricultural statistics. In France, the yearly harvest figures were collected by the municipalities and

8 Guido Cavaglieri, 'Le statistiche agrarie in Italia', *Bollettino quindicinale della Società degli Agricoltori Italiani* 5.24 (1900), p. 894.

9 On Maestri and Correnti as 'patriotic statisticians', see Silvana Patriarca, *Numbers and nationhood: Writing statistics in nineteenth-century Italy*, Cambridge studies in Italian history and culture (Cambridge: Cambridge University Press, 1996), chs 7 and 8. On Correnti's eventual political career, Marco Soresina, 'Cesare Correnti ministro della cultura', *Società e Storia* 114 (2006).

10 MAIC and Divisione di Agricoltura, *Relazione intorno alle condizioni dell'agricoltura nel quinquennio 1870–1874*, 3 vols (Roma: G. Barbera, 1876–1879). On the *comizi*, see Paola Corti, 'I comizi agrari dopo l'Unità (1866–91)', *Ricerche di storia sociale e religiosa* 3 (1973). On their French model and its function for statistics, see Gérard Theodore and Michel Volle, 'Les statistiques agricoles', in Institut National de la Statistique et des Études Économiques, ed., *Pour une histoire de la statistique: Matériaux* (Paris: Institut national de la statistique et des études économiques, 1977), pp. 501–32.

11 A brilliant study of the prefects' role in collecting statistics can be found in Lucio Gambi, 'Le "statistiche" di un prefetto del regno', *Quaderni storici* 15.45 (1980), pp. 823–66. On the Italian prefects in English, see Nico Randeraad, *Authority in search of liberty: The prefects in liberal Italy*, Scrinium 7 (Amsterdam: Thesis Publ., 1993).

then transmitted to the Ministry of Agriculture by the office of the prefects. Every tenth year, the ministry was supposed to carry out an enquiry to establish the 'standard' year. Enquiries of this kind actually took place in 1840, 1852, 1862, 1882, and 1892.[12]

In Italy, just as in France, the prefecture asked municipalities whether the harvest had been above or below the standard year and by what percentage. The base figure was in the *Relazioni.* They then took the average of this percentage and used it as a guestimate of the variation in the whole province. In this way, MAIC could compute the harvest statistics (using the areas given in *Relazione* as the permanent basis). After 1876 these figures appeared in the *Notizie e studi sulla agricoltura.*[13]

It is hard not to see that this method was imperfect, and the statistical work, as a British newspaper put it, 'was done in a very perfunctory way'.[14] Municipalities differed greatly in size and agricultural vocation, even within the same province. What was the meaning of the average of the variations recorded within a province? Very little. The ministry soon realized this, and the Bureau of Agricultural Statistics began applying a special correction to the data of prefects. But it is not clear how the correction was applied.[15] Facing all sorts of criticisms and protests, in 1898, Minister Francesco Guicciardini was urged to discontinue the publication of figures.[16] Publication in a reduced form was resumed shortly afterward and at the beginning of the twentieth century, MAIC published in its bi-monthly *Bollettino Ufficiale* four classes of data directly relevant to the statistics of agrarian production:

1 The Chambers of Commerce of each province reported the economic trends of the province (*Le condizioni economiche della provincia, Relazione della Camera di Commercio*), in agriculture, manufacturing, and trade. The part dedicated to agriculture contained quantitative data on production and prices explained by discursive commentaries.
2 Every four months, the so-called 'Agrarian News' ('Notizie Agrarie') was published in the Bulletin. These short reports were provided (irregularly) by the prefects and contained exclusively qualitative information on three

12 Polzer, *Statistiche agrarie* considers these investigations among the enquiries that compensated for the limits of flawed statistics. In fact, these enquiries were an essential part of the yearly statistics, see: H. Hitier, 'La statistique agricole de la France', *Annales de Géographie* 8.40 (1899), pp. 350–57. For some reason, French secondary literature (for instance, A. Demangeon, 'La statistique agricole de la France', *Annales de Géographie* 37.210 (1928), pp. 554 and Michel Augé-Laribé, 'Les statistiques agricoles', *Annales de Géographie* 54.294 (1945), pp. 81–92) often repeats that the publication of agricultural statistics began in the 1880s, but this is not true.

13 Cavaglieri, 'Le statistiche agrarie in Italia', p. 895.

14 Ibid., p. 893.

15 For a general look at the pre-Valenti statistics of agricultural production, see Giovanni Federico, 'Per una valutazione critica delle statistiche della produzione agricola italiana dopo l'Unità (1860–1913)', *Società e Storia* 15 (1982), pp. 87–130.

16 Cavaglieri, 'Le statistiche agrarie in Italia', p. 893.

elements: the state of cultivation in the four preceding months, the economic and health conditions of the rural classes, the sanitary and commercial conditions of the livestock. ('The state of the countryside, if it could not be said to be bad, was nevertheless not very satisfactory', we read in one of them.)

3 Every ten days, some office inside MAIC (most likely the Bureau of Agraricultural Statistics) provided summaries of other reports originating from the prefectures. They contained qualitative and vague notions on meteorological conditions and the state of cultivations in Italy in general (with some hints of analysis on the scale of regions or compartments).

The reports included under headings 2 and 3 were especially relevant as forward indicators of harvest.

4 Every year, MAIC published draft reports (the 'Notizie Approssimative') on the total production for six commodities: wheat, wine, rice, corn, olive oil and oranges. They included figures of unitary yield and area under crop by province and 'agrarian region' (that is the usual statistical compartments, Piedmont, Liguria, Lombardy, the Veneto, Emilia Romagna, Tuscany, and so on).[17]

In general, an examination of the *Bollettino Ufficiale* gives the impression that these reports, with the possible exception of the 'Notizie Approssimative', were irregular and far from systematic. Moreover, the information seems rather difficult to compare across time for the same province and between provinces or regions. The problem is not that there were no numbers involved (in fact, qualitative labels such as 'good harvest', 'bad harvest', and so on were ordinarily employed within a system of numerical equivalences that allowed them to be turned into index numbers) but that the reference value was not consistent over the years.[18] As a result, most statisticians, in Italy and abroad, were not satisfied with these numbers, which not only came late but were likely to be deeply unreliable. Besides, they concerned too small a number of products, leaving uncovered products of great commercial importance, such as silk, beans of all kinds, fodder and so on

In 1906, for a number of concurrent reasons that we will examine in the next chapter, Minister Francesco Cocco-Ortu (1842–1929), decided to rebuild

17 Around the early years of the twentieth century, the Prefects were also collecting data on agrarian products for the Army Provincial Commissions for Provisions. The municipalities of each *prefettura* were asked to produce data on the areas under crops and total production in 100kg (quintali) together with information on local industries, combustibles, traders, and so on For an example (concerning the year 1903–04), see Archivio di Stato di Roma, Prefettura di Roma, Gabinetto, b. 1085.

18 For the equivalence between qualitative labels and index numbers, see, in general, Umberto Ricci, *Les bases théoriques de la statistique agricole internationale* (Rome: Imprimerie de l'Institute International d'Agriculture, 1914), pp. 197–9, and, for a similar method in Russia, Alessandro Stanziani, 'Les statistiques des récoltes en Russie, 1905–1928', *Histoire & Mesure* 7.1 (1992), p. 77.

the system as radically as the state could afford.[19] To design the new structure, the minister decided to adopt a plan designed by the agricultural economist Ghino Valenti from the University of Padua.

The arrival of Valenti

In the 1880s, when still in Macerata, Valenti had contributed to the Parliamentary Enquiry on Agriculture, called the Jacini Enquiry. The commissioner for the central regions, Senator Nobili Vitelleschi, assigned to Valenti the task of writing a report on the Marche, Valenti's home region, because Valenti was then the secretary of the local *comizio agrario*. His investigations turned out differently from the reports that the commission had received from other compartments. Valenti not only coordinated the group of local informants, but himself wrote an interesting report that strictly followed 'the norms established by Comm[ander] Bodio', who was then the leading Italian statistician (and secretary of the Institut Statistique International). It is important to underline this early research done for the Jacini Enquiry, because it prefigured the way that Valenti decided to organize the activity of the Bureau of Agricultural Statistics when he was nominated to lead it in 1906.

For the Jacini Enquiry, Valenti had elaborated a 'statistics of properties', based on the data offered by the commission charged with the preparation of the CT in the Marche. The CT offered two very relevant sorts of information. First, it kept records of the size of land properties in each municipality. This enabled the enquirer to calculate the approximate number of landowners and the size of properties. Second, the CT attributed each plot to broad classes of productivity and land use. This was a good point from which to develop statistics of agricultural production.

Valenti divided the whole province of Macerata into groups of municipalities, called *zone*. There were four of these: the area of mountains (*zona appennina* or Montagna), the area of high hills (*zona sub-appennina* or Alta Collina), the area of lower hills (*zona delle colline* or Bassa Collina), and the area of plains (*zona delle vallate* or Pianura). In his correspondence with Nobili Vitelleschi, Valenti did not explain how he had drawn up the *zone*, he simply declared that he had applied a 'synthetic' rather than 'analytic' method.[20] It is evident,

19 F. Cocco-Ortu, a Sardinian lawyer, was Minister for Agriculture, Industry, and Trade in the third cabinet presided over by Giolitti, between 1906 and 1909. His successor was Luigi Luzzatti in a new cabinet directed by the (more) conservative S. Sonnino. Maria Letizia D'Autilia, *L'amministrazione della statistica nell'Italia fascista: Il caso dell'agricoltura* (Roma: Gangemi, 1992), p. 13, seems to imply that the Consultative Commission was established by Minister Luigi Luzzatti in May 1910. This is not correct: the commission was already operating in 1907, as it is shown by the records of its meeting in MAIC, ed., *Esperimenti di statistica agraria in alcune province del Regno* (Roma: Bertero, 1907), fasc. I.

20 'Dirò solo che la divisione delle zone è stata fatta con criterio sintetico, non analitico, avendo riguardo alle condizioni prevalenti e trascurando le peculiarità e le eccezioni' letter of Valenti to

though, that the main criterion for the *zone* was altitude. It is likely that this criterion was chosen because of the determining influence of altitude on agricultural production and patterns of land property.[21] In this research, the CT and the agricultural zones were already playing a fundamental role, and Valenti's approach here anticipates the experiments of 1907.

When in 1906 Cocco-Ortu assigned to him the task of reconstructing the Bureau of Agricultural Statistics, more or less from scratch, Valenti first examined the options that the most renowned experts of agrarian statistics had discussed at various congresses of the International Statistical Institute.[22] He tried to evaluate their respective advantages and their applicability to the case of Italy. The first question to settle was whether statistics were the right form of investigation. Valenti, like Salvioni in 1892, distinguished three forms of investigation: enquiries, statistics, and monographs. So far, monographs and enquiries had been the main instrument employed by the Italian state for understanding agriculture.[23] Valenti underlined the differences between monographs and enquiries, on the one hand, and statistics, on the other.[24]

In Valenti's view, neither monographs nor enquiries could adequately replace a permanently established statistical service, although both forms of investigation could complement general statistics. In his plans, the new service must rely on a stable structure at the central and provincial levels and pursue the highest degree of uniformity of data so that the series on crop production could stretch uniformly over many years and many different regions.

In general, the most challenging part of agricultural statistics was the statistics of crop production: wheat, barley, rice, vegetables, fruit, and so on. It accounted for the largest segment of agriculture's gross product. The two key elements of these statistics were the measure of the area under crops and the yield per hectare. For each of these two figures two aspects were usually taken into consideration. The first was the base year of the statistics, its starting point. The second was the yearly variation.

I will explain this in detail, although I have already referred to this method. Yearly variations in the area under crop could be more easily assessed, in practice, as fractions or percentages of the acreage of a specific base year. The same

Nobili Vitelleschi, in ACS, Giunta parlamentare per l'inchiesta agraria e sul le condizioni della classe agricola in Italia, scatola 12, 69.6.

21 The report was republished in Ghino Valenti, *Studi di politica agraria* (Roma: Athenaeum, 1914), *Introduzione* and *Allegati*; a direct trace of Valenti's contribution to the Jacini Enquiry is in ACS, Giunta parlamentare per l'inchiesta agraria e sulle condizioni della classe agricola in Italia, scatola 12, 69.6; see also Daniela Giaconi, 'Dall'inchiesta agraria agli studi sulla proprietà: Le radici del pensiero di Ghino Valenti e l'affermazione di un metodo d'indagine', *Quaderni Fiorentini* XXXII (2003), pp. 375–460.

22 Valenti, *Per l'ordinamento della statistica agraria in Italia*, pp. 8–10.

23 We have seen in Chapter 3 above, the importance of the Jacini Enquiry and the preliminary work done by the *comizii agrarii*.

24 Giovanni B. Salvioni, 'Ai confini della statistica', *Rassegna di scienze sociali e politiche* 218 (1892), pp. 95–107.

held for unitary yields. So, for instance, a good harvest could be 110 per cent of the base yield per hectare, a bad harvest 75 per cent and so on. Conversion into absolute figures was then easy.

As base value, statisticians could choose a 6- or 12-year average of yields or the 'normal' yield. The value of the yield in a 'normal year' was a quantity determined by appraisers, rather than an observable one; it represented the product yielded by the land under standard weather conditions and standard management.[25] Both the problem of knowing the acreage and that of assessing the unitary yield had been widely debated among international experts of agrarian statistics.[26]

The ISI considered two main options for obtaining this information: direct and indirect surveys (the meaning in this case being very different from the meaning of direct and indirect in regard to enquiries). When the investigators obtained the information from the farmers, they were employing direct methods. This was also called the 'census method', because population censuses were done in this way.[27] In 1898 Great Britain, for instance, about twelve hundred officers of the Inland Revenue were in charge of distributing statistical forms to farmers. On these forms the farmers would report acreage under crop, yield per acre and the number and productivity of their livestock. Ninety-seven per cent of the occupiers of more than one acre of land and of the owners of cattle, sheep or pigs completed and returned the forms.[28] Belgium, whose agrarian statistics enjoyed a considerable reputation, held general and annual censuses of agriculture. In the United States, in contrast, the census of the land stock was taken together with the census of the population, every ten years. Every subsequent year, the census data on the use of land were updated by means of a questionnaire that the Bureau of Statistics sent to a restricted group of farmers. Farmers reported the (presumably) small variations that had occurred over the year in the productivity of land and in its use.[29] Sending questionnaires to

25 For a discussion of 'normality' conditions, see Chapter 6. In his work on American agrarian statistics, E. Didier mentions the fact that it had been proven easier for farmers to indicate proportions rather absolute numbers: Emmanuel Didier, *En quoi consiste l'Amérique? Les statistiques, le new deal et la démocratie*, Série Anthropologie des sciences et des techniques (Paris: Éd. La Découverte, 2009), p. 27. A typical mistake of data reports was to confuse the average year with the normal year and the latter with a good year (when no special meteorological event had damaged the harvest), see Federico, p. 110, n. 75.

26 Theodore M. Pilat, 'Rapport sur la statistique agricole', *Bulletin de l'Institut international de statistique* 11.2 (1899), Émil M. Levasseur, 'Les procédés de la statistique agricole', *Bulletin de l'Institut international de statistique* 13.2 (1903), pp. 1–85. Pilat was the director of the Galician office of statistics in the Austro-Hungarian Empire while Levasseur, vice-president of the ISI, was a celebrated French statistician and a member of the Conseil Supérieur de Statistique since 1885.

27 A. De Polzer thus defined direct methods: 'the collection of data by means of declarations issued by producers' ('l'assunzione dei dati a mezzo di denuncie dei produttori'), Polzer, *Statistiche agrarie*, p. 20.

28 Patrick G. Craigie, 'Memorandum on the methods employed in the collection of the annual Agricultural Statistics of Great Britain', *Bulletin de l'Institut international de statistique* 13.2 (1903), pp. 322–4.

29 Didier, *En quoi consiste l'Amérique?* apparently fails to acknowledge the importance of census data, and focuses exclusively on the assessment of yearly variations.

a more restricted range of people, for instance, by asking only large farmers ('because there is not a great number of them') or experienced farmers, was still among the direct methods.[30]

Statisticians agreed nevertheless that direct methods had significant shortcomings. The first was that farmers might tend to conceal the real figures and declare a lower total than they had secured. They were afraid of taxes. Valenti expected this effect to be especially important in the case of Italy 'where farmers, tortured by taxes, see in any request [from the State] a means devised to make taxes heavier'.[31]

Moreover, the practical difficulties of direct methods grew as the number of landowners and farmers increased, properties grew smaller and the average education of the rural population declined. Emile Levasseur, the famous French statistician, observed: 'in a country where property is extremely subdivided, it is very difficult, it would even be impossible, in the present state, to distribute individual questionnaires'. And the Austrian Theodore Pilat acknowledged that 'this system is not feasible in those countries where the land is heavily fractionated and the rural population is not very well educated to compute exactly the area under crop of their own farms'.[32] Valenti points out that the Italian rural world was characterized by small properties and high rates of illiteracy alongside a general mistrust of state authority. Hence, he concludes 'if Levasseur's considerations hold for many foreign countries, they are much more valuable for Italy [. . .]. If we adopted the same system followed in England [. . .] we could be positive that we would not collect a single trustworthy answer even on the part of the most enlightened people'. Valenti resolutely excluded the option of building his statistics on direct methods.[33] On the other hand, he wanted to overcome the traditional reliance on municipalities and incompetent prefects.

The alternative was that investigators assessed the relevant quantities by themselves. Indirect methods were not ignored in European countries. In Great Britain in 1898, for instance, the average produce of crops (the yield coefficients) was ascertained by approximately 250 skilled estimators.[34] By categorically excluding direct investigations, Valenti was forced to adopt indirect methods not only for production coefficients (as in Britain), but also for the survey of areas under crop (the survey in Britain, as we saw, was obtained by direct methods).

30 Levasseur, p. 65. This seems to have been the way in which Russian statistics were constructed. Martine Mespoulet, 'Statisticiens des zemstva', *Cahiers du monde russe Russie, Empire russe, Union soviétique, États indépendants* 40.4 (1999), p. 588. It is worth noting here that questionnaires alone would have counted as an indirect method of enquiry, according to Coletti's categories discussed in Chapter 3, above.

31 Valenti, *Per l'ordinamento della statistica agraria in Italia*, p. 14.

32 Pilat, 'Rapport sur la statistique agricole', p. 67.

33 Valenti, *Per l'ordinamento della statistica agraria in Italia*, p. 14.

34 Craigie, 'Memorandum on the methods employed', p. 323.

At the international level statisticians agreed that the continental *cadastre* (the fiscal land survey done for collecting land taxes, such as the CT) was an excellent starting point for indirect surveys of the area under crops. For Valenti, such international praise for the use of *cadastres* confirmed the value of the practices he had experimented in the Marche during the Jacini Enquiry.

The Italian CT and its potential

It is conventional to start the story of modern Italian *cadastres* with the *cadastre* of Milan that the Austrian administration of the Duchy of Milan began in the early eighteenth century. This *cadastre* was a complete census and measurement of all the land parcels of the Duchy. The government of the Duchy intended to rationalize the land tax by precisely defining the tax base. The Milanese *cadastre* provided a geometric identification of land parcels and was therefore an example of what is called a geometric *cadastre*.[35] Each parcel was reproduced on a map and described on a paper called a *cadastrino* or *sommarione*. The map and the sommarione were prepared by personnel who had been trained in a special school for surveyors.[36]

The Milanese *cadastre* proved a very successful institution and became the model for similar systems all over Europe. Napoleon in particular disseminated the geometric *cadastre* outside Italy. In his time the *sommarione* included seven columns that carried the identification number of the parcel, the name of its owner, the denomination of the property, the quality of cultivation (*qualità*, that is the type of crop), the disposition of the soil (*giacitura*), the class (*classe)* and the area of the parcel. It is very important to understand these distinctions and the related terminology because they passed into the terminology of the CA and will occur repeatedly in this and subsequent chapters. The identification number allowed the *sommarione* to be linked to the representation of the parcel on the cadastral map. The quality of cultivation described in schematic terms some features of the land use, for instance, whether a parcel was sown with herbaceous plants or planted with trees. The disposition indicated whether the parcel was in the plains, on a hill or in the mountains (*Piano, Colle, Monte*). The classes of parcels were distinguished according to their fertility and productivity. The gross product was determined as a function of quality, disposition and class. After subtracting expenses, the appraisers determined the yearly rent.[37] This rent and all the deductions were fictional

35 The alternatives to geometric *cadastres* were descriptive *cadastres* (*catasto descrittivo*) which contained descriptions only and allowed no precise identification of the properties.

36 On the *cadastre* of Milan in the eighteenth century, see: Gian Rinaldo Carli, *Il censimento di Milano* (Milano: Giovanni Silvestri, 1815) and Ivana Pederzani, *Dall'antico regime alla restaurazione: Profili di storia costituzionale in area lombarda tra Sette e Ottocento*, Scienze storiche, filosofiche, pedagogiche e psicologiche 315 (Roma: Aracne, 2008).

37 Antonio Catizzone and Sabatino Di Filippo, eds, *Un tesoro ritrovato: Dal rilievo alla rappresentazione* (Roma: Gangemi, 2009), p. 30.

measures. The gross product was evaluated at prices below market prices, and expenses were intentionally overestimated. Nevertheless the result gave an impressively precise and consistent image of agriculture.

During the nineteenth century, following the Napoleonic example, many Italian states established geometric *cadastres* on this model. With the unification of Italy, the new country had a great number of different *cadastres* (some geometric and some merely descriptive). Such variety made it very difficult to apply a single and fair land tax.[38] Consequently, after long debates, on 1 March 1886 a law was passed that initiated a unified CT. The promoter of the law was the famous economist Angelo Messedaglia, a friend and inspirer of Valenti.[39]

Messedaglia's proposal followed rather precisely the Napoleonic model, and distinguished the qualities, dispositions and classes of the parcels. Considering the complexity of the undertaking, it is no surprise that the operations for the implementation of the law of 1886 proved slow and expensive. The CT was completed only in the 1950s and only thanks to aerial photography.[40] From its beginnings, however, the CT was considered a source of invaluable information on Italy's agriculture.

In the early 1900s, while a professor at the University of Padua, Valenti took advantage of the fact that the Ministry of Finance was carrying out the the cadastral survey of the province of Padua. He asked for access to the survey in order to compile the province's agricultural statistics. When Cocco-Ortu summoned him to Rome, in 1906, Prof. Valenti hoped that the new Italian CT, combined with the geometric *cadastres* of the pre-unification states, would enable him to form a complete inventory of Italy's cultivation by areas and productivity, the CA. In contrast with the CT, the CA served mere statistical, not tax, purposes. It did not report the rent of individual properties, but the area under crops and the unitary yields of municipalities and provinces.

The case of Padua, 1906

Let us examine in more detail Valenti's method for obtaining the areas under crops and per hectare yields from cadastral data. Theoretically, the *sommarione* of the *cadastre* already gave a rough account of the type of crops, but

38 Mario Romani, *Storia economica d'Italia nel secolo XIX* (Bologna: Il mulino, 1982) on the *sperequazione* after the Unification, p. 224ff.

39 Messedaglia was one of the economists of the Scuola Lombardo-Veneta, see: Riccardo Faucci, *L'economia politica in Italia: Dal Cinquecento ai nostri giorni*, Collana di storia dell'economia politica (Torino: UTET Libreria, 2000), pp. 201f. On the economic conception behind the *cadastre*, see, first of all, Angelo Messedaglia, *Il Catasto e la perequazione: Relazione parlamentare, nuova edizione a cura di Luigi Messedaglia, pref. di Giuseppe Tassinari* (Bologna: Licinio Cappelli, 1936) and Luigi Einaudi, *La terra e l'imposta,* Nuova Universale Einaudi 155 (Torino: Einaudi, 1974). On the practice of cadastral estimation at the beginning of the twentieth century, see Vittorio Niccoli, *Economia rurale, agrotimesia e computisteria agraria* (Torino: UTET, 1927).

40 On the complexity of surveying the whole country, see Catizzone and Di Filippo, *Un tesoro ritrovato.*

divided into individual properties. By using cadastral maps to guide the field inspection of the parcels, it was relatively easy to calculate the areas under each crop, to determine, for example, that a parcel that appeared generically as arable land on the *sommarione* of the CT was actually sown with wheat and barley. The information about disposition and classes that the *sommarione* recorded were also useful in dividing the whole stock of land into subsets of roughly equivalent productivity. This was important since surveyors could more easily obtain the per hectare yields for the single classes and dispositions, supposing that each of them gave a more or less equal yield, rather than assessing an average value for a large territory where productivity and yields were likely to vary greatly.

In practice, the work needed for the statistics was more complicated. Surveyors needed bits of information, such as the crop rotation used, that was not visible either in the CT or on a single inspection, but was known only to local farmers and landowners. In 1905, Valenti was able to prepare the CA for the province of Padua and he reported the crops grown and the fertility of the land, but only thanks to the support of the local *comizio agrario* and of the local officials of the ministry of finance, who were compiling the CT.

Once completed, the CA offered a reference term for the area under crops and the unitary yield of the different classes of soil. By assuming this reference term, the making of annual statistics for subsequent years became significantly easier. For the annual statistics, instead of making the complete survey anew (a new CA), it was sufficient to record the variations that occurred in the areas under crops and in the coefficients of yields per hectare.[41] Only after a relatively long period would it have been necessary to repeat the whole operation.

Since the CT recorded all proprietors by municipality, the CA also was to be based on municipalities. Let us examine the sample form that Valenti prepared for the municipality of S. Pietro in Gù in the province of Padua, which he attached to the report to Minister Cocco-Ortu. The first page represents the form to be filled in by the person in charge of the statistics (the so-called commissioner) for ‘herbaceous plants’ (*Modello A*). In the top left corner we see the indication of the province (Padua), while in the top right one, the name of the municipality the sheet refers to (S. Pietro in Gù).

Let us concentrate on the first five columns of sheet 1 (*foglio 1*). The first and second columns list the definition that Valenti found in the CT: the first column reports the qualities of soil where herbaceous plants are grown: arable, irrigated arable, and so on, while the second column indicates the classes for each quality. For some qualities, for instance, arable land, there are five classes (I–V); for others, such as permanent rice fields, there is a single class (*unica*).

41 In fact the difference between the CA and the CT was not self-evident. At the meeting of the Consultative Commission for Agrarian Statistics held at MAIC on 15 January 1907, Antonio de Viti de Marco essentially criticized Valenti for replicating the *cadastre*, MAIC, ed., *Esperimenti di statistica agraria in alcune province del Regno*, p. 339.

The third column (divided into hectares, ares and centares) gives the area according to the CT. These areas are obtained by summing up the areas of parcels belonging to different proprietors that the CT assigned to each quality and class. The fourth column gives the variations possibly registered during the operations for the *classamento* and in this case is blank.

Up to the fourth column all the data are taken from the CT and basically describe the situation of 1886. The fifth column, instead, gives the areas as the commissioner and his collaborator found them in 1905–06, when visually inspecting the fields. Using the *cadastre* for preparing the CA figures on areas meant that Valenti and his team could break down the global survey of the provinces in a great number of smaller and much easier inspections of those individual parcels where variations had occurred since 1886. It was easier to identify small variations than to assess large areas anew. This fact made the CT so important for the CA and, in turn, the CA so valuable for statistics. The work of the commissioner was not limited to assessing the gross areas. The important number was the net area, which is reported in column 13, after different kinds of waste.

On the right of the main frame there is a smaller 'frame n.1', *Production of wheat for the year 1906*. This smaller frame is the first of a series of five, each of which presents the data for a specific crop, out of those that rotate on the different soil qualities and classes (the rotation in use is noted at the bottom of the page). For wheat, for instance, we can read the cultivated area (6 hectares and 50 ares in the case of arable land, class I), the yield per hectare (12 quintals) and the total production obtained by multiplying the cultivated area by the yield per hectare (in the case of arable land, class I, 78 quintals).[42] Coefficients of the yields per hectare were obtained from local correspondents, selected from those who volunteered. Although the commissioner and his collaborator would verify the likelihood of such numbers by direct survey, it was crucial that they could rely on insiders and that they could apply such coefficients to all similar plots with a reasonable degree of approximation in the results.

Very similar forms were devised also for fodder plants (*Modello B*) and arboreal cultivations (*Modello C*).[43]

The statistics for Padua had appeared In the *Bollettino Ufficiale* of MAIC in 1907.[44] The contrast with the more traditional reports from the other provinces was striking.[45]

42 Unitary yields are provided in quintals per hectares, i. e., only in terms of units of areas. This measure derives from the Italian 1886 *cadastre*. Alternative and widespread measures presented the unitary yield per hectare also in relationship with the quantity of sown seeds (the Tuscan *cadastres* for instance worked like this): Marco Marsili Libelli, 'La provincia di Firenze e il nuovo catasto', *Atti della reale Accademia economico-agraria dei Georgofili di Firenze* XC (IX della V serie) (1912), p. 400.

43 Valenti, *Per l'ordinamento della statistica agraria in Italia*, pp. 38f.

44 *Bollettino Ufficiale del Ministero di Agricoltura*, fascicolo VIII, pp. 689f.

45 Valenti, *Per l'ordinamento della statistica agraria in Italia*, pp. 38ff.

The experiments 1907–08

Replicating elsewhere what Valenti had done in Padua was a vast and difficult undertaking. It required collaboration from the competing interest groups that existed in local contexts that differed so greatly from province to province.[46] Valenti and Cocco-Ortu therefore decided to try Valenti's method in a small number of provinces where for various reasons they could rely on local support. They called these pilot projects 'experiments'. The minister was able to funnel into their experiments funds from MAIC's budget ('very modest funds and collected only by means of expedients'), to a total of L. 40,000.[47]

The 15 pilot projects served to check whether Valenti's method for constructing the CA was compatible with the different *cadastres* available in Italy (those made before 1886 in the former Italian states), and in different social contexts. Experiments were undertaken in cooperation with local agricultural associations and prefectures. Valenti directed the central office in Rome, while the minister nominated the provincial commissioners and the committees for 15 provinces.

The situation was far from being the same in the 15 provinces involved. There were dramatic differences in the strength of the state administration and of civil society, but, for the application of Valenti's technique, the most relevant difference followed from the fact that the CT begun in 1886 did not cover all of the provinces. By 1907, in fact, there were three possible situations with regard to the *cadastre*: out of 69 provinces in the whole Kingdom, only 27 could rely (but not always entirely) on the new CT, 23 had older geometric surveys from the pre-unification states (but the Tuscan geometric *cadastre* was unsuitable for Valenti's aims),[48] 19 had only descriptive *cadastres* (without maps). Different operations had to be undertaken in the three cases.

Where some sort of geometric survey was available that could be relied upon (CT or any geometric *cadastre* except the Tuscan one), special effort was put into updating the data, following the method applied in Padua.[49] As central commissioner Valenti prepared the forms, laying great importance on using only one type of form for all the provinces. Although in principle he acknowledged that better forms could be devised by single commissioners or by some local committees, strict uniformity was indispensable for the success of the whole operation.

46 See Chapter 5 below for a more detailed analysis of the network that Valenti put in place.

47 L. 14 July 1907, n. 535, 'On the census of livestock and agrarian statistics'.

48 The Tuscan *cadastres* (the former Grand Duchy had more than one *cadastre* for different parts of its territory) were geometric but it did not present qualities and classes. The parcels were appraised individually to avoid systematic errors; see: Marsili Libelli, 'La provincia di Firenze e il nuovo catasto'.

49 Also for this reason, landowners generally expected that the extension of the *cadastre* would result in many areas in tax reliefs: ibid. Similar claims were also made by southern landowners to the committee of the Faina Enquiry in Abruzzo and Molise. Since it was very difficult to reconstruct the 1886 situation after years or decades, it seems likely that in determining revenue and rent wide margins of bargaining were left to landowners and assessors.

The forms were exactly the same as those we saw used in Padua. For each municipality, the commissioner was supposed to complete one form for each of three main groups of cultivation: form A for herbaceous cultivation (ranging from wheat to beans, corn and tomatoes), form B for fodder (spontaneous or cultivated), and form C for arboreal cultivation (trees and vines).[50] Special forms were distributed among the commissioner's correspondents to gather information. Finally, the commissioners copied all the data onto a summary sheet.[51]

The hardest problem was deciding how to survey those provinces where no *cadastre* could be drawn upon. This was a significant technical problem that had to be solved taking into consideration two major constraints: the survey had to be cheap and it had to be fast. A solution came from Vittorio Niccoli who was in charge of the statistical operations in Florence. He devised a method for compiling the CA that was applicable where Valenti's was not.

In 1907 Niccoli, who taught in Pisa, had become a respected authority in the field of agricultural economics and valuation (*estimo ed economia rurale*).[52] In the province of Florence, the surveys for the CT of 1886 had not yet begun by 1906 (they would start only in 1912) and the Tuscan *cadastre* of the 1830s, although it was a geometric *cadastre* based on maps, did not specify classes and qualities. It was thus meaningless for Valenti's CA. Niccoli, therefore, decided to bypass the cadastral surveys and start directly from the military maps of the *Istituto Geografico Militare* (IGM, the army ordnance survey).

These maps were available at a scale of 1:25,000 and, for certain areas, 1:10,000. The first problem for Niccoli was to know exactly the area of each municipality. The maps came in sheets called *tavolette*. In order to calculate the measurement, the margins of each *tavoletta* and the municipal borders that they included had to be redrawn on a robust sheet of tracing paper. The area could then be integrated either by means of the planimeter or by counting the number of squares that the borders included on the grid of a sheet of graph paper.

Once this preliminary operation had been completed, the territory of each municipality had to be divided into uniform areas according to their destination and cultivation. The maps already roughly recorded the qualities and the disposition *(giacitura)* of the different soils.[53] The surveyors (the commissioner and his collaborators) had to directly register these rough distinctions by means of abbreviations and conventional signs on the tracing paper. Equipped with the tracing paper on which he had drawn the municipal borders, with the map and a notebook, the surveyor was now ready to leave for the field.

50 For the instruction, MAIC, ed., *Esperimenti di statistica agraria in alcune province del Regno* fasc. I, pp. 18ff. On the summary sheet called *Modello II*, see Istituto centrale di statistica, *Le rilevazioni statistiche in Italia dal 1861 al 1956 modelli di rilevazione* (Roma, 1959), p. 19; unfortunately I could find no example of this *Modello II.*

51 MAIC, ed., *Esperimenti di statistica agraria in alcune province del Regno*, p. 25.

52 For Niccoli and appraisal techniques, see also Chapter 6.

53 For the IGM maps and the representation of agriculture on them, see Franco Farinelli, 'La cartografia della campagna nel Novecento', in *Storia d'Italia* (Torino: Einaudi, 1976), pp. 626–54.

It was important for him to acquaint himself with the places and the access roads, so that the operations could proceed smoothly and with the least effort. Wherever possible, Niccoli suggested travelling around by bicycle. The survey operations proper should start from a high point: a hilltop or the top of a tower or bell tower (just like cartographic surveys!) From this vantage point, the surveyor would be able to see a large portion of territory, the limits of which had to be drawn on the tracing paper. Within this territory, the surveyor had to identify areas under similar cultivation. For each he had to indicate the proportions of the whole into in which the different uses of land were divided, for instance: one fifteenth non-productive; one tenth garden; one half sown with vines; the rest pasture.

During the inspections, the surveyors had to ascertain the exactitude of the proportions preliminarily made on the tracing paper and to add more details. By means of a code of abbreviations, all the different crops had to be recorded on the tracing paper. But the surveyor was supposed to supplement information on crops with information on qualities of the sort that Niccoli attributed to agrarian economics proper: 1) the average ratio between the area that was cultivated and the areas used by buildings, roads, bridges and so on; 2) the fertility of the soil; 3) the crops and the crop rotation in use; 4) the average numbers and types of plant for arboreal cultivation (vines and olive trees in particular). Surveyors should note all these data in the field book, at least one page for each class of each quality.

In fact, the surveyor did not observe elements 1–4 over the entire area. He looked only at specific parcels and farms that he characterized as 'typical' and representative for the area. The ratio of the different crops measured for the typical farm would be taken to represent the ratio in the whole area observed. A number, marked on the notebook and repeated on the tracing paper, showed where 'the parcels that were assumed to be of average type [*tipo medio*] and which the notes actually refer to' were located in the map. This allowed the accuracy of the surveyor to be checked. It should be noted that, as Niccoli often repeated, the whole survey operation should not aim at accuracy in its details, but in the general picture. General accuracy, rather than local exactitude was the underlying principle of the entire CA: Valenti and the other experts who participated in the CA were confident that the Law of Large Numbers, the *deus ex machina* of statistics, would make errors irrelevant for the aggregate.[54]

Once all these field operations were completed, the surveyor had two more things to do at his desk: first, integrate the areas of the different qualities; and, second, compute the actual area under each crop and their annual output. The first operation was easily accomplished, as we have seen, by applying a millimeter grid on the tracing paper (in fact, instead of graph paper, Niccoli suggested using special glass slabs on which grids had been drawn). The second operation was achieved by using the notes on the agricultural economy (1–4 above).

54 MAIC, ed., *Esperimenti di statistica agraria in alcune province del Regno*, p. 32.

This meant that the assessment of yearly output required a preliminary operational definition of a typical farm. Only in this way, the surveyors could categorize the land stock according to typical rotations and classes of equivalent productivity.[55] This part of the work could only be done by surveyors trained in land valuation.

As Niccoli explains, for the case of Florence, the achievement of production figures was 'facilitated, [. . .], by the close acquaintance of the surveyor [sc. Niccoli himself] and his main collaborator dott. Tito Pestelli with the way that properties are managed in Tuscany'. Such prior knowledge of local conditions, acquired through many years of fieldwork experience, allowed the agrarian expert to identify 'some typical farms', where he could study 'the annual average subdivision of the land into different crops'.[56]

The data observed in typical farms were deemed representative for what Valenti called '*zone agrarie*'. An 'agricultural zone' (*zona agraria*) was a group of municipalities that shared similar conditions of soil disposition (*giacitura*). These municipalities shared some common patterns of agricultural exploitation, such as the same crop rotation and the same techniques, the same requirements for fertilizer, the same machines, the same contracts, and so on. *Zone agrarie* were the fundamental units of the CA.

The agricultural *Cadastre* nationwide, 1909–10

The pilot projects demonstrated that the agricultural *cadastre*, a huge inventory of the whole stock of Italian land, classified according to crops and fertility and coupled with the production coefficients of each category of land, was feasible. On 1 April 1909, King Vittorio Emanuele III signed a royal decree which charged the Bureau of Agricultural Statistics (Section III of Division VII of the General Directorate of Agriculture) with the task of extending the CA to the whole kingdom. The CA for the whole of Italy was completed between 1907 and 1910, and stretched over 695 agrarian zones and 69 provinces. (In the next chapter, I discuss the network of observers and supporters that made this extension possible.) Once the CA was completed, the Bureau of Agricultural Statistics at MAIC could determine the figures for agricultural output. The agrarian year 1910–11 was the first year when the figures of output were computed using the new system.

After 1910, the commissioners in charge of statistics in each province recorded the changes that occurred in the area under crops and in the productivity per hectare. They did not record all the changes, but only those

55 For the concept of classes of equivalence: see Alain Desrosières, *La politique des grandes nombres: Histoire de la raison statistique* (Paris: La Découverte, 1993).

56 MAIC, ed., *Esperimenti di statistica agraria in alcune province del Regno*, p. 34. Niccoli's system was presented to the consultative commission on 5 November 1907. Niccoli also gave a practical demonstration of the system on 11 November 1907, p. 346.

that they believed would have a permanent and systematic character. Small changes, in fact, due to their idiosyncratic and accidental character, had a very high probability of being offset by other changes happening elsewhere in the same area. It was enough to update the distribution of crops in the different areas and the yields per hectare; thanks to the coefficients of typical farms, the figures of total production for an 'agricultural zone' could be easily conjectured.[57]

The more stable the agricultural world, the more accurate the conjecture was. Smaller variations could be assessed more easily. At the beginning, the CA should have been wholly renewed every five years, but the outbreak of the war in 1915 imposed an indefinite deferral of a new CA. But the system seemed to work fairly well for a while, and Valenti and his collaborators congratulated themselves enthusiastically: 'We remember [. . .] that when the International Institute of Agriculture received the first incoming results produced by the new agrarian statistics of Italy, many said: "Italy, which used to be in the last place, has now taken over the first one"'.[58]

The figures of agricultural output and their analysis were published, together with other related inquiries, in the new *Notizie periodiche di statistica agraria*.[59] In 1911, MAIC began publishing the CA itself, with the volume dedicated to Lazio, Umbria, and the Marche, Valenti's home region. The CA sheets presented the data for the area under crop in the year 1910 and the figures for the unitary yields of the previous years. Moreover, the CA also recorded the unitary yield that the land appraisers attributed to each quality and class as its potential in normal conditions of climate and land management (called normal yield). Valenti would have liked to publish the 12-year average value of the yield rather than this potential yield (which was a theoretical value), but the available historical series was not long enough and the normal value was considered the best solution.

Agrarian zones constituted the first level of data aggregation in the CA. There had been intense discussion among statisticians on whether to provide statistics for administrative (and consequently 'artificial') units or 'natural regions', as proposed by the Bavarian statistician Georg Mayr. Agrarian zones were a sort of compromise between the need to rely on the administrative grid of the state and the wish to describe real phenomena.[60] Agrarian zones

57 In any case, agrarian statistics were considered generally less accurate than other statistics, L. Bodio for instance claimed at the meeting of the Consultative Commission, on 10 February 1907, ibid., p. 340. For the lower degree of approximation in agrarian statistics, see also Polzer, *Statistiche agrarie, cenni storici*.

58 Ghino Valenti, 'La statistica agraria quale rappresentazione dell'economia rurale italiana', in Ghino Valenti, ed., *L'Italia agricola e il suo avvenire* (Roma 1919), p. 73.

59 The *Notizie periodiche di statistica agraria* were originally published by MAIC. In 1923 they migrated together with the service of Agrarian Statistics to the new Istituto di Economia e Statistica Agraria.

60 A trace of this debate can be found in Émil M. Levasseur, 'La statistique graphique', in Statistical Society of London, ed., *Jubilee Volume of the Statistical Society of London* (London, 1885), p. 242.

came to represent the basic units of Italian agriculture in terms of productive conditions and became the basis for subsequent research in agricultural economics.[61]

For each province the agrarian zones combined according to their prevailing geographical character to form three different agrarian regions corresponding to the three possible dispositions of soil (*giacitura*) recorded by the *cadastre*: mountain, hill, or plain. Data were eventually summarized for the whole province. When the CA was generalized, the provinces were aggregated into the usual statistical compartments, the progenitors of the current administrative regions (Piedmont, Lombardy, Liguria, the Veneto and so on). This presentation on multiple layers had many advantages over the presentation by provinces usually offered by the *Notizie provvisorie*. The CA contained more detailed data. The subdivision in agrarian zones showed the inner variability of each province in terms of agricultural economy.[62] The partition by *agrarian regions* corresponded roughly to intuitive realities (the mountains of Pistoia, for instance, or the low plains of Bassano) that were already part of the basic geography of agricultural economists and state administration. Statisticals were thus significant for approaching issues of policy, such as the 'depopulation of mountainous areas' or 'the southern latifundia' and contributed to the typogical narrative with which we begin to be familiar. The aggregation of data into huge statistical compartments followed, instead, representational practices deeply rooted at the political level.[63]

The numbers contained in the CA, and hence the figures provided yearly by MAIC, were conjectures. If we deconstruct, as this chapter attempts to do, the conjectures, we can see that they rested on a multi-layered process. The first layer was constituted by the cartographers and their knowledge of the territory. This ensured completeness. The ancient practices of cadastral surveys, with their numerous staff, formed the second level. They divided the total area of geographers into agricultural categories of class and quality. Then, agricultural economists disaggregated and recombined cadastral data to produce a still image of land, partitioned into specific crops.

They were able to attain such a degree of detail because instead of pursuing a complete survey, they focused on representative types, but by their reliance on the concept of typical, they blurred the distinction between statistics and other forms of social investigation, and an apparent circularity emerges.

61 See for instance, the very influential Arrigo Serpieri, *Guida a ricerche di economia agraria,* Studi e monografie / Istituto Nazionale di Economia Agraria 1 (Roma: Treves Dell'Ali, 1929).

62 G. Valenti, 'Introduzione' to MAIC, Direzione generale statistica e. del lavoro, *Catasto agrario del Regno d'Italia: Compartimento del Lazio* (Roma: Bertero, 1911).

63 On political compartments see Silvana Patriarca, 'How many Italies? Representing the South in official statistics', in Jane Schneider, ed., *Italy's 'Southern Question': Orientalism in one country* (Oxford and New York, 1998), pp. 77–97. Since compartments corresponded to a great extent to the pre-unitary States, they made visible the historical legacy that was thought to weight on the many 'agricultural Italies'.

On the one hand, Valenti argued that monographs needed preliminary statistics in order to identify types. On the other hand, we saw that the entire CA rested on the preliminary identification of typical farms.[64] The contradiction is only apparent, in fact. Agrarian statistics had to start somewhere, and they started with the experience of the practitioners in the field: agronomists, agrarian economist, rural engineers. The CA was realized by involving in its making people (almost invariably men) who possessed a robust knowledge of local conditions. Such an experience, in turn, was validated by the consensus reached among local notables within the provincial statistical committees. Agricultural economists were part of a network of local informants, mostly farmers, and farmers' organizations. Such a network is the object of the next chapter.

64 A contradiction of this kind is actually reminiscent of the dicta of double-headed Janus in Bruno Latour, *Science in action: How to follow scientists and engineers through society* (Cambridge, MA: Harvard Univ. Press, 1987) in particular where the 'science-in-the-making' head states that 'the machine (in our case the statistical service) will work when the relevant people are convinced' (p. 10).

5 Stakeholder statistics[1]

The Italian agricultural statistics of 1910 were the final results of a general mobilization of agricultural élites. It was the political representatives of agriculturalists who insisted in parliament, year after year, that the Ministry of Agriculture, Industry, and Trade should fund finance agricultural statistics. But it was the organizations of agriculturalists that mobilized the expertise that statistics required. Valenti himself occupied his position because of his connections with these organizations. Even more importantly, it was agriculturalists, who, through their local associations, provided the local expertise that, as noted above, Valenti's project needed to draw upon to be successful. The organizations of the landed élites compensated for the proverbial inefficiencies of prefectural offices,[2] and directed the whole effort.

The reorganization of the Bureau of Agricultural Statistics carried out by Valenti and Cocco-Ortu was influenced by two tendencies that dominated Italian statistics after 1901, when Luigi Bodio left the General Directorate of Statistics. One tendency was to spread statistical knowledge within the administration, to create independent statistical offices in the different branches of the administration, and to weaken the General Directorate of Statistics.[3] From this trend arose the specialized and autonomous character of the Bureau of Agricultural Statistics under Valenti. In contrast with the recruitment practices of the Italian ministries of the early twentieth century, still staffed with generic and non-specialist functionaries, the autonomy of

1 An abridged version of this chapter appeared as Federico D'Onofrio, 'Les statistiques agricoles de l'Italie libérale et les porteurs d'intérêts (1907–1929)', in Danielle Fraboulet, Clotilde Druelle-Korn and Pierre Vernus, eds, *Les organisations patronales et la sphère publique* (Rennes: Presses Universitaires de Rennes, 2013), pp. 143–52.

2 Maria Letizia D'Autilia, *L'amministrazione della statistica nell'Italia fascista: Il caso dell'agricoltura* (Roma: Gangemi, 1992).

3 Dora Marucco, *L'amministrazione della statistica nell'Italia unita* (Roma-Bari: Laterza, 1996), pp. 170ff., and Giovanni Favero, *Le misure del regno: Direzione di statistica e municipi nell'Italia liberale,* Ricerche 19 (Padova: Poligrafo, 2001), p. 8.

the Bureau of Agricultural Statistics required it to be staffed with specialized personnel.[4]

The other trend was toward a greater participation of civil society in the production of statistics, either directly (as is the case of the enquiries of the Società Umanitaria di Milano, SUM), or through collaboration with the statistical offices of the state. The autonomy of the Bureau of Agricultural Statistics was, therefore, justified both by the need for specific expertise in agriculture (rather than in statistics) and by its function as a point of contact between the Ministry and the agriculturalists. Agricultural experts who were materially in charge of the compilation of data were at the same time the representatives of an abstract methodology of investigation and the agents of the landed élites and the state.

As in the case of the Milanese *cadastre* of the eighteenth century, the statistical surveys of the CA were executed 'at every stage with the contribution and guidance of those who could have a legitimate interest in the operation', which meant of course prominently the landed classes.[5] In relation to current participatory government, I have called this approach to gathering statistics 'stakeholder statistics'.

The name is somewhat ironic. In the theory of corporate social responsability, stakeholders are convened in order to participate in the decision process, which is usually considered to be an inclusive process. In the case of my stakeholder statistics, it must not be forgotten that the stakeholders were mostly landowners and large tenants who controlled the agricultural organizations: it was their properties and businesses that were at stake. They expressed a demand for statistics, but also demonstrated a certain lack of trust towards the government, and had – or hadn't – the will to participate in the making of statistics.

The existing Italian literature on the country's statistics has stressed the weakness of the Italian state, and has discussed the deviations from a centralized prototype of statistical activity as deficiencies of the Italian administration.[6] The dominating historiographical model has been that of 'statistical observatories',[7] which marked at the same time the centralization of data and the growth of autonomy for statisticians within the administration. According to this view, the creation of the Istituto Centrale di Statistica (ICS, now ISTAT) in 1926 marked the beginning of a more efficient statistical service in the country. The

4 Carlo Desideri, *L'amministrazione dell'Agricoltura (1910–1980)*, Paperback/Officina 9 (Roma: Officina, 1981); Linda Giuva and M. Guercio, 'I ministeri economici', in G. Melis, ed., *L'amministrazione centrale dall'Unità alla Repubblica. Le strutture e i dirigenti* (Bologna: Il mulino, 1992), pp. 69–213.

5 Angelo Messedaglia, *Il Catasto e la perequazione: Relazione parlamentare, nuova edizione a cura di Luigi Messedaglia, pref. di Giuseppe Tassinari* (Bologna: Licinio Cappelli, 1936), p. 33, on the *Cadastre* of Milan.

6 Marucco, *L' amministrazione della statistica nell'Italia unita*.

7 I refer again to Theodore M. Porter, 'The statistical office as a social observatory', *Centaurus* 49 (2007), pp. 258–60.

ICS took over agricultural statistics after a reorganization that we examine at the end of this chapter.

The participative model and the ICS responded to different needs. The choice of participatory statistics was not simply a response to the weakness of the central administration. In the devolution of the most important tasks to local forces we should not see merely a resigned expedient for gathering data, after macroscopic mistakes had discredited the figures of the prefects. The first director of the revitalized Bureau of Agricultural Statistics, instead, expressed a fully fledged 'ethic of producers' and a consistent vision for the civil service. He accused the central administration of being hypertrophic and remote from the interests of the productive classes.[8] Valenti was openly taking sides in a characteristic debate on centralization, coordination, and decentralization.[9]

The direct involvement of local productive classes in the making of statistics was therefore a step towards *discentramento* (decentralization), which brought producers and the administration closer. Moreover, it was an alternative to the wide range of projects that circulated in those years concerning the political representation of agricultural interests.[10] Agriculture and agricultural statistics required proximity and fine-tuned adjustment to local peculiarities. Participative statistics mirrored the desire that the new agricultural statistics should be sensitive to the 'many agricultural Italies' whose existence Stefano Jacini had emphasized.

Unfortunately, the *discentramento* that dominated the making of the CA in 1910 is reflected in the geographical dispersion of the relevant archives. I decided therefore to focus on a few well-preserved archives, in particular, those of the Società Agricola di Lombardia (SAL). My reconstruction of the network behind the CA of 1910 is based mainly on the material preserved there and on the published sources. They were especially valuable because the archives of MAIC at the ACS, and of ISTAT, bear no trace of the Bureau of Agricultural Statistics.

Lobbying for statistics

The allocation of funds from the budget of the Ministry of Agriculture, Industry and Trade to Valenti's experiments and eventually to the nationwide

8 Ghino Valenti, *Per la riforma della pubblica amministrazione: studi* (Unitas: Milano, 1919) and Desideri, *L'amministrazione dell'Agricoltura (1910–1980)*, pp. 26, 28.

9 Jean-Pierre Beaud and Jean-Guy Prévost, 'La forme est le fond la structuration des appareils statistiques nationaux (1800–1945)', *Revue de synthèse* 118.4 (1997), pp. 419–56.

10 On Maggiorino Ferraris' proposal see Sandro Rogari, *Rappresentanza corporazione conflitto: ceti e figure dell'Italia rurale fra Otto e Novecento,* Politica e storia (Centro editoriale toscano, 1998) and Luigi Musella, *Proprietà e politica agraria in Italia, 1861–1914,* Storia 23 (Napoli: Guida, 1984), p. 77f.; Alessandro Garelli supported diverging ideas in Alessandro Garelli, *La rappresentanza dell'agricoltura al Congresso dei comizi agrari in Cuneo, 17 settembre 1905* (Cuneo: Tip. Oggero, 1905) at the National Congress of *comizi agrari* that took place in Cuneo.

reorganization of the service of agricultural statistics was not easy to arrange. Behind the CA of 1910 and the ensuing statistics of agricultural production, we can easily discern a relatively compact interest group. Since the parliamentary debates on the allocation of funding to agricultural statistics did not provoke many contributions, the names of those who spoke in them are significant.

In 1907, in the middle of the Giolittian boom, when Cocco-Ortu proposed the use of part of the budget for the statistical experiments, Giovanni Battista Miliani, praised the initiative of the government in reforming agrarian statistics by arguing that the new statistics would finally allow the nation's agriculture to 'get to know itself'. Hitherto, lacking statistics, MAIC had been something like 'a private firm without its inventory'. When negotiating trade agreements with other countries, Italy had been 'in a condition of inferiority with respect to other countries'.[11]

The year after, when parliament discussed the allocation of 500,000 Lire, not a small sum for MAIC, in order to implement the agricultural *cadastre* nationwide,[12] the proposer of the law in the Chamber of Deputies, Casciani, claimed that 'no country could have a beneficial economic constitution without knowing with the closest possible approximation the extent of her industrial and agrarian production'. Such knowledge was necessary not only 'in order to assess the sum of the annual production which forms the stock of the nation' but also in order to compare it 'with the needs of internal consumption and the demands of the international market to which our product can be easily and profitably sent'. While the government provided more or less reliable statistics of industrial production, Italy 'did not yet possess agrarian statistics compiled with rigorous methods that enable us to know with the degree of exactitude that such investigations permit the extension of various crops, their total and per hectare production, the distribution per region, or the ways they are affected by new methods of cultivation and meteorological events'.

The need for new agrarian statistics could not be contested: 'in the rapid economic transformation that our country underwent in past years, knowledge as accurate as possible of the different trends of our agrarian production is indispensable'. Casciani underlined the fact that agricultural statistics allowed people to compare demand (domestic and international) and supply: for which products there was excessive production, and which products should be encouraged. 'Agrarian statistics can offer useful elements to impress on national agriculture a direction more responsive to the country's economy, and to signal to the

11 Camera dei Deputati, *Atti parlamentari*, 1 tornata del 12 giugno 1907, p. 15750.

12 In June 1908, Cocco-Ortu, the Treasury Minister, Carcano, and the Minister for Post and Telegraphs, Schanzer, presented the measures that became the Law 2.VII.1908, n. 358. The law was promoted in the Senate by Di Collobiano, Bottoni, Colonna Francesco, Sonnino, and Mosso, see MAIC, *L'azione del Ministero nell'ultimo triennio* (Roma: Tip. G. Civelli, 1909).

government in which branches of agrarian industry, in which regions, and by which means, its action has to be intensified'.[13]

In 1908, Miliani and Casciani joined the Agricultural Parliamentary Committee; behind their lobbying we can see the groups of Raineri's Federazione Italiana dei Consorzi agrari and SAI. The leadership of SAI and the Society's president Raffaele Cappelli also used pressure to obtain new and more sophisticated agricultural statistics. From the new statistics, SAI leaders expected much: full knowledge of Italy's production would enable the government to fine-tune its policy of tariffs (a highly relevant issue in those years, given the growth of protection for sugar, and the crisis of old markets for vine products), but it would also inform agriculturalists of the general trends of the market. Moreover, statistics that showed the yearly product of agriculture could be translated with relative ease into statistics of the contribution of agriculture to the national income and wealth and thus show the importance of agriculturalists in the life of the nation, an importance that was more and more frequently called in question during the rapid industrialization of the early twentieth century.[14]

The decisive step in SAI's campaign for agricultural statistics was the creation of the International Institute of Agriculture (IIA). The IIA was the first international institution of its kind, the progenitor of the United Nations' Food and Agriculture Organization (FAO). Although the idea of the organization had been conceived by an American, David Lubin, it was Faina and Cappelli who actually persuaded Vittorio Emanuele III to finance its establishment and support it diplomatically.[15] While Lubin was an enthusiast, Faina and Cappelli imagined the IIA as a sort of 'Agriculturalists' International', by analogy with the Workers' International.[16]

13 P. Casciani, 'Relazione del la Giunta generale del bilancio sul disegno di legge "Provvedimenti per la statistica agraria", presentata al la Camera dei deputati nel la seduta del 15 maggio 1908', in MAIC, ed., *Esperimenti di statistica agraria in alcune province del Regno* (Roma: Bertero, 1907), fasc. II, pp. 28f.

14 Garelli, for instance, in the *Relazione* quoted above (Garelli, *La rappresentanza dell'agricoltura al Congresso dei comizi agrari in Cuneo, 17 settembre 1905*), justified his claim of a prominent role for agriculturalists by arguing that landowners alone owned more than half the wealth of the country. Corrado Gini computed national income on the basis of the figures of agricultural production that were communicated to him by Ghino Valenti and his collaborators Pietra and Gervaso, Corrado Gini, *L'ammontare e la composizione della ricchezza delle nazioni* (Torino: Fratelli Bocca, 1914), pp. 3f.

15 Very few studies have been dedicated to the IIA. Among them, Luciano Tosi, *Alle origini della FAO: Le relazioni tra l'Istituto Internazionale di Agricoltura e la Società delle Nazioni,* Storia (Milano: Franco Angeli, 1989).

16 In 1905 Antonio Agresti published a book with the title: *L'Internazionale Verde, ossia l'Istituto Internazionale di Agricoltura proposto da David Lubin e iniziato dal Re d'Italia*, quot. in Sandro Rogari, *Ruralismo e anti-industrialismo di fine secolo: Neofisiocrazia e movimento neocorporativo cattolico* (Firenze: Felice Le Monnier, 1984). As appears from the documents preserved in the FAO archive, Faina and Lubin struggled for control over the newborn institute. The Italian prevailed and placed Italians in all the relevant positions. In particular, Umberto Ricci and Carlo Dragoni entered the IIA statistical service. In fact, the IIA functioned for Italian statisticians and agricultural economists as a *trait d'union* with international debates.

The tasks assigned to the IIA by the international conference that instituted it related mainly to statistics. Article 9 of the convention signed by Italy and the other member states on the 7 June 1905 contains the following:

> L'Institut, bornant son action dans le domaine international devra: a) concentrer, étudier et publier dans le plus bref delai possible les renseignements statistiques, techniques ou économiques concernant la culture, les productions tant animales que végétales, le commerce des produits agricoles et les prix pratiqués sur les differents marchés.[17]

Obviously, it would have been embarrassing for Count Faina, had Italy been unable to provide reliable statistics for this. At this point, the reorganization of the service of agricultural statistics was as much a matter of interest for Italy's landed classes as it was a matter of international prestige.[18] In a sense, Cappelli and Faina had manoeuvred the Italian government into spending money for statistics.[19]

Valenti's network: devolution

Although the associations of agriculturalists had agreed that there was a need for new statistics, their leadership was well aware that individual members feared that the state might use the information for tax purposes or in some other way contrary to the interests of agriculturalists. The choice of Valenti to lead the Bureau of Agricultural Statistics was reassuring for them.[20] Valenti had been

17 Camera dei Deputati, *Atti parlamentari*, 1 tornata del 2 luglio 1906, p. 9524.

18 That the establishment of the IIA made the renovation of agrarian statistics a 'matter of honour' for Italy, is a view too consistent with the rhetoric of Italy as the 'smallest of the Great Powers' to be adopted uncritically. Nevertheless, Valenti insists on the point: 'the new ordering of the service of agrarian statistics, although invoked for a long time within parliament and outside it, since the time of the agrarian inquiry, [. . .] was only due to a feeling of national *amour propre*', Ghino Valenti, 'La statistica agraria quale rappresentazione dell'economia rurale italiana', in Ghino Valenti, ed., *L'Italia agricola e il suo avvenire* (Roma 1919), p. 72.

19 Cocco-Ortu set the deadline of 1 January 1909 for Valenti to complete the AC and begin the statistical service: 'This deadline is also imposed by the circumstance that the International Institute of Agriculture will then gather and it would be appropriate and decent if Italy could present on that occasion its completed AC and the survey of the harvest for 1908' ('questo limite ultimo è imposto anche dalla circostanza che allora si riunirà l'Istituto Internazionale di Agricoltura a cui sarebbe opportuno e decoroso che l'Italia potesse presentare il suo Catasto Agrario completo e il rilevamento dei raccolti pel 1908'), from the summary of a meeting that took place at MAIC on 19 September 1907, Società Agraria di Lombardia, Archivio Storico, Direzione centrale, Statistica agraria, 1907.

20 The Bureau was formally constituted by Ministerial Decree on 6 March 1907 with the name Ufficio della Statistica Agraria, Sezione III, Divisione VII of the Direzione generale dell'Agricoltura: Giuva and Guercio. Valenti introduced to this office his collaborator G. Zattini, who had been hired in 1907 as inspector for drainage; hence, he belonged to a different directorate Arrigo Serpieri, 'Giuseppe Zattini', *Studi e Notizie Rassegna trimestrale dell'Istituto di Economia e Statistica Agraria* (1926), pp. 5–9.

the Secretary-General of the SAI in the crucial years of its foundation, between 1896 and 1898.[21] Clearly he was well acquainted with the SAI's leadership. The minister selected him from outside the ministry. For the agriculturalists' bloc, putting Valenti at the head of the Bureau of Agricultural Statistics was a successful move: they knew him and they trusted him. But SAI was not Valenti's only connection with the associations of agriculturalists. In Macerata, as we know, he had presided over the local comizio agrario. In 1903, SAI sent him to Ravenna in a failed attempt to moderate the fulminating *Associazione Agraria Ravennate*. In Padua, Valenti counted on the *comizio agrario* for his experiment, in particular on the *comizio*'s secretary, Professor Luigi Basso, who was an agronomist.[22]

His experience in Padua suggested to him that 'from an administrative point of view, agricultural statistics need decentralization, as he thought the system of centralization wrong', as he explained to the representatives of agricultural organizations in Milan. Valenti's *discentramento* responded to the requirements of data gathering, the fears of agriculturalists, and the budget constraints of the government.[23]

According to Valenti, the very nature of agriculture imposed a decentralized action, in contrast with the practice followed for other statistics:

> since we deal in this case, with facts that vary essentially, not only in time, but also in space, and that are subordinated in essence to special, natural and economic conditions of place, not only the collection of data, but also the biggest part of the processing of such data must be carried out by local offices.[24]

Valenti thought it necessary to invert the model of the General Directorate of Statistics, which was top-heavy with employees in Rome while there were none in the provinces. He was aware that it would have been impossible for him to improve on the prefects' statistics, unless he could call upon more qualified observers on the ground. Valenti's observers had to be

21 See Daniela Giaconi, 'Dall'inchiesta agraria agli studi sulla proprietà: Le radici del pensiero di Ghino Valenti e l'affermazione di un metodo d'indagine', *Quaderni Fiorentini* XXXII (2003), pp. 375–460.

22 MAIC, ed., *Esperimenti di statistica agraria in alcune province del Regno.*

23 Valenti's was not an isolated case; Beaud and Prévost in their broad survey of the reorganization of statistical offices in Europe and North America remark that alongside a tendency toward centralization, there was a tendency in favour of decentralization, which 's'appuie d'avantage sur une argumentation en termes de commodité, de naturalité, de proximité, de facilité. Naturellement dans le cours de leur travail, les ministères en viennent à produire des données statistiques. C'est donc aussi naturel qu'ils en contrôlent la diffusion et que la forme de celles-ci leur convienne. C'est dans l'ordre des choses, c'est infiniment plus pratique et surtout cela rend compte d'une manière plus adéquate des aspérités du réel. La décentralisation conduit ainsi à la constitution de séries statistiques adaptées aux besoins de chacun des organes du gouvernement', Beaud and Prévost, 'La forme est le fond la structuration des appareils statistiques nationaux (1800–1945)', p. 443.

24 Ghino Valenti, *Per l'Ordinamento della Statistica agraria in Italia: Relazione a S. E. Il comm. Cocco Ortu, Ministro di agricoltura, industria e commercio* (Roma: Tip. Nazionale di G. Bertero e C, 1907), p. 19.

selected from farmers and local agricultural experts.[25] Moreover, while the General Directorate received raw information from local branches of the administration and then elaborated it statistically, Valenti designed his system in such a way that data were processed locally and the central Bureau of Agricultural Statistics simply fixed the guidelines and assembled the results of provincial activity.

Discentramento also soothed the farmers' anxieties about an inquisitive central state. Information provided to this distant, 'Roman' entity could not be controlled by farmers, and it might be used for threatening tax-related purposes: '[Valenti] wants in this way to avoid the inconveniences that are brought about by the distrust of agriculturalists: it is necessary to inspire trust in order to collect reliable data'. The solution devised by Valenti and the associations of agriculturalists (like SAI, and the local associations) was 'to entrust the survey in every province to a commissioner from the government and keep the information collected within the province [. . .]. To the Ministry the commissioner would send only the aggregated results'.[26]

Finally, there were financial reasons for this 'devolution' of statistical activities. By transferring the weight of statistical surveys to the shoulders of local forces, Cocco-Ortu was free to present parliament with a plan that entailed little permanent cost for the ministry: Valenti imagined that the central office would consist of few 'clever and proactive agents', rather than a plethora of employees. The core costs of the work would be shared between a number of local institutions, making it much more difficult for the conservative supporters of the cabinet to point accusingly at the expansion of the state machinery.[27]

In practice, *discentramento* meant the creation of a network of local statistical centres, close to the farmers whom they had to observe. The documents concerning the establishment of the agricultural *cadastre* of 1910 that are preserved in the archive of the *Società agraria di Lombardia* reveal that Valenti spent the year 1907 in frequent journeys across Italy in order to make contact with the most influential groups of agriculturalists. He travelled between his own city of residence, Padua, the Ministry in Rome, Udine (where the Associazione Agraria Friulana had conducted a second experiment along the lines he set)

25 For Valenti's position on the problems of the administration in Valenti, *Per la riforma della pubblica amministrazione: studi.* Valenti was in favour of a certain degree of decentralization in order to strengthen MAIC and allow it to connect with the vital forces of society. This decentralization ought to be accomplished on one side by equipping the local branches of MAIC with technical personnel, and on the other by involving social forces, Desideri, *L'amministrazione dell'Agricoltura (1910–1980)*, pp. 26–8. It is clear that the renewal of the agrarian statistical service follows these lines.

26 Report of a meeting between Valenti, Alpe, Serpieri, Soresi and others: Verbale del l'adunanza tenutasi il 3 febbraio 1907 presso la Società Agraria di Lombardia per istituire un esperimento di Statistica Agraria nel la provincia di Milano, Società Agraria di Lombardia, Archivio Storico, Direzione centrale, Statistica agraria, 1907.

27 The Ministry of Agriculture represented for old style free-tradists the epitome of state intervention in economic matters. They had obtained Ministry's cancellation in the 1870s, Alberto Caracciolo, *L'inchiesta agraria Jacini* (Torino: Einaudi, 1959).

and some of the other centres where agricultural associations were active and willing to take part in his project.[28]

For his 'experiments', Valenti enlisted the comizii agrarii, chambers of commerce, and other associations (Ortoagricola in Turin, Agraria Lombarda and Umanitaria in Milan, Friulana in Udine, Georgofili and Orticoltura in Florence, Proprietarii e Agricoltori in Naples)[29] in the Provincial Committees for Agricultural Statistics. The associations represented the stakeholders of agricultural statistics and could mobilize the best local experts in agriculture.

In February 1907, for instance, the Annuario della Cattedra d'Agricoltura in Milan, announced that 'His Excellency the Minister of Agriculture, Industry, and Trade, the Honourable Cocco-Ortu has decided to restructure the service of agricultural statistics in a way that responds to the needs of the national economy and therefore he has taken into consideration a study that was presented to him by Professor Ghino Valenti'. Valenti had arrived in Milan from Padua with Luigi Basso and on 3 February he had met in the headquarters of the Società Agraria di Lombardia with Vittorio Alpe, professor at the Scuola Superiore d'Agricoltura and vice President of the Society, with Carlo Stabilini of the agricultural syndicate of Milan, Arrigo Serpieri who was then professor of agricultural economics at the Scuola Superiore, Giuseppe Soresi, who held the Itinerant Chair, Umberto Zanoni who directed the section of Gallarate of the Itinerant Chair, Giovanni Schiavi of the Società Umanitaria, and Guido Barocco, who was the technical secretary of SAL. The result of the meeting was the constitution of a provisional provincial committee that would eventually evolve into the permanent one.[30]

At the Società Agraria di Lombardia, Valenti met the actual decision-makers for agriculture in Lombardy. They represented influential economic groups, but they were also some of the best experts in agriculture. As noted in Chapter 2, some the local associations were at the heart of a number of initatives (*cattedre*, consortia, syndicates, agricultural schools, and so on) in their respective provinces. For agricultural statistics, the associations involved in the 'experiments' mobilized the experts who operated in these initiatives. In more than half of the provinces involved, the commissioners were academics (Padua, Ferrara, Florence, Naples) and directors of the itinerant chairs of agriculture (Milan, Turin, Bari, Ancona). Teachers at the Royal Schools of Agriculture, technical institutes for agriculture, and so on, were represented on all the committees. Many of the most renowned agricultural economists and agronomists (Vittorio Alpe, Eugenio Azimonti, Oreste Bordiga, Nicola Miraglia, Vittorio Niccoli, Arrigo Serpieri, to cite only a few) decided to join the project. Valenti also

28 The documents contained in Società Agraria di Lombardia, Archivio Storico, Direzione centrale, Statistica agraria, 1907, confirm these journeys.

29 MAIC, ed., *Esperimenti di statistica agraria in alcune province del Regno*, fasc. I, pp. 7–14.

30 *Bullettino dell'Agricoltura*, Numero 6, anno XLI, 8 febbraio 1907; see also Società Agraria di Lombardia, Archivio Storico, Direzione centrale, Statistica agraria, 1907, N 139, pos. 11 of 1 March 1907 to the Camera di Commercio di Milano.

recruited the most attentive landowners and agricultural technicians working for the associations.

The result was that Valenti came to occupy the centre of a network with two layers. The first layer was – so to say – political: the associations of agriculturalists. The second layer was technical: agricultural experts, in particular those who cooperated with the associations, for example, Basso in Padua, Serpieri, and Soresi in Milan, Vittorio Niccoli in Florence, and so on. These two layers were echoed by the twofold institutional arrangement that Valenti proposed for his experiments in the provinces. The office of the provincial commissioner for agricultural statistics was a technical one, related to the actual survey. The provincial committee was composed of representatives of different institutions: associations of agriculturalists, local administrations, and other groupings of economic interests. The stakeholders, that is, the agriculturalists, were represented at both levels: directly in the provincial committees, and indirectly by their own experts.

The commissioner received a salary and was in charge of the 'establishment, preservation and updating of the agrarian *cadastre*. He [was to] collect information concerning the forecasts and outcomes of harvests, by compiling statistics for every municipality which he [was to] communicate to the Ministry as soon as possible; he [was to] collect information concerning the livestock, the products of agrarian industries, and domestic trade of agrarian products and livestock, alongside the corresponding prices'.[31] The provincial committees, for their part, had to direct and supervise the collection of data by the commissioners. Actually, such committees certified the trustworthiness of the figures: who knew better than the wealthy agriculturalists, who had so much at stake, which figures would best serve the sector? They were also in charge of all the work of elaborating the data.

As Carlo Stabilini proposed at the already-mentioned meeting in February 1907, whenever possible, the actual survey of the areas under cultivation was best assigned to itinerant chairs.[32] They could take the closest view of the 'special, natural and economic conditions of places', both because of their familiarity with the territory they served, and because they were in direct contact with farmers.[33] For Valenti, the problem was that, although MAIC had recently began imposing some common standards on them,[34] the itinerant

31 Valenti, *Per l'Ordinamento della Statistica agraria in Italia*, p. 29.

32 Verbale dell'adunanza tenutasi il 3 febbraio 1907 presso la Società Agraria di Lombardia per istituire un esperimento di Statistica Agraria nella provincia di Milano, Società Agraria di Lombardia, Archivio Storico, Direzione centrale, Statistica agraria, 1907.

33 On this issue see Chapter 3 above.

34 The measure that generalized the procedure for personnel recruitment was the R.D. 29 novembre 1906 (Norme per le commissioni di vigilanza e i concorsi presso le cattedre ambulanti di agricoltura), in particular art. 1 and 6; the L. 14 luglio 1907 n. 513: 'Le cattedre ambulanti contemplate dalla presente legge sono sottoposte all'alta vigilanza del Ministero d'agricoltura' accounted for the supervision of MAIC over the itinerant teachings.

chairs were still unevenly distributed across regions and provinces. Valenti was thus forced to rely on a different set of organizations in different provinces.

There was a third key element in Valenti's double-layered network. The CA, as noted in the previous chapter, was not a mere survey of areas and crops. It required a great many details on farm life. In particular, the assessment of standard yields per hectare for the different categories of land was a delicate issue. Only local farmers could give the appropriate information. It was therefore the task of each provincial committee to build its own network of informants. The Società Agraria di Lombardia, for instance, addressed potential correspondents with a letter that stated clearly the official character of the inquiry but promised discretion, as follows:

> In agreement with the Ministry of Agriculture, our Society, with the assistance of the Itinerant Chair of Agriculture, has discussed the conducting of an experiment in agricultural statistics in our Province. The enquiry is in no sense a fiscal one. The income from land is not an issue. The enquiry simply wants to ascertain how much is produced in the whole municipality in cereals, fodder, and so on. The purpose is to make up the serious deficiency of statistics in Italy, which, although a predominantly agricultural country, does not know the magnitude of its plant and animal production.[35]

The letter went on to explain that the *società* was addressing its informants because they would be familiar with local conditions, and went on to propose a meeting on a fixed date with a representative of the society.

It has not been possible to find a complete list of correspondents for all the provinces involved in the experiment. We know that there were from one to four correspondents for each agrarian zone in the provinces of Padua, Udine and Trapani.[36] We have only the lists of the correspondents involved in the cases of Padua and Udine.

In the case of Udine (this list being the more informative), the agents and administrators of large landowners are the most represented group of professionals, but there were also foresters, rural teachers, aristocrats, pharmacists, and surveyors.[37] The Associazione Agraria Friulana and the itinerant chair of Udine had been able to mobilize not only large landowners (who were also the leading members of the Associazione), but also the 'reflective' part of the rural population: the backbone of 'civil society'. All those who lived in the countryside were affected by commercial treatises, and by investment and agricultural policies. Statistics were also in their interest.

35 Letter model from the president of SAL, Società Agraria di Lombardia, Archivio Storico, Direzione centrale, Statistica agraria, 1907.

36 MAIC, ed., *Esperimenti di statistica agraria in alcune province del Regno*, fasc. II, p. 65.

37 Ibid., fasc. II, p. 93ff.

Valenti's uncalculating centre of calculation

Devolution was only one aspect of Valenti's strategy for the experiments. Strict standardization was another. When Valenti began his 13 experiments in addition to those already running in Padua and Udine, the agricultural economist was aware that the chamber of commerce in Mantua was trying a method that differed from his own. He decided not to involve them in his experiments because he wanted to standardize the results as much as possible. Local committees had great autonomy in collecting the data, but Valenti allowed no variations of forms.

The standardization of forms produced shortcomings that Valenti was fully aware of, however. Observers on the ground were sometimes inclined to devise forms that better suited the peculiar conditions of their own areas. They might want to ask additional questions or specify entries in a way that answered their particular interests more closely. Yet standardization had its advantages. The main one was comparability of data.

In his instructions Valenti repeatedly stressed this point: 'We recommend the Commissioners to scrupulously follow the present instructions and restrain from modifying in any way the forms sent to them by the central office'.[38] By the emphasis on this recommendation, it seems that the use of standard forms across the nation was in fact a controversial issue.[39]

The homogeneity of the data and standardization of the forms were ensured by Valenti and his Bureau of Agricultural Statistics in Rome. Only the authority that came from his position inside the administration of the state guaranteed that Valenti could enforce standard procedures and forms, and could obtain comparable results in all the provinces involved. Without the Bureau's intervention, the experts mobilized by the associations would most likely have deviated from the standards.

According to the proposal, the central bureau had to be small and flexible. 'The central office should be staffed with only a few, vigorous units, able to guide and control, by means of inspections, what is done in the individual provinces'.[40] Within MAIC, Valenti could not count on a large staff of surveyors. In contrast to the 2000 employees of the Inland Revenue who collected similar data in Great Britain,[41] only a few functionaries could be detached to

38 Ibid., fasc. I, pp. 15ff.

39 P. Brassley has shown that the standardization of methods for making farm surveys was extremely controversial among British agricultural economists, Paul Brassley et al., 'Accounting for agriculture: The origins of the Farm Management Survey', *Agricultural History Review* 61.1 (2013).

40 Società Agraria di Lombardia, Archivio Storico, Direzione centrale, Statistica agraria, 1907, report of a meeting held in Rome on 19 September 1907, at MAIC. The meeting was attended by Oreste Bordiga, Francesco Cavani (who presided over the committee in Bologna), Niccoli, Valenti and Zattini.

41 Patrick G. Craigie, 'Memorandum on the methods employed in the collection of the annual Agricultural Statistics of Great Britain', *Bulletin de l'Institut international de statistique partie II*, 1903, p. 323.

work on agricultural statistics at MAIC. A small and flexible structure would allow Valenti to bypass the bureaucracy of MAIC, 'more sleepy than ever and eager to escape any new work',[42] and also to keep some control over the recruitment of its collaborators. The Ministry, in fact, usually hired generic functionaries who could then be moved to different offices at will.

Basically, the central office was composed of Valenti himself, Giuseppe Zattini, Oreste Narduzzi, Pietro Gervaso, and Umberto Ricci (Luigi Basso, although a close collaborator of Valenti, was not officially at MAIC).[43] The structure of the CA and the support of local institutions were expected to compensate for the small size of the central office.

At the beginning of the experiments, the surveyors of the different participating organizations were asked to visit Padua and Udine, where the new methods had first been tried out, in order to be sure that they understood the way the AC was conceived. In a letter to Vittorio Alpe, for instance, the head of the Bureau for Agricultural Statistics asked the vice President of the Società agraria di Lombardia to send to Padua, Udine and Rome at least one of the young surveyors that the SAL hired, to become familiar with Valenti's guidelines, since 'not everything can be communicated in writing and publicly'. As an alternative, Luigi Basso could go to Milan and train the agricultural engineers who had been hired for the survey.[44] Alpe answered immediately, startled, that he did not see any need for Basso to come to Milan, nor did he think that there was any pressing reason to dispatch two young agricultural engineers to Rome, Udine or Padua. If anybody, it would have been the director of the Itinerant Chair, Soresi, who would go to Rome and meet Valenti.[45] The Società Agraria di Lombardia and its experts tried somehow to retain some autonomy.

42 G. Valenti, 'La statistica agraria quale rappresentazione dell'economia rurale italiana', in Valenti, ed., *L'Italia agricola e il suo avvenire*, p. 72; Valenti belonged to the tradition of classical liberalism. Criticisms of bureaucracy and bureaucrats (as stifling and lazy) are frequent in his work; In *L'agricoltura e lo Stato*, Valenti identified in the nature of State bureaucracy the major source of inefficiency of MAIC: 'we can briefly summarize [them, *scilicet* the flaws of Italian administration] by saying that the organization of services does not follow those economic criteria that are the precondition of success for private enterprises; that the functionaries are on one side badly paid and on the other they bear no responsibility for the outcomes of the public administration and consequently have no interest in making these outcomes positive; and finally that the greater number of functionaries lacks specific competence for their posts. In Italy functionaries are bon à tout faire. Everything is done bureaucratically even when the technical elements are indispensable for the accomplishment of the aims that the function should fulfil'. But the peculiar inefficiency of MAIC was commonplace: see the parliamentary debate over MAIC's budget in 1909 and the harsh attacks of Nitti on Giolitti (Camera dei Deputati, *Atti parlamentari*, tornata del 11 maggio 1909, pp. 590–623), and G. Melis, ed., *L'amministrazione centrale dall'Unità alla Repubblica. Le strutture e i dirigenti* (Bologna: Il mulino, 1992), III, p. 30.

43 MAIC, ed., *Esperimenti di statistica agraria in alcune province del Regno*, fasc. I, p. 6.

44 Valenti to Alpe, 4 August 1907, Società Agraria di Lombardia, Archivio Storico, Direzione centrale, Statistica agraria, 1907.

45 Alpe to Valenti, 5 August 1907, Società Agraria di Lombardia, Archivio Storico, Direzione centrale, Statistica agraria, 1907.

But Valenti insisted: Basso's visit to SAL would, beyond question, be advisable. In other provinces, forms had been interpreted erroneously, and comparability required such differences to be eliminated. Unexpected problems could arise in Milan. Basso had the experience of the work done until then, while the operators in Milan had the specific knowledge of local conditions. A meeting to coordinate local peculiarities in a nationwide format could be very helpful.[46] Clearly *discentramento* was made possible by Valenti's dedication to keeping potential sources of divergence under control. But Valenti was not left alone at the head of the office. Before Cocco-Ortu approved his plan of 1906, the minister asked the budget promoter Casciani and Luigi Bodio for advice, as Valenti recalled shortly after.[47] Following these discussions, the minister established a different advisory board, an *ad hoc* Consultative Commission. Consultative Commissions were standard practice in Italian ministries and the High Council of Statistics had been one such. Important academics usually took part in such commissions alongside senior officials from the ministries involved and ministers themselves.[48] The Consultative Commission for agrarian statistics was composed of the minister Cocco-Ortu, Senator Luigi Bodio, Paolo Casciani MP, Antonio De Viti De Marco MP, Prof. Maffeo Pantaleoni, Prof. Montemartini, Commander Bartolomeo Morelli, inspector of MAIC, while Umberto Ricci served as secretary.[49]

The Consultative Commission gave a larger institutional framework to the Bureau of Agricultural Statistics. It gave the experiment the greatest scientific legitimacy, since Bodio, De Viti De Marco and Pantaleoni were celebrated academics, and Giovanni Montemartini was a statistician with a good reputation. It also shielded the initiative from attacks that could be made by the bureaucrats of MAIC itself because its members were top officials or MPs.

46 Valenti to Alpe, 9 August 1907, Società Agraria di Lombardia, Archivio Storico, Direzione centrale, Statistica agraria, 1907, this time typed (rather than handwritten) on the official paper of the General Directorate of Agriculture.

47 Valenti to Alpe, no date but January 1907, Società Agraria di Lombardia, Archivio Storico, Direzione centrale, Statistica agraria, 1907, Numero d'ordine 62a, posizione 11.

48 On the Consultative Commission for Statistics, which eventually became the Superior Council for Statistics, see Marucco, *L' amministrazione della statistica nell'Italia unita*; Beaud and Prévost, 'La forme est le fond la structuration des appareils statistiques nationaux (1800–1945)', attribute this model of organization to Quételet, but it actually derived from a more general practice; in those very years, the Superior Council of Statistics included members such as Rodolfo Benini, Napoleone Colajanni, Francesco Coletti, Luigi Einaudi, Maffeo Pantaleoni, whom M.L. D'Autilia qualifies as 'i personaggi più rilevanti del mondo accademico e della nuova burocrazia tecnica', D'Autilia, *L'amministrazione della statistica nell'Italia fascista*, p. 12.

49 Bodio was the most illustrious Italian statistician, who had been Secretary-General of the International Statistical Institute and led MAIC's general directorate for statistics until 1898, see his biography Marco Soresina, *Conoscere per amministrare: Luigi Bodio: statistica, economia e pubblica amministrazione,* Studi e ricerche storiche (Milano: Franco Angeli, 2001); De Viti De Marco and Pantaleoni were economists; Montemartini was a statistician stemming from the Società Umanitaria di Milano, becoming director of general statistics in 1911; Ricci, a statistician as well, was to move very soon to the IIA as director of the statistical service there.

To face objections from the Consultative Commission, on the other hand, the head of the Bureau of Agricultural Statistics could rely, in addition to his closest collaborators (Basso and Zattini, in particular), on a smaller group of provincial commissioners: notably, Niccoli, Bordiga, Francesco Cavani and Pecile; he consulted them whenever specific difficulties emerged.

On 11 October 1907, Valenti began confidentially communicating the results of the experiments to the provincial commissioners, in the form they would be published in the *Bollettino Ufficiale* of MAIC. They had done most of the work, so out of respect he kept them informed. The experiments seemed to be a great success. The great number of committees, commissions and commissioners who took part in the undertaking and the Minister himself seemed to have been satisfied: the statistics were deemed reliable, quickly done, and complete.[50] There was still the matter of costs to be resolved. The central commissioner therefore required all the provincial committees to estimate the costs incurred by them in the process. From the data collected, Valenti and Zattini expected that the whole CA would cost 555,000 Lire, out of which 55,000 already spent on the experiments. This was a huge sum, but the two assumed that once this initial work had been done, the Ministry would then save on the yearly statistics.[51] When Cocco-Ortu, jointly with Finance Minister Carcano, required funding from parliament for the statistics, in July 1908, he forecast that the first implementation of the AC would cost 500,000 Lire, while the annual statistics would cost around 120,000 Lire yearly.[52]

On 1st April 1909, King Vittorio Emanuele III signed a Royal decree by means of which the Bureau of Agrarian Statistics (Section III of Division VII of the General Directorate of Agriculture) was put in charge of extending to the whole kingdom the survey already completed in the 15 provinces where experiments had been performed. In the statistical year 1910, the first statistics of agricultural production based on the CA were published. The whole CA had cost slightly more than expected. But in the end the enterprise was hailed by the main group of agricultural experts as a remarkable improvement. Immediately after the conclusion of the survey Valenti was able to add the results of his statistics to the stream of publications that marked the 50th anniversary of the unification of Italy.[53] Retrospectively, agricultural

50 Exactitude (*esattezza*), timeliness (*rapidità*) and completeness (*completezza*) were the three basic characteristics that statistics should possess according to Valenti.

51 Società Agraria di Lombardia, Archivio Storico, Direzione centrale, Statistica agraria, 1907: report of a meeting held in Rome on 19 September 1907 between Valenti, Zattini, Bordiga, Niccoli, and Cavani.

52 Prospective costs were presented by Valenti at the meeting of the Consultative commission for agrarian statistics that was held with the participation of Minister Cocco-Ortu, Senator Bodio, Prof. Pantaleoni and others on 5 November 1907, MAIC, ed., *Esperimenti di statistica agraria in alcune province del Regno*, fasc. I, p. 344. Actual costs ended up being higher for the establishment of the AC.

53 Ghino Valenti, 'L'Italia agricola dal 1861 al 1911', in R. Accademia Dei Lincei, ed., *Cinquanta anni di storia italiana*, (3 vols, Roma: Tip. della R. Accademia Dei Lincei, 1911), II, p. 2.

experts celebrated the achievement in a collective volume published by the Federazione Italiana dei Consorzi Agrari in 1919: *L'Italia agricola e il suo avvenire*, a book whose publication signaled the post-war consolidation of the group gathered around the old scholar.[54]

Valenti's departure: centralizing statistics after the Fascist takeover

Notwithstanding the positive beginning, the history of the publication of the projected volumes of the CA shows that the effectiveness of the Bureau of Agricultural Statistics was far from established. Publishing began with the volume concerning the Marche, Lazio and Umbria in 1912, but stopped after two more volumes and was never resumed, probably because the data for many provinces were incomplete and also because the publication itself was very expensive.[55] Meanwhile, and after only two years, Valenti had been forced to resign. The new minister of agriculture in the fourth of Giolitti's cabinets, Francesco Saverio Nitti (1858–1953), decided, against Valenti's advice, that the Bureau for Agrarian Statistics should be removed from the General Directorate for Agriculture, and merge with General Statistics in the revitalized Labour Office.[56] Valenti strenuously opposed this change; for him, agrarian statistics required more competence in agrarian economics than in statistics. By placing the Bureau of Agrarian Statistics under the aegis of General Statistics, Nitti would have emptied it of its specialized staff and best collaborators. When Nitti ignored the protests, Valenti resigned.[57]

There were personal reasons for Nitti's hostility towards Valenti, as the two had violently clashed in 1896 over the chair of Political Economy and Science of Finances at the University of Naples, but the contrast between them may have been more substantial. Nitti, a radical, was a vociferous advocate of industrial development and technical *dirigisme*, and among the statisticians he protected was Alberto Beneduce, who was later one of the founders of the industrial state holding, IRI.[58] The activity of the Bureau of Agrarian Statistics, instead, depended on the collaboration of landowners and landowners' associations and

54 Valenti, *Per la riforma della pubblica amministrazione: studi.*

55 Istituto centrale di statistica, *Catasto agrario, 1929* (Roma, 1929–39), 'Introduzione', p. 4.

56 On the Labour Office, Riccardo Johnson, 'Amministrazione e organizzazione delle informazioni: Il ministero dell'agricoltura e i problemi del lavoro', in Istituto per la scienza dell'amministrazione pubblica, ed., *L'Amministrazione nella storia moderna*, II; see also: Manfredi Alberti, *La scoperta dei disoccupati: Alle origini dell'indagine statistica sulla disoccupazione nell'Italia liberale, 1893–1915,* Premio tesi di dottorato 34 (Firenze: Firenze University Press, 2013).

57 This is at least how Valenti himself recalled the story: Valenti, 'La statistica agraria quale rappresentazione dell'economia rurale italiana', pp. 77ff. n. 1, where Valenti published a letter from him to Nitti, complaining about dispersal of the statistical personnel to other offices.

58 On Nitti's clash with Valenti, see Francesco Barbagallo, *Francesco S. Nitti,* La Vita sociale della nuova Italia 33 (Torino: UTET, 1984), pp. 75ff; on Nitti's attacks on the Bureau of Agrarian Statistics in 1907, p. 144; on his favouring Beneduce, p. 167.

carried the traditional agricultural elites. Moreover, by putting agricultural and general statistics under the Labour Office, Nitti refocused statistics on areas of social conflict. In the strained social climate that followed the strikes of 1909, this meant that the new cabinet, or at least MAIC, was steering to the left precisely at the moment when the associations of agriculturalists were radicalizing their opposition to the demands of the workers.

The political shift that was brought about by the fourth cabinet of Giolitti determined not only the end of the climate of cooperation of the government with the agricultural elites but also serious fractures within the representation of agriculturalists themselves. Local associations (as in Bologna and Ravenna) became fierce opponents of Giolitti's policies, while the Society of Italian Agriculturalists (SAI) still tried to mediate. In these conditions, Valenti's position was undermined by the fact that Nitti looked for statistics that focused on workers rather than production, but also by the weakening of the group of agriculturalists who had supported his project, that is the moderate leadership of SAI and the founding figures of the Agricultural Parliamentary Committee such as Pantano, Ottavi (president of SAI since 1911), Faina, and Luzzatti.

Valenti was succeeded by his closest collaborator at MAIC, Inspector Giuseppe Zattini (1861–1926).[59] But Zattini was unable to maintain the office's working capacity and lacked both the political support and the ramified network that had guaranteed the success of Valenti's experiment. Personnel was transferred to other offices, funds shrank, the reliability of the statistics fell. Nevertheless, in one form or another, Zattini and his remaining collaborators continued to provide figures and update the agricultural *cadastre* wherever possible. The itinerant chairs, for instance, were given instructions to recalculate the areas again in 1916.[60] Somehow the network of agricultural experts created by Valenti in academia and in the institutions of technical assistance survived the war (for instance in the Ufficio Tecnico per L'Agricoltura of the National Committee on Trade Tariffs and in the Ufficio Tecnico of the Federazione Italiana dei Consorzi Agrari), but its ability to control the creation of statistics was undermined.[61]

After Valenti's death, in 1920, the network came to be dominated by Arrigo Serpieri, especially after 1923 when he entered the cabinet and created the Istituto di Economia e Statistica Agraria. Serpieri has often been connected

59 Giuseppe Zattini was an engineer. After his graduation in Bologna (1885) he worked for many years at the administration of the *cadastre*. Valenti called him to the newly formed Bureau of Agricultural Statistics.

60 MAIC Ufficio di Statistica Agraria, *Norme e istruzioni pel servizio di statistica agraria* (Roma: Tip. ditta L. Cecchini, 1914); the Milan's chair reported its activities in Cattedra di Agricoltura per la Provincia di Milano, *Annuario della cattedra di agricoltura per la provincia di Milano, anno 1916* (Milano: Tipografia agraria, 1917).

61 Salvatore Adorno, 'L'Italia agricola e il suo avvenire: Note sul ruolo della Commissione di studi tecnici ed economici della Federconsorzi', in Severina Fontana, ed., *La Federconsorzi tra stato liberale e fascismo*, Biblioteca di cultura moderna 1084 (Roma, Bari: Laterza, 1995), pp. 61–108.

with Nitti by previous historians. D'Autilia and Melis for instance call him 'un tecnico nittiano' due to the commitment to modernization that Nitti and Serpieri both shared, and to the similar view they held on state intervention.[62] Yet, Serpieri, through Valenti, was introduced to other, if anything more influential, circles, such as the Federazione Italiana dei Consorzi Agrari, SAI, and so on. There was a strong sense of community among the agricultural experts that belonged to or collaborated with these institutions, thanks in particular to the common effort made for Valenti's agricultural *cadastre*. The Istituto di Economia e Statistica Agraria capitalized on this network and was an attempt at giving it an institutional form.

At the death of Zattini, nevertheless, Serpieri's idea of keeping together agricultural economics and agricultural statistics, came into conflict with the hegemonic designs of Corrado Gini. Since 1926, Gini had been the head of the newly founded Istituto Centrale di Statistica. In the politics of the Fascist regime, the Istituto Centrale di Statistica (now ISTAT) corresponded to the pivotal role of Mussolini, the leader and ultimate decider. ICS directly responded to the chief of government and was in principle intended to be the sole supplier of statistics for all the ministries of the cabinet. In the struggle between Gini and Serpieri, the statistician had the upper hand: the Istituto di Economia e Statistica Agraria ceased to exist, and all its statistical tasks were transferred to the ICS.[63]

In 1928, under the direction of first Carlo Dragoni and then Nallo Mazzocchi Alamanni, the ICS began the collection of data on areas and yields for the new agricultural *cadastre* of 1929 (whose ponderous volumes were published throughout the 1930s). If the general concept remained the same as had inspired the agricultural *cadastre* of 1910, the Fascist regime transformed the collection of data. Rather than exploiting the cooperation of state and local elites on an equal footing, the ICS designed a centralized system. The itinerant chairs were transformed into local agents of the Ministry of Agriculture and Forests, losing their autonomy completely.[64] The responsibility of collecting the data would now rest exclusively with the itinerant chairs, thus excluding the larger network that

62 The link between the two would be confirmed by the fact that it was Nitti who called Serpieri to Florence to lead the Istituto Agrario Forestale of Vallombrosa, a prestigious position, D'Autilia, *L'amministrazione della statistica nell'Italia fascista*, Lea D'Antone, 'Politica e cultura agraria: Arrigo Serpieri', *Studi Storici* 20.3 (1979).

63 Istituto centrale di statistica, 'Il progettato trasferimento degli uffici di statistica agraria', *Annali di Statistica: Atti del Consiglio superiore di statistica* VI (1930) expresses the point of view of Gini.

64 Regio Decreto-Legge, 6 dicembre 1928 n. 3433 (*Gazzetta Ufficiale del Regno d'Italia*, n. 50, 28 febbraio 1929, I) stated that 'the chairs perform the tasks of the Ministry of National Economy concerning . . . agricultural statistics and others' (titolo I, art.3). It ruled that there would be one itinerant chair per province, that there would be up to three representatives of the Ministry of National Economy in the board of directors of the chair (while MAIC used to have only one representative) and increased the authority of the chairman of the board of directors (appointed by the Minister of National Economy); the Legge 13 giugno 1935 no. 1220 abolished the chairs and created the Ispettorati Provinciali dell'Agricoltura.

had cooperated in the AC 1910. The collation and manipulation of the data, instead, was to be the exclusive domain of the statisticians in Rome.[65]

Conclusions: building the observatory

The renovation of Italian agrarian statistics that took place between 1906 and 1910 shows some interesting aspects, both in terms of the organizational forces involved and for the techniques, methods and concepts that it required. I now list some of them as they emerged in this and in the previous chapter. The organizational plan shows at least two interesting elements. The first is the interaction between experts (technicians inside the administration and academics) on one side, and the government (the ministers but also the MPs who took part in the Consultative Commission). In this case the two central elements are the Consultative Commission and Valenti's own network. The Consultative Commission was explicitly conceived as the crossroads of scientific expertise (Valenti, Pantaleoni or De Viti De Marco) with the administrative experience of functionaries (Inspector Moreschi, for instance). Luigi Bodio in this case was the amphibious figure of a scientist who had served in the administration. The minister was the arbiter.

Valenti himself was at the centre of a scientific network of connections. We have seen that he managed to mobilize all the leading experts of his field: Alpe, Bordiga, Miraglia, Niccoli, Peglion, and Serpieri, who all had different roles and different specializations (although most of them were expert in valuation and rural economy). In a sense this undertaking contributed to unify the field of agrarian economy by grouping its practitioners together.[66] Next to the economic and agronomic expertise of the academics, the CA required the collaboration of more 'technical' experts whose formation and training had developed inside the office of CT and the IGM. At their best, such technicians were represented by Ing. Zattini, but less qualified land surveyors are also included in this category.

65 Comparing the CA 1929 and the CA 1910, Mazzocchi Alamanni wrote: 'Il fatto che la rilevazione sia stata totalitariamente affidata ad una unica categoria di tecnici specializzati, quelli delle Cattedre ambulanti di agricoltura (oggi, Ispettorati agrari) – categoria particolarmente organizzata e rafforzata ai fini della specifica e vasta opera di rinnovamento rurale della Nazione – ha indubbiamente costituito ulteriore ed importante elemento di tranquillità circa la 'sufficienza' dell'approssimazione potuta raggiungere dall'attuale catastazione a confronto con la prima, la cui esecuzione fu, di necessità, affidata a rilevatori i più disparati: società di agricoltori, privati studiosi, qualche cattedratico', Istituto centrale di statistica, *Catasto agrario 1929*, I, p. 10.

66 After the war, most of these men (Serpieri, Peglion, Alpe) contributed to Ghino Valenti, ed., *L'Italia agricola e il suo avvenire* (Roma, 1919). The problem of defining 'agrarian economists' (as opposed to 'agronomists') drives Francesco Lechi, 'Réflexions sur l'évolution de la pensée économique agricole en Italie', *Économie rurale* 200 (1990), pp. 36–9, and Giancarlo Di Sandro, *Gli economisti agrari italiani tra Otto e Novecento,* Collana di economia applicata 6 (Bologna: Clueb, 1995), Giaconi vindicated the inclusion of Valenti in the group of 'agrarian economists', in Giaconi, 'Dall'inchiesta agraria agli studi sulla proprietà'.

The third element of interest is that the gathering of statistics involved some of the 'stakeholders' of statistics: the agrarian associations, the landowners, all the possible 'experts' regarding local conditions who could be induced to participate as representative of their area alongside the public administration. Through their associations and representatives in parliament, groups of agriculturalists had been campaigning for new statistics long before 1907. For them, statistics were part of the overall modernization of the country, would enable the government to better adapt its policies to the actual needs of agriculturalists, and would give agriculturalists themselves a better understanding of their economic conditions. The participation of associations of agriculturalists in the making of the CA was therefore motivated by an interest in securing better statistics, as well as by the desire to control the statistical survey.[67]

Such participation was supposed to compensate for the weakness of the public administration itself, which was unable to run the machine on its own through its provincial branches (prefects and municipalities). Local associations and the experts whom they could involve in the project replaced the peripheral offices of government that lacked the knowledge needed. The result was a network of observatories made up of informants, commissioners, and associations, kept together by Valenti. The core of the empirical work was done by itinerant chairs, thus beginning the evolution that ended in 1935 with their transformation into the territorial offices of the Ministry of Agriculture. But in the 1900s, itinerant chairs still had a double nature, as both organs of the state and private organizations. Agricultural experts themselves, led by Valenti, moved rather frequently from business organizations, to academia, to business-friendly administrative offices.

Although Valenti's were 'participative' statistics, they were not democratic. His project excluded direct investigations based on a general census. Not everybody had their say in the final figures, as they would have done by filling out forms themselves. Only some respondents were considered reliable enough to provide sound numbers, and even fewer took part in the sort of state or civil society *fora*, the Provincial committees, where wealthy agriculturalists exerted a high degree of hegemony.

The organization of the service moreover had to be configured differently in every province, according to the way landowners and tenants exerted such hegemony. Informants had to be contacted on a semi-personal basis by provincial commissioners and the final statistics rested on the work of very different people in the different provinces. Here again, Valenti's network was probably an essential starting point. As former Secretary-General of the Società degli Agricoltori Italiani he was in contact with most of the associations, and a member of several.[68]

67 During the war, Valenti's *reseau* was mobilised by SAI for a series of surveys that should prepare for the post-war management of the sector, see Ghino Valenti, ed., *L'agricoltura e la politica commerciale dell'Italia* (Roma: Bertero, 1917) Comitato nazionale per le tariffe doganali e per i trattati di commercio.

68 He was a member of the Accademia dei Georgofili, for instance.

The CA mirrors the forms of political representation that characterized 'liberal' Italy before the extension of the suffrage enacted in 1911.[69] The Bureau of Agricultural Statistics was a 'privileged contact point' of agricultural interests and the state.[70] The harmonious composition of interests within MAIC became more difficult when Nitti became minister. Fascism formally imposed a clear division between state officials and representatives of economic interests, thus severing the links between statistics and stakeholders, while the state reinforced its role in the countryside.

Charles S. Maier defined corporatism as a system of brokerage between interest groups, somehow incorporated in a permanent fashion, in the decision-making process of the state. Interest groups were very much represented in the Giolittian era, but what changed with Fascism was the role of the state, which acquired an overwhelming predominance, precisely because the regime managed to organize and absorb all interest groups: landowners, trade unions, and experts. When the Fascist regime ordered a new CA in 1928, the Central Statistical Institute replaced all such forms of participative statistics with a centralized structure. The itinerant chairs of agriculture (which had themselves meanwhile undergone a process of bureaucratization) became the only bodies responsible for the collection of raw data while the ICS took over the whole task of elaborating them.

The CA was not a practice that could be exported to a virgin and unknown land. The importance attached to the participation of local élites in the undertaking was precisely motivated by the need to grasp the reality of something local, something singular, but also something essentially beyond contingencies, which was revealed only by long acquaintance and familiarity. The skilled surveyors, with their theoretical basis in valuation and agronomy, were entitled to select and describe the typical farms, and their constitutive elements. The provincial committees, as a sort of statistical parliament, set the limits on what was acceptable in the resulting image. The 'normal' features, identified by skilled surveyors and checked by way of discussion within provincial committees, offered the least bad starting point. The correction of mistakes was entrusted to the law of large numbers.

69 On the mistrust of Italian élites for the people: Alberto Baffigi, *Cultura statistica e cultura politica: L'Italia nei primi decenni unitari,* Quaderni dell'Ufficio Ricerche Storiche / Banca d'Italia 15 (Roma, 2007), and the first essay in Roberto Vivarelli, *Il fallimento del liberalismo: Studi sull'origine del fascimo* (Bologna: Il mulino, 1981).

70 Guido Melis, 'Amministrazione e mediazione degli interessi: le origini delle amministrazioni parallele', in Istituto per la scienza dell'amministrazione pubblica, ed., *L'Amministrazione nella storia moderna,* II.

6 Observing typicality

The second half of the 1920s, with foundation of the National Institute for Agricultural Economics (INEA) and the assignment of the tasks of the Bureau of Agricultural Statistics to the ICS, marks a turning point in the evolution of the methods of the agricultural economists and of their role. The personal struggle between the founder of the Institute for Agricultural Economics and Statistics (IESA), Arrigo Serpieri, and the president of the Central Statistical Office (ICS), Corrado Gini, was only the surface of a deeper dispute over the significance to be attributed to the different forms of observation. Agricultural economists on the one hand defended the combination of essentially qualitative forms of observation, such as surveys and enquiries, with quantitative statistics of areas and yields, in the name of the unity of the subject matter of observation, namely agriculture. Statisticians, instead, aimed at imposing statistical methods as the only legitimate way of investigating economic subjects, and wanted to impose this monolithic view of data.

In the end, both groups were partially disappointed. Apparently, the ICS at first expected to take over the whole IESA. Inside the ICS, what had been Valenti's and then Zattini's Bureau of Agricultural Statistics would carry on updating the agricultural *cadastre* and provide, on this basis, the statistics of yearly output, while the research in agricultural economics would be attributed to the Ufficio Studi of the ICS. Serpieri could not accept this radical loss of autonomy for agricultural economists. Instead, the tasks of the IESA were split between the ICS and the INEA. The way the tasks were divided between the two institutions is revealing of the way in which statistics and competing forms of investigation came to be conceived in the 1920s.

As we know, the ICS took over the functions of Zattini's Bureau of Agricultural Statistics: the update of the agricultural *cadastre* and the making of the yearly harvest statistics, based on surveys of yields and areas. This corresponded to the narrow interpretation of statistics that had slipped into the language of the time. Valenti and his parliamentary supporters had attached the name of 'agricultural statistics' (*statistica agraria*) to the figures that concerned the yearly agricultural production, the areas under crop, and the yield per hectare. Such has been the definition of agricultural statistics used throughout the previous chapters, its key elements being the comprehensive study of the whole population and its quantitative character. To this we must add the census of agricultural businesses that was eventually made for the first World Census of Agriculture of 1930.

The INEA inherited everything that fell outside this definition of statistics, which was considered a matter pertaining to agricultural economics proper. The INEA claimed for itself the investigation of farms by means of surveys and through the analysis of account books (*osservazione contabile*). Such observations were to be made by the central structure of the institute with the help of a network of local 'observatories' (*osservatori*): 'The principal task of the INEA is to carry out and promote studies – prevailingly surveys – on the economy of agricultural production, and to collect, coordinate and elaborate the accounting data of agricultural businesses'.[1]

In the eyes of the statisticians of ICS, the subjects the INEA was prepared to investigate (prices and costs of production, the distribution of income, and the effect of the reclamation policy over farms and families) required statistical methods, were statistical in nature, and therefore should be kept under the control of the ICS itself. In their view, agricultural economics and agricultural statistics were inseparable: 'The economic investigation has a concrete and practical value if it is supported by statistical data, which are a precondition for it. Agricultural statistics have an effective value, if their data make the economic investigation possible'.[2] They also believed that agricultural economists were unaware of statistical methodology, and used outmoded methods. They contested the representativeness of surveys and accounting studies.

Agricultural economists, instead, were willing to narrow the tasks of the ICS down to the production of statistics about yields and the CA. In their view, statisticians should provide a general quantitative framework. Studies in agricultural economics would complement such general figures. Such research required a more specific training in agricultural economics than statisticians had. The practices of investigation of agricultural economists, in general, relied upon a fundamental notion of 'farm types' (*azienda agraria tipica*), whose validity was heavily questioned by statisticians because of the difficulty of its mathematical treatment and its dependence on the judgment of experts. In Chapter 3, above, I briefly introduced the concept of the typical farm. In this chapter I want to make this concept more explicit.

This chapter and the next deal with farm surveys and their evolution into accounting-based statistical texts. They explain how the division of tasks between INEA and ICS was justified by the practices of agricultural economists. While Chapter 7 is dedicated to the institutional framework of surveys and accounting studies, mostly after the foundation of INEA, here I investigate

1 Arrigo Serpieri, *Guida a ricerche di economia agraria,* Studi e monografie / Istituto Nazionale di Economia Agraria 1 (Roma: Treves Dell'Ali, 1929), p. vii.

2 Istituto Centrale di Statistica, 'Il progettato trasferimento degli uffici di statistica agraria', *Annali di Statistica: Atti del Consiglio superiore di statistica,* VI (1930), p. 240.

the roots of these forms of observation, and the different traditions of thought that determined their development between the nineteenth and early twentieth centuries, and show how they differed from what was conventionally called 'statistics'.

Surveys and types

As we have seen, in his report to Cocco-Ortu, Ghino Valenti lists three methods for observing agriculture from an economic point of view. He mentions the general statistics of production that his office was to publish (these he called agrarian statistics proper), enquiries (*inchieste*), and farm surveys.[3] Farm surveys derived in part from family surveys, which had been popularized – if not invented – by the French engineer Frederic Le Play in the second half of the nineteenth century.[4] Le Play and his collaborators interviewed working-class families and undertook surveys that focused on the family budget. By means of family budgets, family surveys described the living conditions of a family, their sources of income, their expenses, and the workforce available to it. Everything was computed in the assets or liabilities of the family's balance sheet.

A similar method of compiling surveys was also applied to farms. Farms were often run by individual families and it was easy to move from the study of a family's expenses to the study of the productive unit from which the family earned its income. Farm budgets were the central elements of such farm surveys: they showed how gross production was divided in order to remunerate all the factors of production and compensate for the amortization of capital. The study of gross production and its inputs revealed the technical features of agricultural production, such as crop rotation and crop specialization, and also the technical efficiency of farms. Two disciplines with which agricultural economists were familiar, land valuation and accounting, became the lenses through which the distribution of income and poverty could be observed. Together, family surveys and farm surveys respectively represented the two elements of a country's agrarian economy: demand and supply, the workers and the farms. For this reason they were often included in socioeconomic enquiries. Problems of production (inputs, outputs, and technologies) and of distribution (the distribution of social product and net product) could be reduced to a familiar accounting framework. In this way, phenomena could be investigated in a limited number of individual *specimina*, rather than in terms

3 Ghino Valenti, 'Per l'ordinamento della statistica agraria in Italia', *Bollettino Ufficiale del Ministero dell'Agricoltura, Industria e Commercio* II (1907); It should be noted that, for Valenti, farm surveys were only significant when the farms were selected on the basis of previously existing statistics. In fact, appropriate statistics were often unavailable and surveys worked as substitutes rather than as complements to statistics.

4 An interesting (but teleological) history of the evolution of budget enquiries from family to farm budgets is given by Aleksandr V. Čajanov, *O budžetnikh issledovanjakh* (Moskva: Izdatel'skij Dom Tonču, 2006).

of empirically and theoretically troublesome macroeconomic concepts. The analysis of the farm included determining the productivity of inputs and hence fixed the general frame (and in some cases the boundary curve) for discussing issues of distribution and production.

There was a variety of reasons to focus on businesses. The micro-level allowed investigation of the various forms of contract that ruled agricultural businesses as economic living organisms. It also responded to a long tradition of economic thought that had started with the Physiocrats, if not before, and took individual farms and eventually firms as the site where the product was distributed among factors of production.[5] Around the turn of the nineteenth century Marshall's theory of representative firms simply provided an updated theoretical justification for observation methods focused on individual businesses. Finally, farm analysis was consistent with the technical tools that agricultural economists learned in universities. Since they were basically trained to be farm managers, accounting and management provided them with basic economic categories and frameworks.[6]

Agricultural economists, in adapting Le Play's *monographie de famille* to farms, translated Le Play's fundamental concepts into their own terms. The typical family that Leplayan surveys studied became a typical farm, the representative instance of a way of combining the factors of agricultural production. What I would call the agronomic concept of farm types was characterized by two dimensions: a first dimension was productive orientation (dairy farm or crop farm, and so on), a second dimension was that of local peculiarities, which involved both adjustments to climate and geography and social factors, such as tenancy contracts. Farm types were hence usually labelled with names that reflected both dimensions, such as 'Lombard dairy farm'.

Farm types (and, as a consequence, typical farms) were abstractions that conceptualized the interaction of farming systems and concrete social, and natural contexts. This view of farm types was relatively old, dating back at least to the German agronomists of the early nineteenth century. The *Norfolk* and *three-field* rotation schemes that were discussed and compared in nineteenth-century agronomic debate were farming systems, or, in other terms, specific combinations of technical factors and managerial principles. Farming systems resulted in

5 For the Physiocrats and their farm accounts see, Christine Théré and Loïc Charles, 'The Writing Workshop of François Quesnay and the Making of Physiocracy', *History of Political Economy* 40.1 (2008) and some of their recent most works; on Ricardo's analysis of farms, see Mary Morgan, 'Experimental Farming and Ricardo's Political Arithmetic of Distribution', *Amsterdam WP Series* 3 (2008).

6 Serpieri's reconstruction of the history of farm studies is significant, as he sketched a line that goes from Cuppari, to Oreste Bordiga, to Niccoli, to himself and ends with Perini, see Arrigo Serpieri, 'Sui concetti di impresa marginale, impresa ordinaria e azienda tipo', *Rivista di Economia Agraria* 2.2 (1948). Giancarlo Di Sandro, *Gli economisti agrari italiani tra Otto e Novecento,* Collana di economia applicata 6 (Bologna: Clueb, 1995), convincingly argues that the analysis of individual farms, what he calls 'agronomy', lay at the basis of agricultural economics as a discipline.

different levels of productivity, and for this reason it was important to establish which type was better for farmers and estate owners, given different social, economic, and natural conditions. Was the *Norfolk* better than the *three-field* type as Albrecht Thaer claimed for Germany?[7] Answers were not unanimous.

The geographically differentiated approach proposed by Johann Heinrich von Thünen with his famous model of the *Isolierte Staat* gave a theoretical rationale for the variety of regional farm types.[8] As a consequence, the school of von Thünen often engaged in descriptions of farm types across Europe. But before Thünen, Arthur Young (the main influence on Thaer) had already popularized in Europe a geographical approach, centred on the description of the agricultural traditions that he encountered in his travels. Almost in response to Young, Jean Charles Simonde de Sismondi published his celebrated description of Tuscan agriculture that extolled the Tuscan tradition of sharecropping (a farm type) as the best way to promote social peace and economic prosperity.[9]

Farm surveys typically contained the survey of a farm type, the description, that is, of a typical farm, either a real or an idealized one. Pietro Cuppari from the 1850s,[10] and later Vittorio Niccoli set the model for studies of this kind in Italy.

At the core of farm surveys lay the farm budgets, since the budget clarified the relationship between the inputs and the outputs of the farm. Surveys showed the monetary values of the farm's assets and liabilities, revenues and expenses, which formed the budget, and they also included such physical quantities as the area under crop, the number of hours worked, the gross product or the livestock that corresponded to such monetary values.

But the budget was only part of the farm survey. It usually included an account of the land tenancy contract and of the physical composition of the farm (area, buildings, and so on), the prevailing crop rotations and the farm's

7 Albrecht Thaer, *Einleitung zur Kenntniß der englischen Landwirthschaft und ihrer neueren practischen und theoretischen Fortschritte in Rücksicht auf Vervollkommnung deutscher Landwirtschaft* (Hannover: Gebrüder Hahn, 1804); on this debate see Joosep Nõu, *Studies in the development of agricultural economics in Europe,* Lantbrukshögskolans annaler, v. 33, nr. 1 (Uppsala, 1967) on Thaer and von Thünen.

8 Thünen, Johann Heinrich von, *Der isolierte Staat in Beziehung auf Landwirtschaft und Nationalökonomie, oder, Untersuchungen über den Einfluss, den die Getreidepreise, der Reichthum des bodens und die Abgaben auf den Ackerbau ausüben* (Hamburg: Verlag Wirtschaft und Finanzen, 1826); Thünen is particularly celebrated for his theory of land use in concentric rings in relationship to distance from urban centres. He is now considered one of the founders of economic geography; Paul Krugman for instance declared his debt to von Thünen in his seminal paper Paul Krugman, *Increasing Returns and Economic Geography* (Cambridge, MA: National Bureau of Economic Research, 1990).

9 Jean Charles L. S Sismondi, *Tableau de l'agriculture toscane* (Genève: Paschaud, 1801); Bernardino Farolfi and Massimo Fornasari, 'Agricoltura e sviluppo economico: il caso italiano (secoli XVIII–XX)', in Massimo Canali et al., eds, *L'agricoltura e gli economisti agrari in Italia dall'Ottocento al Novecento* (Milano: Franco Angeli, 2011), pp. 13–70, use Sismondi's *Tableau* to demonstrate the existance of 'the awareness of the peculiarity of the agriculture of the peninsula', p. 16.

10 Pietro Cuppari, 'Spese e proventi di una famiglia colonica', *Giornale agrario toscano* 3 (1860); on Cuppari's method, see also Alberto Gabba, '"Lo studio di un'azienda rurale", in una lettera di Pietro Cuppari a Francesco Brioschi', *Aestimum* 39 (2000).

various enterprises.[11] In an area where small farms predominated, the typical farm had a small amount of land. In an area where sharecropping contracts prevailed, the typical farm was leased to sharecroppers. Where fertilizers were used in limited amounts, the typical farm used them sparingly, and so on. The farm type was characterized by both qualitative (tenancy contracts, for instance) and quantitative elements (area, the relative importance of enterprises on revenues, and so on). The study of farm accounts therefore contributed to the crystallization of farm types. In turn, the representativeness of farm accounts depended on the assumption that farm types existed and real farms conformed to the type.

As noted above, investigators could proceed in two ways. They could either devote a survey to an ideal farm constructed by them or describe an actual farm, thought of as representative of its type. The early investigators, such as Cuppari, preferred the first method. The relatively reduced number of farm surveys available, the wish to illustrate synthetically the general forms of agriculture that prevailed over relatively large areas, induced them to integrate different features from actual farms into a single typical one. Just as the famous painter Zeuxis had created an image of Helen by copying the best parts of the most beautiful women of Kroton, so agricultural economists could combine the most characteristic features of different farms into a typical one.

It could be very difficult to find a real farm that reflected the type in all its details. The importance of observing actual instances, nevertheless, was stressed abundantly by Le Play and his followers and became commonplace among investigators in the second half of the nineteenth century.[12] We see in 'Surveys, enquiries, and statistics', below how Italian social scientists interpreted these directions. The choice of an existing representative farm, however, and the combination of typical features of different farms, both relied on the 'good intuition of the investigator'.[13]

In contrast with the most important supporters of the survey method, such as Le Play, Duplectiaux and Ernst Engel, Cuppari did not plan to collect large numbers of surveys. Cuppari and his followers claimed that, by carefully selecting the farms to be investigated, the resulting farm surveys would be able to offer a good description of a country's agriculture through its prevailing farm types.[14] The investigator's experience was sufficient for discounting the irrelevant or misleading elements and selecting the right farm to represent the dominant characteristics of a region's farms. For Cuppari: 'A clear concept of the rural economy of a country can be offered only by the description

11 See, for instance, Comizio Agrario di Bologna, *Monografia del podere bolognese* (Bologna: Società tip. già compositori, 1881).

12 For the positive and concrete character of Le Play's method, see Maria R. Protasi, 'Tra scienza e riforma sociale: Il pensiero e il metodo d'indagine sociale di F. Le Play e dei suoi continuatori in Italia (1857–1914)', *Studi Storici* 37.3 (1996), pp. 816–17.

13 Arrigo Serpieri, *Istituzioni di economia agraria* (2nd edn, Bologna: Edizioni agricole, 1950), p. 486.

14 Pietro Cuppari, *Manuale dell'agricoltore* (Firenze: Barbera, 1869); see Arrigo Serpieri, *Principi di economia corporativa* (Firenze: Barbera, 1938).

of specific farms; among which to select a certain number of types [. . .]. The overall physiognomy – so to say – of the local rural economy will emerge from comparing the various types'. Farm and family surveys alike were inspired by the assumption that the family or the farm to be studied could be selected in such a way as to represent the families or farms of its area or a specific class of them. They were the types of their class.

For agricultural economists as well as for politicians interested in agriculture at the beginning of the twentieth century, the framework for thinking about Italy's regionally differentiated agriculture was provided by Vittorio Niccoli's *Manuale dell'agronomo e dell'ingegnere agrario* (1897). He studied in detail three types of farm, each roughly significant for a specific region of Italy: the irrigated farm of Lombardy, the *podere* of Val d'Elsa, and the latifundium of Maremma. For each type, Niccoli addressed the issue of gross product, expenses and interest costs on capital, in order to compute the rent, the rate of return on the purchase of land and the value of the farm.[15] Agricultural economists could refer to the three types sketched by Niccoli when investigating different areas and farm typologies, by exploiting likeness and variation. Niccoli's *Handbook* provided in this way a sketchy atlas of Italy's agriculture in economic terms: rent, the expected returns on land investments, and some technical coefficient. Onto this atlas, other researchers could map their own local studies.

Investigators could *a posteriori* determine the position of a real individual farm on the grid of types, using the data collected.[16] This was especially useful for valuation, where an individual farm had to be assigned to the appropriate type in order to determine its value. Each of Niccoli's three types was intended to represent different forms of agriculture, and could serve as a reference point during the valuation of farms of the same type. The irrigated farm of Lombardy gave a general scheme for the understanding of capital intensive forms of agriculture, the *podere* of Val d'Elsa represented labour intensive forms, and the latifundium of Maremma stood for all similarly extensive farms in central and northern Italy as well as the south.[17]

Typical farm as ordinary farm

Studies such as Niccoli's rested on the appraisal of different elements of the economic structure of farms and estates that characterized each farming system. The most important was the determination of the value of land as it varied between farming types. High unitary values of land seemed to be an index of the high productivity of an area and its prevailing farming system. There was a

15 Value was obtained by capitalizing the expected rent; Vittorio Niccoli, *Prontuario dell'agricoltore: Manuale di agricoltura, economia, estimo e costruzioni rurali* (Torino: UTET, 1897); Niccoli also applied his type-based analysis in the creation of Italy's CA in 1910, on the basis of harvest statistics until the 1930s, see Chapter 4.

16 This was especially the case for E. Laur's celebrated farm accounting statistics.

17 Serpieri, *Istituzioni di economia agraria*, p. 481 n. 2.

general consensus that the value of land was to be computed as the capitalized value of yearly rent. Land valuation hence depended on the assessment of rent. But what was rent, and how was it assessed?

In Italy, already in the *cadastres* of the eighteenth century, the rent (*rendita* or *beneficio fondiario*) was considered the part that remained to the landowner once all the expenses for cultivation were subtracted from the land's gross product. But whenever for some reason no full actual rent was paid by tenants to landowners, this was a notional rather than an actual value, and it was difficult to assess it accurately. Once the expenses were detracted from the gross product, the result did not include the rent alone. It was the sum, instead, of the rent (*beneficio fondiario*) and the return for the entrepreneurship of the farmer (*beneficio industriale*).[18] Expenses included the remuneration of managerial work and the interest paid on capital other than land, together with the cost of seeds, insurance against bad weather, fertilizer, labour, and so on. There were two problems to be solved, and both involved the identification of typical farms. The first issue was how the farm gross product was to be assessed. A furious debate raged up until the end of the nineteenth century between two schools of valuation in Italy, the *suscettivisti* and *attualisti*. The whole point in the argument between *suscettivisti* and *attualisti* was about what counted as a legitimate basis for the computation of rent. A second problem was how to distinguish *beneficio fondiario* and *beneficio industriale*.

Although appraisal and land valuation were very general practices, Italian agricultural economists of the nineteenth and twentieth centuries were convinced, almost unanimously, that appraisal was an 'Italian science'. The Italian tradition of appraisal was for them the oldest and the most thoughtful in Europe. For Niccoli, after the Romans and their principles of land valuation, the modern bibliography on appraisal began in 1755. 'The first stone of the scientific building of valuation' according to him was the *Trattato sulle stime dei beni stabili* by Cosimo Trinci.[19] Trinci listed three classes of element that had to be considered when estimating the land value: the area, the quality of land, the position. But what was he estimating? Was he appraising land on the basis of its current, actual, production, or instead on the basis of its potential production, given the land's best foreseeable use? Trinci was in favour of considering the dispositions of the soil, its potential, as the basis of land value. Niccoli saw in Trinci's work the very beginning of a debate between *attualisti* and *suscettivisti*.

Attualisti claimed that, in assessing the value of a specific plot, it made no sense to consider also the income that could be obtained by additional investments.

18 Di Sandro, *Gli economisti agrari italiani tra Otto e Novecento*. It is worth noting that the *beneficio industriale* was distinct from the returns on capital. It represented rather the reward for the entrepreneurial ability of the farmer.

19 Vittorio Niccoli, *Bibliografia dell'estimo ordinario in Italia fino al 1856* (Verona-Padova: Drucker e Tedeschi, 1889), p. 19.

Land had to be appraised for what it was when it was bought, not for what it could have been according to the estimator if all sort of counter-factual conditions were fulfilled in the future. The *suscettivisti* claimed instead that the dispositions and potentialities of land (*suscettibilità)* should not be ignored, because the buyer of the land could have exploited them. There was a great variety of positions within these two battling groups. Adamo Fabbroni, for instance, held a position that was somehow in between the two (but the dispute had not yet reached its climax): while private investors should take into account only the current, actual, rent, states should tax land according to its potential, in order to stimulate improvement.

Melchiorre Gioia, the reference point of the *suscettivisti,* suggested that the crops with the most stable prices, rather than the crops actually growing on the land, should serve as the starting point for land appraisal. But after expressing so strongly the position of the *suscettivisti*, he limited its radicalism by adding:

> If an appraiser is asked to evaluate a plot which yields but a minimum rent, due to very bad methods of cultivation, he shall ignore the current rent, and look for the value by assuming that the plot was already worked according to better methods and the standard ability [of the farmer]. For the very same reason he shall not attribute to the plot a value that results from an extraordinary enterprise or abundant capital.[20]

Gioia introduces here a limitation to the position of the pure *suscettivisti* that eventually led to the final solution of the debate. He introduces the idea of the standard ability of the farmer. Since it is the land, and not the ability or negligence of the farmer, that is transferred with the purchase, it would be wrong to assess production on the basis of something exceptional.

This idea was soon to be generalized. Not only the farmer's ability, but also the techniques and even the crops considered for appraisal must be those prevailing in the area where the plot is situated. Hence Nicola Cavalieri San Bortolo in 1821 distinguished transitory from permanent rent. The transitory rent was only the rent computed on the basis of the product of the years preceding the appraisal. The permanent rent, instead, depended 'on the internal natural, social and economic conditions of the plot itself, according to the *ordinary system of cultivation* and the structure of the land'.[21]

With the works of Giuseppe Borio, who left a lasting mark on the landscape of the science of appraisal in Italy (a small but pugnacious territory), the debate between *suscettivisti* and *attualisti* reached its conclusion along the lines traced by Nicola Cavalieri. A farm should be appraised neither by assuming its potential production, nor considering its actual production. The appraiser, instead, should compute the farm production as if the farm was an ordinary farm,

20 Gioia (1817), quot. ibid., p. 39.
21 Nicola Cavalieri San Bortolo (1821), quot. ibid., p. 49 (my emphasis).

where the standard techniques of the area were applied, and the area's standard system of farming adopted.[22] Such an ordinary farm was, in fact, a typical farm, which represented the prevailing type, or one of the prevailing types in its area. Beyond considerations of soil, exposure, area, that could apply to a great many different areas and regions, appraisers should consider the farming types that prevailed in their area, that is, the standard crop rotations, the traditional techniques. They served as the reference points for land valuation.

This implies that appraisers must have been able to identify the typical farms of the areas in which they operated. Unfortunately, manuals of appraisal usually took this ability for granted. While they devoted a great many pages to accounting formulas for capitalization and discussed in detail the different elements that had to be taken into consideration in specific cases, they never discussed how to identify the ordinary farmer, techniques and farming system in practice.[23] Prevailing farm types probably seemed self-evident to people with localized knowledge. The ordinary farmer (for private purposes or for the *cadastre*) must have been recognizable as such by locals and the criteria of ordinariness emerged from within the local community.[24]

The second problem mentioned above was not so much a problem in practice (the reason why will emerge below), as it was a tormenting riddle for the theory of appraisal: how to separate *beneficio fondiario* (B_f) from *beneficio industriale* (B_i), the revenue of the entrepreneur and that of the landlord? In 1916–17 Arrigo Serpieri, who became the most influential agricultural economist in Italy for decades, published a long paper proposing to reframe the notion of the ordinary farmer in a marginalist framework, inspired by Vilfredo Pareto, Enrico Barone, Léon Walras and above all by Alfred Marshall and his theory of

22 In the early 1900s, Marenghi wrote: 'We are perfectly aware that in many agrarian reasons the rent of plots under ordinary farming systems is much lower than what could be achieved with a few and simple modern practices. Yet we capitalize the rent that corresponds to usual farming systems'. Within the neoclassical Walrasian framework, this meant that the rate of profit tended to become uniform and equal to zero, because the ordinary farm was, by definition, not innovative or privileged, Mario Polelli and Guidi Sali, 'La valutazione dei capitali fondiari', in CESET, ed., *Aspetti evolutivi della scienza estimativa: Seminario in onore di Ernesto Marenghi* (Firenze: Florence University Press, 1995), p. 92.

23 See as an example the textbooks by Cesare Tommasina, *Corso di estimo civile industriale rurale: Teoria dell'estimo razionale e tecnica estimativa con esercizi numerici, esempi di stima e tavole finanziarie,* Grande biblioteca tecnica 10 (Torino: S.T.E.N., 1912), and Giulio Fettarappa, *Nozioni di economia politica: intorno alla produzione, allo scambio, al valore, al capitale ed all'interesse: Come introduzione a un corso d'estimo ad uso degl'ingegneri, geometri e periti catastali* (Torino: Camilla e Bertolero, 1887), the main names, with Borio of 'scuola di estimo torinese'.

24 On the consensual formation of cadastral estimates, see Giuseppe Tassinari, *Frammentazione e ricomposizione dei fondi rurali,* Pubblicazioni del R. Istituto Superiore Forestale Nazionale Firenze N. 8 (Firenze: Tip. M. Ricci, 1922), on the combination of plots in Austria; for the *cadastre* in Milan, the already mentioned Ivana Pederzani, *Dall'antico regime alla restaurazione: Profili di storia costituzionale in area lombarda tra Sette e Ottocento*, Scienze storiche, filosofiche, pedagogiche e psicologiche 315 (Roma: Aracne, 2008) and Gian Rinaldo Carli, *Il censimento di Milano* (Milano: Giovanni Silvestri, 1815).

the representative firm. Serpieri assumed that, for an ordinary farmer who lacked any special managerial ability or extra capital (or who was not particularly incapable nor deprived of capital), P (production) equalled K (expenses, including rent) and B_i (the industrial profit of the farmer, *beneficio industriale)* was absent. For him, this was the consequence of an equilibrium market where competition ate up economic profit, but not rent. In fact, if $P = K$, since all expenses except rent (B_f) are supposed to be known, it is enough to reverse the equation as $B_f = P - K'$ (expenses except rent), in order to obtain the rent itself (*beneficio fondiario*).[25]

The theoretical premise for estimating rent was thus the existence 'of a widespread ordinariness (*ordinarietà diffusa*) in the use of production factors such as can be considered the analogous Walras tendency towards the offset of profit'.[26] The ordinary farm was characterized by the ordinary combination of production factors and corresponded to Alfred Marshall's representative firm. The empirical identification of ordinary methods of cultivation was the task of the appraiser. For the area where the farm was situated, he had to fix, first, the ordinary farming system, i. e. the combination of crops, the way the products were marketed, the organization of labour, the area of each enterprise; and, second, the way the farming system was applied, that is, the fertilization methods, the methods of executing technical operations (machines, and so on).

Although Serpieri refrained in this contribution from giving practical guidelines for determining an area's ordinary farming system, he noticed that this was hard to determine whenever (and wherever) agriculture was undergoing systematic transformation, but was relatively evident to the eyes of appraisers when agriculture enjoyed periods of relative immobility and stability.[27]

The theory of appraisal translated the concept of typical farm into that of ordinary farm and therefore decisively contributed to determine, for agricultural economists, what a typical farm was. By the First World War, the typical – that is, the ordinary – farm was, for Serpieri, the agricultural equivalent of the representative of Marshall's 'firm': being incapable of particular innovation and safe from extraordinary losses, it was a price-taker without (economic) profit. This idea also implied that farms, at least locally, must have similar cost structures; this tended towards a similar use of production factors, since the market pushed all farmers in the same direction. Statistically, this meant that farms would be distributed normally around a central average size for all the relevant quantitative factors (area, use of fertilizers, hired labour, and so on). Although they did not have empirical evidence, agricultural economists were fairly confident that this must be so.

25 Arrigo Serpieri, 'Il metodo di stima dei beni fondiari', *Annali del R. Ist. Superiore Forestale Nazionale* II (1916–17), p. 35f., §11, §17, §22.

26 Polelli and Sali, 'La valutazione dei capitali fondiari', p. 92.

27 Serpieri, 'Il metodo di stima dei beni fondiari', p. 84f.

Surveys, enquiries, and statistics

Until the 1920s, the relationship between surveys, enquiries, and statistics seemed relatively simple to economists and statisticians alike. Surveys provided the detail, and the other two forms of investigation, each of them in its own way, provided the general picture. Like Le Play's pupil, Emile Cheysson, Italian agricultural economists assumed that:

> La statistique officielle va donc en avant-garde et dégage les moyennes qui conduisent le monographe à son type. A son tour la monographie lui rend le service de vérifier par une étude détaillée les résultats généraux de l'enquête.[28]

Statistics, in particular, studied the whole relevant population, while surveys studied a limited number of well-chosen cases. The choice of such cases rested on the general features of the population as a whole, such features being known to the investigators from available statistics.

Their relationship with statistics rested, at this time, on the principle that statistics were actually a precondition for surveys. Valenti's comments on the plan of the minister of agriculture who preceded Cocco-Ortu are revealing. Pantano, the minister, held that farm surveys could be a cheap substitute for statistics of agricultural production, thus saving the government the effort of asking parliament for significant funds.[29] Surveys of typical farms represented local variations of the nation's agriculture in more detail than any nationwide statistics. They described crop rotations and production coefficients that the static character of output figures would not fully represent. And surveys were obviously cheaper than statistics, since they did not require a permanent or semi-permanent institutional setting. Moreover, Belgium had already started the publication of collections of farm surveys describing different regional types of agriculture.[30] To Pantano and his staff, this seemed to be the Columbus' Egg of statistics and they ordered farm surveys to represent each of Italy's 69 provinces.

Valenti had been chosen to prepare the survey for the province of Padua, where he was teaching, but as soon as the cabinet fell and the incoming

28 Emile Cheysson, quoted in Alain Desrosières, 'La partie pour le tout: comment généraliser? La prehistoire de la contrainte de représentativité', *Statistique et analyse des données* 13.2 (1988), p. 97; on Cheysson as the reconciliation of Le Play and Quételet, see Protasi, 'Tra scienza e riforma sociale'; and Giovanni Favero, 'Business Attitudes Toward Statistical Investigation in Late Nineteenth Century Italy: A Wool Industrialist from Reticence to Influence', *Enterprise and Society* 12.2 (2011), pp. 265–316.

29 The agricultural enquiry that the Italian parliament undertook in 1876 also included farm surveys. The analysis of individual farms was thought to be the right way to reveal the dominant traits of the types, agricultural businesses in each area (a province or a smaller unit). They were expected to distinguish what Jacini himself called 'the many Italies of agriculture'. Not enough effort was made to institutionalize the collection of such data; see Chapter 3.

30 Belgium: Ministère de L'Agriculture, *Monographies agricoles,* 1–4 (Brussels: Ministère de l'agriculture, 1899–1901).

minister, Cocco-Ortu, selected him to reorganize the Office for Agricultural Statistics, he voiced his dissent from the project. Valenti, like Cheysson, was convinced that surveys and statistics were complementary to each other, and one could not substitute for the other. He stressed the difference by claiming that only the availability of good statistics could provide adequate information for formulating the appropriate typology.

Only when the general figures representing the agriculture of a province ('the average ratio of areas of different crops and relative productions, the average revenue of the land, the average number of livestock, and so on and so on') were known, was it possible to judge which farm was close to typical. However, 'a farm survey [. . .] will give a much more robust idea of the agrarian organism than that formed by considering the results of direct investigation alone, since they cannot offer but the general schematic lines'.[31] His criticism of Pantano's plan was confirmed by a closer examination of the latter's Belgian model. The Belgians prepared their surveys on the basis of the general agricultural census of 1895 (Recensement général agricole). This meant that 'statistics preceded, rather than followed, surveys'.[32]

The Italian and French statisticians, after Adolphe Quételet, thought that when the data concerned were distributed approximately along the curve of a normal distribution, they revealed the existence of a single underlining cause of the phenomenon observed. They thought that the average datum revealed an essential feature of the population studied, and that divergence from the mean, on one side or the other, meant some sort of error or deviation from such essence. The 'typical value' was taken to be the most frequent value:

> [Anyone] who wants to study, for instance, a professional group from the point of view of the number of children of each member of the group, will ask: how many individuals in the group under examination have no child; how many of them have 1; how many have 2 children; how many have 3, and so on and will determine in this way the typical value. The group of Italian miners discussed in 1907 in an enquiry of the Bureau of Labour is distributed under this respect, as follows: 4526 with no child; 4167 with 1 child; 4954 with 2 children; 4188 with 3 children; 3158 with 4 children; 3633 with 5 children or more. We will therefore say that the typical value of the phenomenon

31 Ghino Valenti, *Per l'ordinamento della statistica agraria in Italia: Relazione a S.E. Il comm. Cocco Ortu, Ministro di agricoltura, industria e commercio* (Roma: Tip. Nazionale di G. Bertero e C, 1907), p. 26; on this see also the discussion between Bodio and Montemartini at the Consultative commission, where Montemartini argued that surveys were intended to select the most profitable sources on which statistics could rely, and were thus preliminary to statistics, while Bodio answered that surveys (as practised by Cheysson, Le Play and Cuppari) could provide only the coefficients that need to be multiplied by the large numbers obtained through statistics, MAIC, ed., *Esperimenti di statistica agraria in alcune province del Regno* (Roma: Bertero, 1907), I, p. 340. Bodio's remark seems to consider surveys only good to provide the coefficients of conjectural statistics.

32 Valenti, *Per l'ordinamento della statistica agraria in Italia*, p. 12.

observed (family status concerning number of children) is represented, at least in the rough series presented here, by the miner with 2 children.[33]

But a population could show more than one type. This was the case, for instance, when instead of normal, the distribution was bimodal, that is, instead of showing a single central value in the proximity of which observations thickened, it showed two such values. In his studies on the height of Greek statues in the collection of the Louvre, for instance, Quételet had observed a similar distribution: the heights observed clustered around two values. He assumed that there had been two types of Greek statue: a bigger and a smaller one, most likely with different destinations.[34] The typical emerged from the analysis of the statistical distribution of masses of data as the average or also as the mode (which in a normal distribution coincide): 'What's the aim of Statistics? It aims at discovering what is typical beyond variability, what is definite in the indefinite mass of social facts'.[35]

In principle, Cheysson was confident that types that emerged from statistics could well serve survey investigations. In practice, however, the guidance offered by statistics in the choice of the type for the survey was less straightforward, and Le Play's followers were always forced to adjust their notion of typical to the real needs of the investigation.[36] For agricultural economists, Cheysson's concept of 'typical' (a concept shared by many statisticians at the end of the nineteenth century) also interfered and combined with the older notion of farming type and typical farm. When it came to actual research, agricultural economists thought that their own typologies, developed according to agronomic categories and already applied in land valuation, would coincide with the typical instance of Cheysson's surveys and hence with the average individual of the type. As we saw in Chapter 4, the lack of previous reliable statistics induced Valenti to combine Cheysson's systematic view of the typical with Niccoli's agronomic view of farming types. Coletti's methodological guidelines for the Faina Enquiry, discussed in Chapter 3, above, should help set out the multiple ambiguities in the concept of typical.

In the next chapter I show how the growth of data on individual businesses that was made available to agricultural economists with the expansion of farm accounting services, made a rigorous definition of type necessary,

33 Alfredo Niceforo, *Il metodo statistico: Teoria e applicazioni alle Scienze naturali, alle Scienze sociali, e all'Arte* (Messina: Casa Editrice Giuseppe Principato, 1923), pp. 39f. Niceforo's treaty is relatively recent, but it expresses the received view of Italian statisticians; see also Alberto Baffigi, *Cultura statistica e cultura politica: L'Italia nei primi decenni unitari*, Quaderni dell'Ufficio Ricerche Storiche / Banca d'Italia 15 (Roma, 2007), p. 42f.

34 Niceforo, *Il metodo statistico*, p. 54.

35 'A che mira la Statistica? A scoprire il tipico nel variabile, il definito nell'indefinito di numerosi fatti sociali', Giovanni B. Salvioni, 'Ai confini della statistica', *Rassegna di scienze sociali e politiche* 218 (1892), pp. 97–8.

36 Bosco quot. in Baffigi, *Cultura statistica e cultura politica*, pp. 42f. and Protasi, 'Tra scienza e riforma sociale'.

while statisticians increasingly criticized the methods of fieldwork based on types. For the first decades of the twentieth century, the confidence in surveys was shared, nevertheless, by statisticians and agricultural economists alike.

In the parliamentary enquiry of 1906–11, on the conditions of the peasants in the southern provinces and Sicily (the Faina Enquiry), surveys complemented the parliamentary enquiry and served as 'a synthesis and an index' – in Coletti's words – of what was happening to a class, that of peasants or that of landowners, and in specific areas. Francesco Coletti recommended the preparation of family and farm surveys for typical families and farms.[37] While Coletti's alleged models, the 1902 Irish and British enquiries on income and wages in agriculture, and the German enquiries on income and labour conditions,[38] were based on the collection of a large number of budgets, in practice, Coletti's technical delegates were able to collect only a few detailed budgets.

Coletti summarized and published in 1907 Cheysson's directions for the compilation of surveys as methodological guidelines for the Faina Enquiry. In 1929 Coletti's *abregé* of Cheysson was extensively quoted by Arrigo Serpieri in his *Guida a ricerche di economia agraria* which remained the basic textbook for empirical research in agricultural economics until after the Second World War. First of all, the survey method rested upon the presupposition that there existed a pre-ordered division of all elements of a class into 'typical categories'. This categorization depended on factors that the researcher must have known already (for instance from an equivalent of the Belgian *Recensement Général*, mentioned above). Coletti gives this example, concerning the choice of typical peasant families:

> In a *circondario* (. . .) there are two distinct agricultural zones: the zone of hills, and that of mountains. In each zone, there are peasants who cultivate the land as sharecroppers, others as tenant farmers, others, finally, as free wage labourers. In one of these categories, say for instance among the tenant farmers, there is a visible difference between a group of well-to-do tenants and a group of tenants who can barely subsist. We thus have for each agricultural zone four types of family: sharecroppers, fat tenants, meager tenants, wage labourers. In the whole of the *circondario*, eight types.[39]

It will be noticed that some of these family types are rather farm types, and that they all spring from the agricultural conditions of the area (which makes types dependent on the preliminary division of the country into agricultural zones).

37 Francesco Coletti, *Come si compilano le monografie di famiglia: Estratto dallo Cheysson e Focillon* (Roma: Bertero, 1906).

38 Among the enquiries to which Coletti referred are the following: Great Britain – Board of Trade: *Earnings of agricultural labourers: 2nd report by Mr. Wilson Fox on the wages, earnings and conditions of employment of agricultural labourers in the United Kingdom, with statistical tables and charts*, London 1905; Germany – the enquiry of the Verein fuer Sozial Politik, *Die Verhältnisse der Landarbeiter in Deutschland, Leipzig 1892; Dettweiler, Die Handarbeit in der Landwirtschaft*, Jena 1905.

39 Coletti, *Come si compilano le monografie di famiglia*, p. 153.

Within each type so defined, the researcher could choose a larger or smaller number of typical families according to the resources available. But in general in the original practice of Le Play and his school, it was the village notables – the social authorities – who selected representative individuals for Le Play's envoys: types could be identified through their environment.[40] Coletti, who was a reforming socialist, did not expect researchers to rely absolutely on social authorities (he claimed that Le Play's political principles had been generally discarded) but he nevertheless based the choice of typical instances on the mobilization of 'all the expert and practical individuals who will be found in each *circondario*, i.e., in the small area that will be taken as the scope of the enquiry'.[41]

For Coletti, their choice of the typical is what distinguishes surveys from statistics. While statistics surveyed a population, and extracted the typical from the mass or series of data, by computing the average and the mode of the population, the enquiry and the survey fixed their attention immediately on the cases that were considered typical and representative of a particular class of phenomena. On the basis of the features observed in such cases, they directed their observations and developed their inductive reasoning.[42]

Surveys as a unifying language

In practice, the choice of typical instances, and the study of such typical instances for the compilation of surveys rested, to a great extent, on the enquirer's ability to establish relationships and mobilize resources during his or her fieldwork. Selecting and studying a typical farm or a typical farmer's family required a sort of empathy (It. *immedesimazione*) between the researcher with the object of his/her research. This argument had already been developed by Luigi Einaudi.[43] In the case of Italian agricultural economists, this meant attributing great importance to the institutions that formed an intermediate level between science and peasant life, such as the *cattedre ambulanti di agricoltura.*

Professors and assistants of the *cattedre ambulanti* lived amidst the farmers: they knew what was typical and how to build the area's farming types, because they experienced every day the fine grained differences between types of agriculturalists. The more or less explicit hope was that the results of the survey method either coincided with the typical obtained by means of statistics, or allowed the researcher to verify the results of the statistical method.[44]

40 Bernard Kalaora and Antoine Savoye, *Les Inventeurs oubliés: Le Play et ses continuateurs aux origines des sciences sociales,* Collection Milieux (Paris: Champ Vallon, 1989), a praiseworthy attempt at recognizing the scientific character of Le Play's methodology beyond Le Play's (and his pupils') ideological allegiances.

41 Francesco Coletti, *Programma questionario dell'inchiesta per i delegati tecnici* (Roma: Bertero, 1906), p. 61.

42 Ibid..

43 Protasi, 'Tra scienza e riforma sociale', p. 816.

44 Favero, 'Business Attitudes Toward Statistical Investigation', p. 276.

Investigators in general compensated for the small number of surveys with the high degree of detail collected. Each survey required a very skilled investigator, with a good knowledge of agricultural techniques and a certain familiarity with specific local conditions. In these conditions, therefore, they could not be collected in great numbers. But this was not even necessary, since investigators assumed that they were representative enough, precisely thanks to the careful choice of the farms described. For Coletti, farm surveys served more as an illustration of the conditions of the area, than as an inductive base.

This wealth of detail was not strictly speaking limited to economic factors. Next to the study of land use (the main concern of agricultural statistics), investigators observed peasant mores, production technology and institutional arrangements (contracts, relations with the state and among private individuals). Agronomic and social aspects closely intertwined in the farming type. Farming depended on contracts, on the relations between peasants and landlords, on the morality of the peasants, on their degree of literacy, their openness to new techniques, their spirit of enterprise and other sociological and anthropological categories. State enquiries usually dedicated a consistent space to this kind of investigation because they were expected to produce at the same time knowledge on social problems and on the economic environment that limited the possibility of their solution.[45]

When the Faina Enquiry was launched in 1906 it was an enquiry that programmatically concentrated on the condition of peasants and smallholders. The focus naturally was on typical peasants and typical farms. When instead of the agronomic elements of the farm type, the investigators stressed social and ethnographic facts, such as peasant mentality, housing, living standards, and so on, almost inevitably their research, while keeping them still within agricultural economics, came close to the research of ethnographers and sociologists. In both disciplines, surveys of farms were considered the best way to capture farm types. Since agriculture was described by means of typical farms, and typical farms presupposed typical farmers, great importance was attributed to the description of living and working conditions of typical farmers. These were described through the selection of documents: contracts, photographs, drawings, witnesses' statements, and budgets. Agricultural economists shared these methods with ethnographers or scholars of folklore, who transcribed the legitimate traditions of a population. All these factors were regarded as part of economics, since they affected the economy. Contracts, for instance, were the cornerstone of the economy and determined by their prescriptions the prevalence of certain farming types.

45 For some aspects of the rising importance attributed to the interconnection between moral elements and economic milieu, and economics as a middle ground for facing the social question in France, see Paul Rabinow, *French Modern: Norms and Forms of the Social Environment* (Chicago: University of Chicago Press, 1995).

Ernesto Marenghi, who was the enquiry's technical delegate in Calabria, documented tenancy contracts in the area. They usually followed standard types with similar modes of renewal, payment structure, and so on. Sometimes they were made on blank forms that the parties themselves could fill in with suitable specifications. In other cases, contracts might be regulated by conventions, transmitted orally, and generally respected. Marenghi collected examples of written types and transcribed oral contracts (discussing their possible variations).

Other areas where the enquiries of the economist and of the ethnographer overlapped were the study of agricultural techniques and housing. The volumes of the Faina Enquiry contained a great many photographs of houses (typical houses, of course) and peasants engaged in agricultural activities. This was the same kind of material that agricultural economists who worked for local extension offices (*cattedre ambulanti*) also collected in their daily work. Only pictures could properly reproduce the different typologies of ploughs and the different ways of using them. They thus constituted invaluable documents.[46]

The investigators of the Faina Enquiry also took a great many photographs that delineated population types in terms of their traditional clothing and physiognomy. Types could and should be exhibited. This obviously left open the problem of selecting the truly typical costume, tool, village structure, and so on, a problem equally confronted by ethnographic collectors of the same period.[47] In some cases, agricultural economists organized displays of the life of villages for the benefit of the visitors to national or international fairs.[48]

This sociological-ethnographic approach to farm types shows the cross-contamination between strictly agroeconomic studies and anthropology and linguistics. The overlapping was mutual and, in parallel with the field work of agricultural economists, anthropologists investigated the possible causes of poverty in southern Italy. In the study of southern Italy made by Alfredo Niceforo, the investigation of socio-economic factors combined the 'physical study, the pathological-physical and the psycho-physical study of the individuals who constituted the population studied'.[49] Ethnic types were identified by a plurality of elements, cultural and physical. For Niceforo, as for his teacher Cesare Lombroso, anatomical types demonstrated socio-economic characteristics.

46 See also Giuseppe Šebesta, 'Fotografia e disegno nella ricerca etnografica', *La Ricerca Folklorica* 2 (1980). It should be noticed that in the same years, a group of Swiss linguists was preparing an atlas that recorded, among other things, the shape take by agricultural tools in the various regions and the names given to them in local languages across Italy: K. Jaberg and J. Judd, *Sprach- und Sachatlas Italiens und der Südschweiz* (Zofingen: Ringier, 1928).

47 Sandra Puccini, *L'itala gente dalle molte vite: Lamberto Loria e la Mostra di etnografia italiana del 1911* (Roma: Meltemi, 2005), p. 32, recalls the concern for representativeness expressed by Lamberto Loria in organizing the collection of folk objects for the Universal Exhibition of 1911, in Rome.

48 Laur prepared a fake 'typical village' in Switzerland to exhibit local life, Ernst Laur, *Erinnerungen eines schweizerischen Bauernführers: ein Beitrag zur Wirtschaftsgeschichte* (Bern: Buchverlag Verbandsdruckerei, 1943).

49 Alfredo Niceforo, *Antropologia delle classi povere, Trattato di medicina sociale* (Milano: Vallardi, 1910), p. 16, quot. in Protasi, 'Tra scienza e riforma sociale', p. 824.

Photographs or even physiognomies described by means of police methods of identification offered material for overall judgment. Niceforo was highly influential on Italian public opinion and in 1920 became a member of the Council for Statistics, which superintended Italy's statistical works.[50]

Although not everybody agreed on the racial explanation of southern Italy's economic destitution, reasons for this backwardness were inevitably attributed to a plurality of causes that included not merely economic facts but traditions, (material) culture, and mental habits.[51] Ethnography, physical anthropology and economic investigation could combine and types should be able to summarize populations that were supposed to be homogeneous and often became stereotypes.[52]

Farming types – farming styles

In the period discussed in this chapter, different definitions of type competed and overlapped. A rigorous formalization in the language of statistics proved hard to obtain. This very indeterminacy allowed researchers to bend the typical to answer a variety of needs. Together with the physical elements of crop rotation and area, farming types could not avoid including other elements: techniques, technologies, contracts, family structure, and so on that were difficult or impossible to quantify, but were part of the expertise of agricultural economists in particular places. The farming type therefore had an agronomic and a social dimension: it existed empirically but it was also a prevailing style or a set of values diffused across the agricultural population.[53]

Probably the most emblematic of the Italian farm types was the Tuscan sharecropper, the veritable myth of which focused not so much on the physical, agronomic data of the Tuscan *podere* but on the moral values of the sharecropper (*mezzadro*): the steady family, social peace, personal

50 On Niceforo and the Italian anthropologists, see Peter D'Agostino, 'Craniums, Criminals, and the "Cursed Race": Italian Anthropology in American Racial Thought, 1861–1924', *Comparative Studies in Society and History* 44.2 (2002).

51 For a survey of different interpretations of Southern backwardness, see Giuseppe Galasso, *Passato e presente del meridionalismo,* 2 vols, I Tascabili (Napoli: Guida, 1978), pp. 14–30, while, on the early stereotypes on southerners, see Marta Petrusewicz, *Come il Meridione divenne una questione. Rappresentazione del Sud prima e dopo il Quarantotto* (Soveria Mannelli: Rubbettino, 1998). An interesting example of the persistence of categorizations based on farm types is to be found in Paolo Macry, 'Rethinking a stereotype: Territorial differences and family models in the modernization of Italy', *Journal of Modern Italian Studies* 2.2 (2008).

52 On homogeneity, see Niceforo, *Il metodo statistico,* and also Baffigi, *Cultura statistica e cultura politica* for a thorough discussion of the importance of such a concept in Italian statistics.

53 On farming styles, see the seminal Jan D. van der Ploeg, 'An Introductory Note on Concepts and Methodology', in Jan D. van der Ploeg and Ann Long, eds, *Born from Within: Practice and Perspectives of Endogenous Rural Development,* European perspectives on rural development (Assen: van Gorcum, 1994), pp. 7–30, and a reassessment of the concept in Frank Vanclay et al., 'The Social and Intellectual Construction of Farming Styles: Testing Dutch Ideas in Australian Agriculture', *Sociologia Ruralis* 46.1 (2006).

engagement in the enterprise, and so on. So vivid was this myth that sharecroppers from central Italy would be dispatched to the most destitute areas of the south to export their techniques and values in so-called internal colonization.[54] It was this wide range of components that made the concept of type so valuable.

The social dimension connected immediately research in agricultural economics with ethnography and anthropology. There was a sort of methodological *koiné* (common language) in theory and practice that embraced such disciplines as anthropology and agricultural economics. This *koiné* was not necessarily the product of diffusion from one discipline to another; it could also be the result of a polygenesis (as the importance of farming types in appraisal practices sufficiently documents) that eventually led to phenomena of contamination. The common language centred on types allowed, in the view of the investigators, a grasp of local differentiation along multiple dimensions of analysis (economic, but also social, and so on). Hence the attention paid to representative individuals capable of summarizing and displaying the (blurry) type, rather than statistics. In agricultural economics, types also possessed a geographical character; they served to systematize structural differences induced by the adaptation to climatic, hydrographic, orographic and geological conditions. This adaptation extended to purely social facts, to the mores of the population.

The practices of agricultural economists, land valuation in particular, played a great role in the construction of types of farms. In field research, recognizing types was a matter of the eye, of *coup d'oeil* rather than of information, something that could only be learned by practice, and by experience.[55] Statistics, doctrine, the science taught in university were preliminary to but not a replacement for fieldwork.

Notwithstanding this close link with expertise and practice, agricultural economists did not abandon a theoretical framework for their typical farm. Cheysson, in particular, provided the statistical framework: the farms selected for the investigation should display the characteristics that prevailed in the population according to the statistics available. In the first decades of the twentieth century, agricultural economists combined rather uncritically Cheysson's criteria of choice with their own disciplinary tradition of farm studies. Since the 1920s, the viability of Cheysson's view of type has been questioned and the confidence in its results shaken, but, as Serpieri's *Guida* witnesses very well, farm types still responded to the methodological needs of agricultural economists.

54 Eugenio Azimonti, *Il Mezzogiorno agrario quale è: relazioni e scritti* (Bari: G. Laterza & figli, 1919) sceptically described the arrival and subsequent failure of settlers from central Italy.

55 On the history of *coup d'oeil*, see Valeria Pansini, 'Pour une histoire concrète du "talent": les sélections méritocratiques et le coup d'oeil du topograph', *Annales Historiques de la Révolution Française* 354 (2008) which focuses on military engineers and topographers.

In practice, the debate in agricultural economics on the respective roles of statistics and surveys, of average and type, ended with the marginalization of type but did not lead to the disappearance of surveys and types. The INEA systematically collected farm surveys all through the 1930s, while surveys of farm types remained an important component of enquiries and had a role in the making and updating of the agricultural *cadastre*. From the 1910s in Italy, agricultural economists also began to focus on the budget of farms and from farm surveys originated the budget studies that I discuss in the next chapter. It was through research in rural sociology that farm types (or farming styles) adapted to the new environment and survived.

7 Budget studies

The relationship between surveys and statistics was in no way straightforward. Surveys could also turn into statistics. As Salvioni noticed, once a sufficient number of surveys had been accumulated, it was possible and meaningful to apply the methods of statistics to them.[1] There was a quantitative element in surveys that lent itself very well to statistical treatment. The most important quantitative feature of farm and family surveys was the budget. The budget entries were monetary values representing the incomes and the expenses of the farm or the family studied. Ernst Engel, for instance, discovered his celebrated law (that the proportion of expenditure devoted to food decreased as income grew) by examining family budgets collected in Saxony.[2] This way of approaching social issues was very successful for the investigation of socioeconomic phenomena and was applied everywhere in Europe, to investigate, in particular, the conditions of the lower classes and their levels of consumption.

In Italy, Giolitti's policy of neutrality in social conflict – which most landowners in the countryside opposed, as vehemently as factory owners opposed it in the cities – induced part of the landed classes to look for the peaceful solution of disputes in scientific investigations of the agricultural economy. Tensions in the countryside revolved around the issues of tenancy, wage, and labour conditions. Agricultural economists, thus, focused on the micro-level of farms in order to analyse the way that the product was affected by the different factors of production: labour, land, capital, and entrepreneurship. In this way, they sought to find out how farmers could bring about changes in the distribution of gross product without affecting production. Agrarian economists and progressive members of the liberal ruling class thus hoped that statistics might serve as a common ground for landowners, tenants, and trade unions. The study of farm budgets seemed to be a way to give scientific foundation to the

1 Giovanni B. Salvioni, 'Ai confini della statistica', *Rassegna di scienze sociali e politiche* 218 (1892), p. 98.

2 Ernst Engel, 'Die Lebenskosten belgischer Arbeiter-Familien früher und jetzt. Ermittelt aus Familien-Haushaltrechnungen und vergleichend zusammengestellt', *Bulletin de l'Institut International de Statistique* 9.1 (1895), pp. 1–124, which also contains Engel's previous work on Saxony, together with long discussions on data collected by Le Play and Duplectiaux.

Giolittian compromise, by analogy with the growing importance of scientific management during the taylorist moment of the early twentieth century.[3]

Agricultural economists thus saw their discipline and observational techniques as the starting point in the quest for solutions to social controversies, and implicitly claimed for themselves the role of impartial observers. The data provided by agricultural economists seemed to account for Giolitti's policy of neutrality before and shortly after the Great War. Coletti's approach was nevertheless insufficient to address such questions appropriately. The task required many more standardized budgets to be collected, as Engel had done. Only in this way could agricultural economists make their case convincingly and claim impartiality in a world of polarized class struggle.

The apparent impartiality of numbers, however, could exist only as a combination of different elements. The ideal of 'mechanical objectivity' dominated the natural sciences, and its principles extended to the collection of numbers in different fields. It seemed to offer a good solution to the issue of impartiality. As described by Daston and Galison in the case of the natural sciences, mechanical objectivity is the ideal of observing phenomena without interference from the subjectivity of the observer.[4]

Such an ideal was to be pursued by means of machines (the camera, the spectrometer, and so on). In social sciences, a close equivalent for mechanical objectivity was the rise of statistical observatories, whose data were collected almost mechanically by low-skilled data gatherers and could be freed from idiosyncrasies and aberrations by statistical manipulation.[5] Standardization, sheer quantity as regards the sample, and the machinery of the institutional framework stood for the machine component of mechanical objectivity.[6]

Mechanical objectivity in itself, however, was not an issue for early twentieth-century agricultural economists who thought it absolutely natural for investigators to select their material on the basis of their acquired skills. But the

3 The reference to Taylor's texts was not explicit, but it seems to me that the mediating role attributed to agricultural economists fits well with a broad definition of social Taylorism: 'What was novel about Taylorism was the application of the supposedly machine-oriented discipline of engineering to labour relations', Charles S. Maier, 'Between Taylorism and Technocracy: European Ideologies and the Vision of Industrial Productivity in the 1920s', *Journal of Contemporary History* 5.2 (1970), p. 30.

4 On objectivity in terms of the mechanical reproduction of phenomena, freed from the perturbing influences of the scientist's choices, see Lorraine Daston and Peter Galison, *Objectivity* (Cambridge, MA: Zone Books, 2007).

5 Theodore M. Porter, 'The statistical office as a social observatory', *Centaurus* 49 (2007), pp. 258–60, Theodore M. Porter, *Trust in Numbers: The Pursuit of Objectivity in Science and Public Life* (Princeton: Princeton University Press, 1996).

6 The phenomenon of a growing mechanization and 'Taylorization' of statistics has been observed in recent works by Thomas A. Stapleford, *The cost of living in America: A political history of economic statistics, 1880–2000* (Cambridge: Cambridge University Press, 2009) and by Emmanuel Didier, *En quoi consiste l'Amérique? Les statistiques, le new deal et la démocratie,* Série Anthropologie des sciences et des techniques (Paris: Éd. La Découverte, 2009), for different aspects of American agricultural statistics.

conception of 'selection of observers on the basis of their position', as I defined it in Chapter 3, was not very convincing when it came to discussing extremely conflictual topics. The quest for impartial numbers, and for a general consensus on the results of their investigation, therefore, induced an increasing concern with subjectivity. For budget enquiries, the primary effect of this concern was an increase in the number of budgets collected. Since growth in scale would have been meaningless without standardization, agricultural economists also tried to impose rules to standardize account books. Finally, to make the data collection easier and more constant, they looked for institutional frameworks that allowed them to pursue their research. These developments were costly and, to be accomplished, required agricultural economists to form alliances with different social forces.

The institutional model for the collection of farm budgets was Ernst Laur's Accounting Office at SBV. We can call this metaphorically an 'observatory' for the economic life of the countryside since it was able to collect significant numbers of budgets every year. In the words of Ernesto Marenghi, similar institutions 'mark the beginning of a new period in the history of agricultural economics, in the same way as the invention of the weighing scale marked the beginning of a new and glorious period in the history of chemistry'.[7]

In Italy, as Giolitti's neutrality experiment came to an end, and the rise of the Fascist regime froze social conflicts, the forces that supported inquiries into distribution weakened, and agricultural economists tried to redirect their methods of investigation along productivist lines, in agreement with the new interests of some of the most advanced groups of the landed elite. How agricultural economists tried to reclaim safe neutral ground out of the muddy marshes of political partisanship, and why they failed in the Italian case is the main point I hope to clarify in this chapter. I will thus examine different ways of dealing with farm budgets, from Serpieri's experience at Società Umanitaria di Milano to the INEA's series on farm budget statistics. Through such cases, I trace the effort to make numbers more objective (and less reliant on individual experts), the way in which this effort responded to dramatic political changes, and how, in the end, Italian agricultural economists fell short of their alleged models.

The data provided by the observatories of agricultural economics, nevertheless, were not without effect. In the fourth section of this chapter, I discuss how the definition of 'typical' was questioned when statistics based on the observation of a significant number of farms were made available by the observatories.

7 Quot. in Istituto centrale di statistica, 'Il progettato trasferimento degli uffici di statistica agraria', *Annali di Statistica: Atti del Consiglio superiore di statistica* VI (1930), p. 240: 'segnano una nuova epoca nella storia dell'Economia agraria, nella stessa guisa che la introduzione della bilancia e del metodo ponderale ha segnato un nuova e gloriosa epoca nella scienza chimica'.

Serpieri and the peasants of Alto Milanese

In 1904, the Società Umanitaria di Milano (SUM) promoted an inquiry on the land-leasing and labour contracts that involved peasants in the area of Milan. The SUM had been established thanks to the legacy of Prospero Moisè Loria in 1902 'as a Red Cross, which rescues and assists those who have been injured on the battlefield of industry'. In Loria's mind the activity of assistance could not be disjoined from a positive understanding of the 'factual conditions determining its activity'.[8] The SUM hence dedicated a great deal of its activity to the investigation of the conditions of the working class, in both its Labour and Agrarian Offices.

The two offices launched a joint enquiry on the living conditions of the peasants of the Milanese region (the Labour Office, directed by Giuseppe Lorenzoni, took part in the preparation of questionnaires).[9] The wave of strikes and acts of sabotage that hit that area in 1901 had been impressive (64 strikes in 48 municipalities[10]) and had been followed by substantial changes in the tenancy and labour contracts of peasants.[11] In order to study such changes and their effect on the conditions of the peasants, the SUM charged Serpieri, who was then a young professor of Appraisal and Agrarian Economics, with the task of investigating the situation, 'by surveying the actual conditions of a great number of real cases, that is, a great number of estates and peasant families'.[12]

This enquiry marked a turning point in the use of farm surveys. Although surveys of farms could still be woven into a wider inquiry, as in the Faina Enquiry, in Serpieri's work they formed the empirical basis of the analysis. Farm surveys were here employed in a way closer to that of Dettweiler's *Die Handarbeit in der Landwirtschaft*.[13] Instead of referring to them as 'indices' or 'episodes' (as Coletti had done), Serpieri wanted to replace, by means of farm surveys, 'qualitative, generic terms whose interpretation wavered with the mood of individuals, by quantitative, specific, exact terms'.[14] The macroscopic effect of this desire was a growth in the number of farm budgets collected and a focus on a relatively small

8 Quot. in Ivano Granata, *In difesa della terra: l'Ufficio agrario della Società Umanitaria 1905–1923* (Milano: Franco Angeli, 2003).

9 Giovanni Lorenzoni, *Le inchieste statistiche dell'ufficio del lavoro* (Milano: Ufficio del lavoro, 1903); on the Labour Office of SUM, see also Maria Letizia D'Autilia, *Il cittadino senza burocrazia Società umanitaria e amministrazione pubblica nell'Italia liberale* (Milano: Giuffrè, 1995).

10 Arrigo Serpieri, *Il contratto agrario e le condizioni dei contadini nell'Alto milanese* (Milano: Ufficio agrario della Società Umanitaria, 1910), p. xii.

11 On the evolution of peasant life in the area, see Paul Corner, *Contadini e industrializzazione: società rurale e impresa in Italia dal 1840 al 1940,* Quadrante (Roma) (Laterza, 1993).

12 Serpieri, *Il contratto agrario e le condizioni dei contadini nell'Alto milanese*, p. xii.

13 Dettweiler had collected very specific questionnaires from a relatively large number of farms in order to determine how manual labor was used in agriculture: how many working days per year, what were average wages, and so on. He had elaborated the data in order to reach some kind of general conclusion by computing means and dividing the population into classes.

14 Rodolfo Benini, *Principi di statistica metodologica* (Torino: UTET, 1906), quot. in Serpieri, *Il contratto agrario e le condizioni dei contadini nell'Alto milanese*, p. xii.

and homogeneous geographical area. The survey of individual estates (each of which contained a number of farms leased to peasant families) and the collection of peasant budgets in the Upper Milanese took almost three years. Serpieri and his two assistants visited 114 estates in 95 out of the 169 municipalities in the area studied and investigated 206 families in 89 municipalities and 129 estates (94 of them included in the 114 mentioned above).

Estates' owners or administrators were asked to reveal to the investigators as many details as possible concerning the organization of the estate. The questionnaires covered three points. The general description of the estate came first: its extension and the different crops that were cultivated, but also the systems adopted to administer it, the composition of capital (land, trees, and buildings), the productivity of the soil and the way the estate was divided into different farms. Second, there was the investigation of the economic budget of the estate. The third question covered by the questionnaire for the survey of estates concerned the relationships between the owner and the peasant families, and, in particular, the contracts that bound the two. By law, landowners had to keep an updated account of the exchanges occurring between them and their peasants, called the *Libretto Colonico* (a record of all the exchanges of services and money between the sharecropper and the landowner), but landowners kept such accounts very irregularly or unreliably, preferring to be 'fair' in their own way or deliberately taking advantage of the ignorance of the peasants. This was nevertheless the element in the estate organization on which most data were available.

The questionnaires for families aimed at describing the peasant family in its composition (number of family members and housing), and the farm they worked on (use of farm land and respective extension of different crops), including the capital they had invested in the farm (*capitale d'esercizio*), the ways in which the land was cultivated, the amount of work they did on the farm, and the final economic results. The farm budget was intended to determine 'the net income of the peasant family, that is, how much they earned in remuneration for the labour they expend on the farm and the capital they invested (in the form of livestock, tools, and so on)'. We can treat these surveys as farm surveys: the budgets Serpieri collected were the peasant farms' budgets, where peasant families themselves were entered only as the source of inputs (management, labour and part of the capital) and as the recipients of the remuneration of such inputs.

From a statistical point of view the main result of this impressive empirical work are the six tables that conclude the discussion on 'the income of tenants'. The scientific 'neutrality' of Serpieri's position manifested itself in the economic analysis of contracts that he conducted on the basis of the data collected. The way in which the gross product of farms was split between landlords and tenants, which was discussed in the text by means of idealized and generic examples, is displayed in these tables. Three of them concerned contracts that involved at the same time payments in kind (forms of sharecropping) and in money (*contratti misti*), the other three concerned farms whose rent was paid exclusively in money (*affitto in danaro*). For each of these two macro-types, the first table showed how the farm gross product was divided between the different co-operators of production. Serpieri and his collaborators computed the gross value of production for each farm. They estimated a 'standard' annual yield and multiplied it for the prices they judged to be reasonable (slightly lower than current prices, to account for transportation and storage expenditure).

This was a complicated operation that involved plenty of discussions with peasants, inspections and conjectures. From the ensuing value, a quota was subtracted immediately because it was due to the landlord (sharecropping). Other expenses due from peasants according to their contracts (*oneri colonici*) were easier to determine because they were recorded by landlords in a special booklet (the *libretto colonico*), whereas it was much more complicated to estimate the production expenses proper. Only the investigators' knowledge of agricultural production processes and their appraisal skills made estimates credible. Finally, the difference between the value of gross product that was left to the tenant and the sum of *oneri colonici* and production expenses yielded the average yearly income of the tenant family under the hypothesis that all of its labour force and capital were invested in the farm and in the farm alone (which in many cases was not true).

The annual average income so obtained was then divided by units of workforce (mens', womens', and children's work was made comparable by means of a special conversion coefficient) to show the returns of labour. This was a very significant datum since a low return per unit of labour was taken as a symptom of some pathology in the farm. If a low price of land generally meant that capital and labour were scarce (given certain assumptions), low returns of labour meant that the distribution of land was not optimal.

In the case of the Upper Milanese, Serpieri interpreted the low values reported in some areas as an effect of ongoing industrialization: as more and more family members entered factories, agriculture was confined to older marginal labour, plots grew smaller, and mulberry trees declined.[15] Income from industrial wages was factored into the tables that showed the family income divided by numbers of consumers (here, again, made comparable by appropriate coefficients). Similar data are displayed for the farms leased in exchange for a monetary rent (the computation of detractions from the gross product was obviously different in this case).

These tables showed the basic facts about the gross product of agriculture and its distribution that any decision on modifying tenancy contracts had to take into consideration. In themselves, these figures were the result of painstaking activity. The survey (*bilancio economico*) was more difficult to complete for estates. Most landowners were not easily persuaded to provide the investigators with confidential information: 'asking straightforwardly for the estate's budget

15 On the decline of silk production as tenants gained contractual power, Corner, *Contadini e industrializzazione: società rurale e impresa in Italia dal 1840 al 1940.*

was often perceived by the interviewee as exceedingly indiscreet for us to insist on', wrote Serpieri.[16]

But lack of confidence in the investigators was only part of the problem. Most landowners and their administrators plainly lacked the information asked for by the investigators: 'in how many cases', complained Serpieri, 'the landowners themselves do not know and do not care to know the composition of the peasant families that live on their estate! In how many cases they do not even know exactly the estate's total area nor how much of it is dedicated to the different crops!'[17] Part of these data could be 'stressfully' retrieved from 'messy logbooks and account books' whose accuracy was often questioned by Serpieri's team. Faced by information that they judged 'approximate and incomplete', nevertheless, Serpieri and his team remained confident that the pieces of information collected would 'check each other' and a consistent synthetic picture would result.

Moreover, for individual farms and tenant families, in the absence of account books, the collection of such minute information presented special difficulties. Peasants were 'ignorant', 'rude', 'diffident', and tended to complain about the owners more than they should have, but Serpieri assumed again that such a method could 'find in itself control and correction when extended [. . .] to a great number of family farms'. Moreover, the investigator, 'an expert investigator, not lacking knowledge of agriculture', should be able, in his opinion, to 'exert on the answers a sufficiently critical spirit, being able to discuss and eventually contradict [the interviewee], and so on'.[18]

Difficulties also involved the reliability of the information collected. This depended not only on matters of precision, but also on larger social issues. Most of the families to be interviewed were chosen with the help of the owners themselves and the interviews were held in the presence of the owners or their representative, so that peasants – this was Serpieri's explanation – would not exaggerate the misery of their conditions. In some cases, the participation of peasants was not totally spontaneous, but in others, peasants themselves were eager to attract the attention of the investigator. Serpieri, for instance, interviewed a significant number of peasants when a competition was held in Desio for the best farm (*colonìa*); on this occasion, the tenants disclosed a great deal of information for the competition 'under the incentive of prizes'.[19]

All this was openly stated, as the investigators were members of an educated class and their social stance allowed them to relate to peasants in an openly paternalistic manner, in particular in a book – such as the enquiry's proceedings – that was destined for other members of the educated classes and would never fall into peasant hands. But landowners were equally liable to manipulate information,

16 Serpieri, *Il contratto agrario e le condizioni dei contadini nell'Alto milanese*, p. 54.

17 Ibid., p. 54.

18 Ibid., pp. 204ff.

19 Ibid., p. 205.

although Serpieri was less vocal in his criticisms. He expressed scepticism about the information they provided, criticized the way they recorded the debts and credits of the peasants; he assumed that only by cross-checking and comparing the data they provided could he paint a satisfactorily lifelike picture

In fact, Serpieri and the economists of the SUM tried to achieve a neutral point of view, somewhere between the claims of the peasants or factory workers and that of the agricultural or industrial owners, but no purely mechanical procedure made the information they collected fully free of lies, omissions, and manipulation on the part of their informants. 'Scientific neutrality' had to navigate between the Scylla of landowners who were willing to resolve social contrasts without great interference from economics (and more interference from the army), and the Charybdis of peasants who trusted their own resistance leagues and trade unions much more than they trusted agricultural economists.

Farm accounting services and accounting statistics: Laur

Serpieri's use of farm surveys in *Il contratto agrario e le condizioni dei contadini nell'Alto Milanese* shows most of the difficulties that Italian agricultural economists, among others, faced when they wanted to collect a significant mass of detailed data on the fine-grained structure of farms. The precision, comparability, and reliability of the data each constituted a problem. Moreover, long and painstaking enquiries such as Serpieri's focused on small areas and restricted periods of time. To extend them across space and time, to build what we would now call historical series, radically new institutions were required. In 1901, shortly before Serpieri began compiling his surveys in Milan, Ernst Laur, then a *Privatdozent* at the ETH in Zurich, established an Office of Farm Accounting (*Abteilung fuer Rentabilitaetserhebungen*) in Brugg. The Office was a branch of the Secretariat of the League of Swiss Peasants (SBV) and was partially funded by the Swiss Federal government. Its aims were at least twofold: on the one side, its task was to disseminate accounting techniques among peasants so that they could manage their farm more rationally; on the other, the resulting accounting books were to serve as the basis for detailed statistics of agriculture.[20]

Year after year, the office instructed dozens of peasant-farmers so that they could keep the accounts of their farms (on average each year 55 farmers for the German cantons, 40 for the French, and 20 for the Italian). For years after the course, the peasants so instructed collaborated with the Farm Accounting Services, by compiling their accounting books and sending them to the office in Brugg. In a few years, Laur had collected hundreds of farm accounts from all over Switzerland, all compiled according to the standard criteria of the office (which Laur himself had

20 On Laur see Werner Baumann, *Bauernstand und Bürgerblock: Ernst Laur und der Schweizerische Bauernverband, 1897–1918* (Zürich: Orell Füssli Verlag, 1993) and Laur's own autobiography, Ernst Laur, *Erinnerungen eines schweizerischen Bauernführers: ein Beitrag zur Wirtschaftsgeschichte* (Bern: Buchverlag Verbandsdruckerei, 1943).

devised for his aims and whose application was verified by employees of the office who visited the farms in the survey to check for errors[21]). Land, inventories, and stocks were assessed, by the Appraisal Office of the Secretariat, according to shared principles, thus offering a reliable and comparable starting point for the following budgets. By 1922, Laur had 6063 farm accounts from 2280 farmers.[22]

On the basis of these data, Laur and his collaborators elaborated a vast mass of statistics 'able to measure – in time and across economic groups of farms – the economic structure of enterprises and their economic results and also, consequently, the fluctuations determined by natural or economic factors: statistics suitable, thus, to serve as the basis of certain comparisons, and to provide a systematic economic illustration of Swiss agriculture'.[23]

Monitored farms were attributed to different classes according to their dimension, the prevailing regime of soil use (the s.u.r. or *Bodennutzungssystem*, of which there were 26 typical ones in Laur's system[24]), and the relationships with the milk processing industry (*Betriebsrichtung*). The classes corresponded to categories (geographical and productive) that were considered agronomically and socially significant. They were thus conceptually analogous to farm types, as discussed above for Coletti. To be true, though, Laur's results were heavily criticized by statisticians, who thought that the vast mass of farm accounts collected could not be representative of Swiss agriculture: the self-selected sample seemed likely to include the best farms in Switzerland.[25]

For all classes, alongside other figures, the office provided three sets of fundamental indicators of economic activity: the gross return, the sum of expenses, and the income or net return. The gross return was 'a very carefully recorded and as carefully appraised account of the increases in values due to the operations of the farm plant for the time period involved'.[26] It included not only operations in cash, but also contributions in kind and appraisals of the variations in the inventory. The same held for the expenses, which included not only cash outlays and outlays in kind, but also 'the appraised value of the labour time of the farmer and his family' and 'a nominal charge for the farm operator's management'.[27]

21 Laur's accounting system is in Ernst Laur, *Landwirtschaftliche Betriebslehre für bäuerliche Verhältnisse: Lehrbuch für den Unterricht an landwirtschaftlichen Schulen un für den praktischen Landwirt* (8th edn, Aarau: Wirz, 1927); for Italian agricultural economists it was summarized by Ernesto Marenghi, *Lezioni di contabilità agraria* (Milano: Libreria editrice Politecnica, 1922).

22 O. Howald and Schweizerischer Bauernverband, *Der Schweizerische Bauernverband: 1897–1922: Festschrift herausgegeben zum 25jährigen Jubiläum des Schweizerischen Bauernverbandes* (Schweizerischer Bauernverband, 1922).

23 Alessandro Brizi and Alfredo De Polzer, *L'Ufficio di contabilità agraria e l'Ufficio di estimo rurale dell'Unione svizzera dei contadini*, Studi e monografie (Roma: INEA, 1938), p. 15.

24 Laur, *Landwirtschaftliche Betriebslehre für bäuerliche Verhältnisse*.

25 Such criticisms to the method of Laur's accounting statistics are hinted at in Istituto centrale di statistica, 'Il progettato trasferimento degli uffici di statistica agraria', p. 241.

26 Walter J. Roth, 'Farm accounting in Switzerland', *Journal of Farm Economics* 13.4 (1931), p. 562.

27 Ibid., p. 563. The rejection of this aspect of Laur's method was the starting point of A.V. Čajanov's theory of the family farm; for him, it made no sense to assign a monetary value to a working

The resulting income of the family was 'that share of the gross return which, within a given time period, has become the property of the operator and may be consumed by the operator and his family without reducing the family's farm assets during the same period'.[28] There were four measures for it, the first three more appropriate to smallholdings, the fourth to larger farms:

1 Family Farm Earnings, reported as (a) a total money figure and (b) per man-day of labour.
2 Family Labour Earnings, per man-day of labour.
3 Family Capital Earnings, reported as (a) a total money figure and (b) as a percentage of family capital invested.
4 The Net Return (on total farm assets), reported as (a) a total money figure and (b) in per cent of total invested capital.

By means of his accounting definitions, Laur and his collaborators determined for each class of farm and for different years the distribution of total product in remuneration of the different factors of production. In particular, they showed how the gross product was divided between the abstract economic characters of capitalists, entrepreneurs, landowners, workers, on the one hand, and, on the other, the average incomes perceived by concrete combinations of such abstract characters as they concretely manifested themselves in Switzerland: entrepreneur-capitalist-worker (a farmer who was working on a farm that belongs to somebody else but who has invested his own capital), entrepreneur-worker (a farmer who borrowed his capital and leased the land), entrepreneur-capitalist (a farmer who leased the land and hired labour), and so on. By so doing, Laur provided a conceptual (and statistical) framework in economic terms for the understanding of economic contrasts in agriculture.

From a scientific point of view, the figures made it possible to identify relationships between phenomena, for instance between classes of area and income, by means of a method intuitively similar to correlation.[29] A key result concerned, for instance, the so-called social income per hectare. This was defined as gross product minus all the expenses but those for labour and taxes, that is, all that was left for distribution among the human co-operators in production (the

time which lies outside the category of wage labor; A. V. Čajanov, 'Peasant farm Organization' (Organisacija Krest'janskogo Khozjajstva, 1925) in Aleksandr V. Čajanov, *A. V. Chayanov on the theory of peasant economy*, ed. Daniel Thorner et al. (Manchester: Manchester University Press, 1986), pp. 29–270 and Basile Kerblay, 'A.V. Chayanov: Life, career, works', ibid., p. xxxiv.

28 Laur quoted in Roth, 'Farm accounting in Switzerland', p. 563.

29 A discussion of the limits of this view is to be found in Brizi and DePolzer, *L'Ufficio di contabilità agraria e l'Ufficio di estimo rurale dall'Unione svizzera dei contadini*, p. 97: 'When – to take only one example – we elaborate the resulting incomes by classes of area, we are actually considering as a unique cause, what is in fact – however important and influential – only the result of a complex of causes (the area under crop). Nothing guarantees – in each individual farm – that these causes really affected the result or that they always affected the result positively'.

owner, the entrepreneur and the workers). The office's statistics showed that social income per hectare was larger for the classes of smaller farms, and that, moreover, small farmers achieved larger levels of production per hectare and sold more of their production per hectare on the market with respect to larger properties, thus contributing more to the welfare of cities. The results I have just mentioned motivated Laur's support for farmers rather than large estates: smallholdings (if not too small!) were socially more efficient than large properties. Laur thus offered sound statistical arguments for the idea that relatively small farms formed the backbone of a healthy agriculture and that family farmers were an asset that European states should protect against the temptations of cities and fluctuations of world markets.[30]

It must be stressed, nevertheless, that Laur and the Secretariat of the League of Swiss Peasants were more concerned with conflicts between agriculturalists and industrialists, between producers and purchasers of agricultural products, than with distributive struggles within agriculture (day labourers and small tenants against landowners, for instance).[31]

Alongside the scientific ones, these numbers also served practical purposes in defense of SBV associates. On the one side, they influenced the political debate, motivating requests for subsidies and protectionist tariffs. On the other, they were intended to guide the specific decisions of farmers. On the basis of these data, the Office for Land Valuation (another branch of the SBV's Secretariat), for instance, computed for perspective purchasers of land the appraised value of plots (*Ertragswert*) and their *Existenzwert*. What was called the *Existenzwert* was the maximum theoretical value that a peasant family could pay for land without reducing its wealth and possessed a clearly prescriptive value, forming the basis of Laur's 'economic education' of peasants.[32]

Very early, Italian groups of agriculturalists developed an interest in Laur's experience. The International Institute of Agriculture (IIA), which at that time was led by Marquis Raffaele Cappelli and was heavily under the influence of Italian concerns, despatched Ernesto Marenghi to Brugg. Marenghi, who taught accounting, appraisal and agricultural economics in Milan until his early death in 1926, prepared a detailed report for the IIA in which he described Laur's activity (as well as other institutions promoting accounting among farmers)

30 Ernst Laur, *Einführung in die Wirtschaftslehre des Landbaus: Unter besonderer Berücksichtigung der Landarbeitslehre*, 2nd rev. (Berlin: Parey, 1930).

31 In his autobiography Laur connected the birth of the SBV with the protectionist wave of the 1890s, and the activity of the Secretariat bore this mark; Baumann, *Bauernstand und Bürgerblock: Ernst Laur und der Schweizerische Bauernverband, 1897–1918* shows how the SBV lobbied in favour of agriculturalists and against industrial lobbies. On the combative politics of the SBV see also Werner Baumann and Peter Moser, *Bauern im Industriestaat: agrarpolitische Konzeptionen und bäuerliche Bewegungen in der Schweiz 1918–1968*, Zeitgeschichte: O. Füssli (Orell Füssli, 1999), especially Teil II.4.

32 On Laur's methods for appraising properties, see Ernst Laur, 'Die Schaetzung des Ertragswertes von Landguetern nach dem Rohertrage des landw. Betriebes', *Archiv fuer exakte Wirtschaftsforschung* 4.2 (1912).

and its advantages for understanding the problems of agriculture. The report focused on the two sides of Laur's work: the dissemination of accounting techniques among farmers and the usefulness of aggregate statistics that by means of accounting data could display indicators for the structure of agricultural business. Although it was published complete only after the war, Marenghi's report was ready by 1914 and had already begun circulating in Italian during the war, immediately making Laur's office a standard reference point for statistics of agricultural businesses.[33]

Observatories of agricultural economy

Since Serpieri and his school – after the earlier Cuppari and Niccoli – had put the study of farms (*azienda agraria*) at the core of the interests of Italian agrarian economists for generations,[34] they were among the first to seize upon the potential of Laur's statistics. They thus began a series of attempts to extend the investigation of farm budgets to the whole of Italy and to an ever-increasing number of farms and farm types.

Data from farm budgets responded to two different research interests: a productivist and a social one. Serpieri pursued these two lines together. Because he stressed the role of entrepreneurs (*imprenditori agricoli*) in almost Schumpeterian accents,[35] only the analysis of accounting data made it possible to describe the different combinations of inputs of production and resulting outputs. But, as we have seen, he also resorted to farm budgets in order to observe the conditions of peasants and determine the range of possible variations that could be introduced into tenancy contracts. When Serpieri moved from the Scuola d'Agricoltura of Milan to Florence, his pupils in northern Italy concentrated on farm accounts in order to evaluate the economic results of different regimes of land use. It was in particular Giuseppe Tassinari who pushed forward this line of research at the University of Bologna (while the myth of sharecropping induced Serpieri's school in Tuscany to pay more attention to social and even sociological aspects of agriculture).[36]

33 Ernesto Marenghi, 'Organizzazione ed importanza degli Uffici di contabilità per lo studio dell'economia dell'azienda agraria', *Rivista Italiana di Ragioneria*, n. 4, pp. 162–75; n. 5, pp. 201–4; n: 6, pp. 241–6; n. 7, pp. 289–301; n. 8, pp. 329–38; n. 9, pp. 386–90 (1914); Institut International d'Agriculture, *Les offices de comptabilité agricole dans les divers pays*, 3 vols (Rome: Institut International d'Agriculture, 1920–24).

34 A. Serpieri's books were reference textbooks for agricultural economists until the 1960s, and I can say from direct experience that Serpieri's books are still often out on loan at the library of the Faculty of Agricultural Sciences in Florence! See Giancarlo Di Sandro, 'La manualistica di economia agraria da Cuppari a Serpieri', *Il pensiero economico italiano* 14.1 (2006), pp. 173–212.

35 See Arrigo Serpieri, *Sui metodi di determinazione del profitto nelle imprese rurali: Analisi di stima e conti colturali* (Milano: tipo-litografia agraria, 1901) and id., 'Il metodo di stima dei beni fondiari', *Annali del R. Ist. Superiore Forestale Nazionale* II (1916–17).

36 The myth of Tuscan *mezzadria* runs as a red thread from Sismondi's *Tableau de l'agriculture toscane* in 1801 and Sidney Sonnino to R. Putnam's analysis of Tuscan civism and social capital in the 1990s,

Tassinari began collecting farm accounts from various parts of Italy in 1912, just after the social struggles reached their pre-war peak in the area of Bologna.[37] His work, suspended during the war, was resumed in the early 1920s when strikes and social protests reached culmination point and violent repression began. The research was finally published in 1926 with the support of the Federazione Italiana dei Consorzi Agrari, the spearhead of agricultural modernization in Italy, as a synthetic view on the effects of the Great War on Italy's agricultural businesses.

Tassinari's *Saggio intorno alla distribuzione del reddito nell'agricoltura italiana* resembled, in principle, the work done by Luigi Einaudi's group a few years earlier. In Turin, Einaudi's pupils had collected accounts of joint stock companies in order to 'ascertain how economic results varied across time, sectors and firm size'.[38] Tassinari, instead, examined variations of economic results according to farm size and crop specialization. His analysis, however, was complicated by issues of sample size and completeness. While the results of joint stock companies were relatively easy to get, gathering a statistically significant sample of farm accounts would have been unfeasible.

Tassinari, thus, centred his analysis on farm types and after a short general introduction, he presented a number of surveys of farms, each representative of different regions of Italy and different productive specializations: there were three farm types for the irrigated areas of Piedmont and Lombardy, two types for the dry farms of Emilia, two for Monferrato's vines, and so on, for a total of 20 types covering most of Italy's regions. For each type, the book offered a survey of a single actual farm, which was described in its inputs and outputs, often for both periods 1912–14 and 1921–22. Although Tassinari acknowledges that his types did not represent the whole existing variety of farms (the south was in particular underrepresented), he built in this way a 'geography' of farm types that followed the lines traced by Niccoli's *Manuale* of 1897.[39]

Robert D. Putnam and R. Leonardi, *Making Democracy Work* (Princeton University Press, 2002); farm surveys in Tuscany produced, in the 1930s, the image of happy and blessed families that appear in the INEA surveys (recently republished in Roberto Tolaini, *Contadini toscani negli anni Trenta: Monografie di famiglie dell'INEA 1931–1938,* Collana del Centro di documentazione e ricerca sulla storia dell'agricoltura e della società contadina 0002 (Ospedaletto, Pisa: Pacini, 2005)).

37 On the increasing difficulties encountered by intermediate positions in social struggles around 1910, see Sandro Rogari, *Proprietà fondiaria e modernizzazione: La Società degli Agricoltori Italiani 1895–1920,* La società moderna e contemporanea Analisi e contributi 40 (Milano: Franco Angeli, 1994); for a typical reaction of landed interests to strikes and legislators' reformism, see the report that the Agraria di Ravenna addressed to the government, Associazione Agraria Ravennate, *Condizioni del lavoro e della produzione nell'agro ravennate e l'agitazione agraria del 1910: Memoriale presentato dall'Associazione Agraria Ravennate all'On. Commissione d'Inchiesta nominate da S.E. il Presidente del Consiglio* (Bologna, 1910).

38 Francesco Forte, 'Cesare Jarach e Achille Necco', in Roberto Marchionatti and Giandomenica Becchio, eds, *La scuola di economia di Torino: Da Cognetti de Martiis a Einaudi* (Torino: Leo S. Olschki, 2005), p. 156.

39 Giuseppe Tassinari, *Saggio intorno alla distribuzione del reddito nell'agricoltura italiana* (Piacenza: Federazione italiana dei consorzi agrari, 1926).

After the presentation of the individual types, Tassinari discusses the most relevant economic issues. The key numbers for him were the net product of the farm, and the rent; the first being the portion of gross product that is available to the agricultural classes (workers, entrepreneurs and landlords) after subtracting production expenses, and the latter being the return on land. Tassinari compared the result of the investigation for 1912–14 and for 1921–22, in order to discuss the changes brought about by the war with special attention to the distribution between landlords (the rent) and tenants (profits and wages). It is to be noticed that the figures he presented were not averages. They refer, instead, to the individual farms presented in the surveys, whose 'typical', representative character had to be assumed beforehand.

That Tassinari limited his research to a few typical farms, instead of collecting a large mass of data, did not result from deliberate methodological reasoning. As Serpieri states in his preface to Tassinari's book, the investigation originally began with the aim of providing 'research on the economic structure of agricultural living organisms' for the 'solution of disputes' between wage labourers and landowners. This meant that the whole research was initially dominated by urgency:

> every time necessity was impending and new positive information urged, researchers would be called upon for help, in order to investigate and prepare the elements for judgment (such was the case with the agricultural unrest of Bologna, Tuscany and Soresina; with the update of the *cadastre*'s valuations; with the crisis of wheat in 1923 and the more recent crisis of beetroot).[40]

Tassinari himself acknowledged in the introduction that he could study only those very few farms whose owners decided to cooperate, but his work was a beginning.

Statistics of accounting allowed him to focus on both distributive and productive issues, and were stimulated by contingent situations of disorder, either social or economic. If Tassinari's collection of farm surveys was, initially, driven by the will to find a solution to the social turmoil that was compatible with the necessity of production, eventually it attracted the attention of powerful Federconsorzi also for a different reason. It offered a starting point for an analysis of the effect of the agricultural crisis of the 1920s on agricultural business.[41] The demand for budget statistics did not disappear when the Fascist regime put an end to strikes. On the contrary, the relative social peace induced

40 Ibid.

41 Salvatore Adorno, 'L'Italia agricola e il suo avvenire: Note sul ruolo della Commissione di studi tecnici ed economici della Federconsorzi', in Severina Fontana, ed., *La Federconsorzi tra stato liberale e fascismo,* Biblioteca di cultura moderna 1084 (Roma, Bari: Laterza, 1995), pp. 61–108, described the relationship between Serpieri, Tassinari and the Federconsorzi.

the Federconsorzi, and other organizations to plan the establishment of permanent institutions for the collection of accounting data with a stronger focus on agricultural systems (*sistemi agrari*) and their respective economic results.

When Serpieri entered Mussolini's government as vice-minister for agriculture, and established IESA as the new nationwide research centre for agricultural economics, he included among the tasks of the new Institute the creation of local offices for farm accounting: the Observatories for Agricultural Economics. The aspiration was to replicate in Italy Laur's Office for Farm Accounting. The first of such observatories to be created was that of Bologna. The creation of the observatory was promoted by the Società Agraria della Provincia di Bologna, an old institution of the landed patricians who had sided with the Fascists since their appearance in Bologna.[42]

Like its model in Brugg, the Bologna office also combined in principle scientific tasks ('it will update the surveys of agricultural businesses that already exist and will undertake the missing ones [. . .]'; 'elaborate data resulting from accounting for research in agricultural economics'; 'cooperate [. . .] with the service of agricultural statistics') with practical ones ('elaborate a method of accounting suitable for the peculiar local conditions'; 'keep the accounting books of all the smallholders and tenants who required its assistance').[43] The Società Agraria invited Tassinari himself to lead the observatory. Under the latter's guidance, Dario Perini carried on Tassinari's work on farm accounts within the institutional framework of INEA's Observatories for agricultural economics.

In 1932, INEA began publishing the statistical series *Risultati economici di aziende agrarie*. In these reports Perini published a vast collection of data taken from the accounting books of hundreds of farms from all over Italy.[44] As the omnipresent Serpieri puts it in his preface to the first volume of the series, Perini's work was the first comprehensive collection of statistics based on accounting data available for Italy's agriculture. Since by that time many other countries had been publishing their data regularly in a series coordinated by the IIA and inspired by Dr Laur,[45] Serpieri emphatically declared that Perini was finally filling a gap.

42 On the Società Agraria Bolognese, its role in bringing about the regime change in Italy, and the type of technologically advanced agriculture it promoted, see Anthony L. Cardoza, *Agrarian elites and Italian fascism: the Province of Bologna, 1901–1926* (Princeton University Press, 1982).

43 Funding was provided by the Cassa di risparmio di Bologna and by the government: *Annali della Soc. Agr. Di Bologna*, 56, 1925, p. 49.

44 In Perini's first volume (Dario Perini, *Risultati economici di aziende agrarie,* Studi e monografie 18 (Roma: Treves Dell' Alii, 1932)) there are budgets for 110 farms compared to the 65 of Giuseppe Tassinari, *La distribuzione dell reddito nell'agricoltura italiana* (Piacenza: Federazione Ital. dei Consorzi Agrari, 1931), which cover the years 1925–28 (and is actually a second updated edition of Tassinari, *Saggio intorno alla distribuzione dell reddito nell'agricoltura italiana*).

45 Laur's importance is witnessed by his report to the IIA, Ernst Laur, *Directives générales pour les travaux de l'Institut International d'Agriculture rapport presenté par M. le Prof. Laur,* à la Ière Session du Comité économique agricole, 1 Octobre 1929, D5 comité économique agricole, 1928–1935, FAO Archive, by his address to the Agricultural Congress in Bucharest, and also the repeated mentions of him

The observatory, however, was never able to instruct peasants or landowners in accounting techniques, in part because it lacked adequate financial resources but also because of a certain lack of interest on the part of agriculturalists.[46] As a consequence, although Perini was able to collect a much larger number of account books than Tassinari, such books were still kept according to different methods and definitions, and the lack of standardization made them ineligible for statistical analysis: Perini renounced any elaboration of the kind provided by Laur's team, and simply presented the data for each individual farm, adding only a synthetic comment on the trends of Italian agriculture.

Giuseppe Medici, with the assistance of the Federconsorzi, was the first to attempt a statistical elaboration of farm surveys on a large scale. Medici, who after the war launched a land reform that increased the number of smallholders, used these data to question the very existence of typical farms.[47]

Medici and the typical farming business

The young Giuseppe Medici (later Minister of Agriculture in the De Gasperi cabinets after the Second World War) took part in the collection of data for Lower Lombardy. He accumulated a significant mass of figures concerning the use of land, farm revenues, and so on, during the collection of data for the First World Agricultural Census. In 1933, he published a paper in the proceedings of the Observatory of Bologna, *Ricerche intorno alla azienda agraria tipica*. This lengthy contribution discussed whether 'there exists a typical farming business, from a purely statistical viewpoint or [whether] the concept of typical should be limited to only certain specific factors or ratios'.[48] This discussion was intended to move the concept of typical farm from qualitative to quantitative: was 'typical' to be used in the proper statistical sense or in the 'qualitative sense proper of some sciences or arts which consider the typical as a model or a paragon'? The apparently neutral concept of 'typicality' had come under fire from statisticians.

Medici fundamentally questioned the relationship between statistics and surveys as it had been theorized by Cheysson and Coletti. Typical, in statistics,

and his results in Alessandro Brizi, *Enquetes complémentaires sur les conditions générales de l'Agriculture et documentation ordinaire de l'Institut*: rapport presenté par M. le Prof. Brizi à la Ière Session du Comité économique agricole, partie IIème, 3 Octobre 1929, D5 comité économique agricole, 1928–1935, FAO Archive.

46 See Perini, *Risultati economici di aziende agrarie*, since I was unable to document the activities of the Observatory otherwise (the Bologna branch of the INEA was somewhat uncooperative). Moreover, the *Annali dell'Osservatorio di economia agraria per l'Emilia* do not contain many details on the extra-scientific work done.

47 Giuseppe Medici, *Richerche intorno all'azienda agraria tipica* (Faenza: F.lli Lega, 1933); id., *L'azienda agraria tipica: Nuove ricerche* (Faenza: F.lli Lega, 1945). A less theoretically ambitious work, based on the data collected for the *second* World Agricultural Census, is Paolo Albertario, 'Le "fattorie" dell'Italia centrale', *Annali di Statistica* III (Serie VII) (1939), pp. 103–91.

48 Medici, *Richerche intorno all'azienda agraria tipica*, p. 7.

meant 'the most frequent value'. Statistical textbooks of the age used the typical value to indicate the value of the mode.[49] The whole point of the quest for the typical in the social sciences, however, was to find a value 'which could replace or summarize the whole population under consideration', and for this task the mode was not always appropriate. In particular, it was not appropriate whenever the distribution was not normal. The representativeness of the typical value (in the statistical sense, that is, the mode) was hence 'a function of the regularity of the phenomenon': the closer the most frequent value was to the average value, the more representative the statistically typical value would be of the whole population.[50]

There was an additional problem. Adolphe Quételet had assumed that it was possible to construct a statistically typical man by taking the average measure of each body part: the arm, the head, the trunk, and so on But, while the composing elements of a man seemed to be intuitively clear, what did a farm consist of? Not to say that this was an operation that transfigured a mass of data empirically gathered into a totally ideal image: was it legitimate? Could a similar ideal man, or an ideal farm, obtained by adding up average parts, really exist? It could well be that an average area is incompatible with an average revenue, and so on. Even if the quest for the typical farm was reduced to a small homogeneous agricultural zone (by analogy with the search for average men limited to individual races), the relationships between the different components of the farms were in no way easy to understand.

In order to solve these problems, Medici divided the characteristics for which he had data available into two groups: the physical and economic features of farms. The first group consisted of 13 items ranging from area, to yield per hectare, number of working hours spent on the farm, number of machines, and so on. The economic features (nine items) consisted of the gross saleable production, the net product, the value of stock, and so on. Medici argued that, for agricultural businesses (*aziende agrarie*), the physical quantities were often more significant than the economic quantities. The fact was that the latter were functions of the former.[51]

Excluding economic quantities from consideration meant reducing the importance given to the personality of the agricultural entrepreneur, since this was reflected mostly in the commercial action, and constituted the most relevant determinant of irregularity in the data. Moreover, the lack of uniformity in accounting principles would not have hindered the analysis of physical data. But reducing the

49 Benini, *Principi di statistica metodologica*, p. 6: 'Gli statistici alla loro volto considerano tipico il carattere che appartiene alla classe di maggior frequenza, alla varietà più comune fra molte varietà più o meno rare, talora anche la semplice media risultante da un gran numero di osservazioni', Alfredo Niceforo, *Il metodo statistico: Teoria e applicazioni alle Scienze naturali, alle Scienze sociali, e all'Arte* (Messina: Casa Editrice Giuseppe Principato, 1923).

50 Medici, *Richerche intorno all'azienda agraria tipica*, p. 8.

51 To understand this, it is enough to consider, for example, that the net value of product per hectare was obviously a function of the farm area and of the total product in physical units.

analysis to physical data alone was also relatively harmless for Medici's argument since, if he found great irregularity (that is a non-normal distribution) in physical factors, how could he expect to find more regularity in the economic features that derived from them but incorporated also the variations of the market?

Medici proceeded to the analysis of the physical data available. He had data for five relatively similar agricultural zones (Ferrara and Alagna, Alto Pavese, Basso Pavese in Destra Ticino, Basso Pavese in Sinistra Ticino, Basso Pavese Vitato), that he considered separately. The classification of the farms according to their productive area turned out to be far from the bell curve of normal distribution.

The same held for the area dedicated to each crop. The distribution was consistently irregular. The typical farm seemed not to exist even when the smallest and largest farms were excluded (in particular the former, a huge group of farms). In contrast to this result, however, the graphs displayed a regular curve when Medici examined the percentage of area dedicated to each crop, instead of the absolute figures. Here finally the distribution appeared close to normal. This meant, for Medici, that it was statistically meaningful to speak of typical farms.

In this case, the conclusions of statistics were far from unexpected for the agricultural economists. Even though the use of fertilizers and the increasing dependence of farms on the market made crop rotations less regular, inevitably each agricultural zone was characterized by a succession of crops gravitating around one or two types. In the area of Alto Pavese, for instance, the prevailing types of crop rotation were two: the most common included rice fields, the less common excluded them. Independently of statistical data, this was easily observable for agricultural economists, almost at a glance.

Moreover, the persistence of conventional types of tenancy contract determined the prevalence of a symmetric (roughly normal) function for the distribution of the percentage of net product received by each factor of production (labour, land, agricultural capital, directive work) in each year in each farm (for these data, Medici relied on works by Giuseppe Tassinari and Stefano Perdisa).[52] Contracts prescribed precisely the way that the product was divided between the farmer, the landowner, and the hired workers. The model contract acted persistently and determined a central pattern of income distribution with minor variations in one or the other direction.

In these two cases, although the normal distribution only approximated to the empirical curves, it nevertheless came reasonably close. For such features, the representative value of a typical farm, selected statistically, was relatively high.

Once reassured about the existence of typical farms, Medici confronted his results with economic theory to show their importance. Serpieri had assumed, in agreement with theoretical economists such as Walras and Marshall, that market forces drove entrepreneurs towards the typical farm. Their varying

52 Giuseppe Tassinari, *La distribuzione dell reddito nell'agricoltura italiana* and Luigi Perdisa, 'I redditi dell'agricoltura emiliana: I risultati economici di 40 aziende nel settennio 1925–1931', *Annali dell'Osservatorio di economia agraria per l'Emilia*, 1933.

degrees of ability determined the distribution of farms along a normal curve of efficiency. As for the use of the single most important production factor, land, the statistics should have shown a central (typical) value representing the size of a typical farm, but they did not. According to Medici, they could not, since it was impossible to assume equal cost curves for each farm. Marshall, according to Medici, had already been forced to define his representative firm in contradictory terms. Just like the theoreticians of appraisal, Marshall (according to Medici) had in mind a theoretical construct, but he also wanted to give it flesh and find an empirical counterpart:

> Our typical firm must have lasted for a reasonable time, experienced a discrete prosperity, it must be managed with normal ability, it must be able to obtain, in a normal measure, such internal and external economies as are appropriate for the total volume of production.[53]

Although Medici's data confirmed the possibility of singling out some typical features, they also showed that an overall typical farm, obtained by assembling average values for each feature into an artificial construct, was a monstrosity and ran into contradictions:

> In the end, the agricultural economy of a territory, the result of the activity of individual businesses, cannot be replaced by an average datum, however clever and refined the statistical methods employed. And this because the 'agricultural business', as a fact, is neither individually typical nor collectively typical, but atypical par excellence; it is an individual fact that bears the deletable traces of an unmistakable personal work, the product of the contrast between well-defined natural elements and the man who manages the farm.[54]

But if the type could not be constructed statistically, how was the agricultural economist to proceed? He will use, following Medici's suggestion, real cases that he will then 'ideally link with all the other farms wherewith the farm is connected in the reality of agricultural life'. If a statistical definition of 'typical' was not viable, the cases that presented themselves to the attention of the researcher (for contingent reasons) had to be surveyed and critically analysed on the basis of the researcher's 'intimate knowledge of the environment that he describes and which he only can thoroughly grasp so that difference and likeliness will emerge'.

Calling Marshall's definition of a typical or ordinary firm into question meant, in the end, casting a shadow not only on the survey method, but also on those methods of appraisal that assumed the existence of an ordinary farm (that is an attack on Serpieri). Neither Medici nor Serpieri seem to have fully

53 Marshall, quot. in Medici, *Richerche intorno all'azienda agraria tipica*, p. 106.

54 Ibid., p. 113.

appreciated the consequences for appraisal and research, with the dominance of Serpieri's paradigm remaining unshaken for decades,[55] but the introduction of statistical methods in the study of farms paved the way for important changes. Although it was still necessary to induce individual farmers to open their account books, the treatment of masses of data, instead of individual surveys, made the results and the very science of agricultural economics more impersonal, more 'mechanically objective', and widened the gap between farmers and economists, between the observed and those observing them.

An international trend

I have been trying to sketch the evolution of Italian research studies based on farm budgets and accounts. There are at least three lines of development that I would extract from this dash through 30 years of statistics. First of all, a tension existed between different ways of considering statistics. In the myth of Laur's office can be discerned a general tendency towards data that emerge almost mechanically from the processes of the economy. What the Swiss had achieved was the standardization of accounts, the institutionalization and regularity of their collection, and their collection in large numbers. This ideal did not respond to an abstract desire for objectivity alone. Smooth, standardized data spontaneously flowing from business to statisticians permitted much better analysis and displayed the attractive properties of large numbers that the few surveys collected by field-experts could never show.[56]

A second tendency, that partially contradicts the first one, was at work in the investigations directed by Coletti and Tassinari. Whenever significant quantities of farm budgets could not be collected, or could not be collected in time (as it was the case with parliamentary enquiries or with any other investigation dominated by the urgency of action), then a well-chosen example, a typical specimen, was considered to serve as well. Actually, the most influential guide to fieldwork for agricultural economists consecrated surveys of typical farms as the working paradigm of the category.[57] The analysis of typical farms, thus, was not simply a

55 Giuseppe Medici and William G. Murray, *Principles of appraisal* (Ames, Iowa: the Iowa state college press, 1953); Arrigo Serpieri, *L'azienda agraria* (Bologna: Edagricole, 1946); id., 'Sui concetti di impresa marginale, impresa ordinaria e azienda tipo', *Rivista di Economia Agraria* 2.2 (1948); and id., *Istituzioni di economia agraria* (2nd edn, Bologna: Edizioni agricole, 1950), in particular ch. XV. As already mentioned, Marco Zaganella, *Dal fascismo alla DC: Tassinari, Medici e la bonifica nell'Italia tra gli anni Trenta e Cinquanta,* I fatti e la storia 4 (Siena: Cantagalli, 2010), greatly stresses the methodological opposition between Serpieri and Tassinari-Medici. Right after the Second World War, Medici give vent to his discomfort with Serpieri's method in Giuseppe Medici, 'Stato e problemi degli studi di economia agraria in Italia', *Rivista di Economia Agraria* 1.2 (1946), pp. 124–34.

56 But on the subjectivity of appraisal in business statistics, and in particular of inventory, see Alain Desrosières, 'How real are statistics?', *Social Research* 68.2 (2001), pp. 339–55.

57 Arrigo Serpieri, *Guida a ricerche di economia agraria,* Studi e monografie / Istituto Nazionale di Economia Agraria 1 (Roma: Treves Dell' Ali, 1929); the extreme defence of a well-chosen sample brought forward by Corrado Gini against Anders N. Kiaer's random sampling (for instance in

cheaper substitute for statistics of farm accounts. Its main concerns, as it emerged from being employed in parliamentary enquiries, was with regional differentiation, with mapping local types and with doing these quickly.

The long-term tendency towards Laur's model that nevertheless dominated the field of budget and account research implied high financial costs. Offices for farm accounting required a heavy structure, a consistent number of employees and a permanent organization. But they also required social forces determined to engage in the process. The tenants and smallholders who went to attend a three-day crash course in accounting and who submitted their accounts to the office in Brugg every year willingly sacrificed their time and energy to the cause of statistics. This was made possible by the specific social configuration and pervasiveness of the SBV. Seemingly impartial numbers were actually the result of engagement.

Italian agricultural economists made their investigations in a changing political environment where there was nothing comparable to the SBV.[58] They initially exploited the opportunities that the social reformism of Giolitti's era offered them and focused their use of farm budgets on issues of distribution of income. In part, their attempts fell victim to the failure of such reformism. After the war, alliances shifted, as Serpieri and Tassinari at different times prepared to enter Mussolini's cabinets.[59] For statistics based on farm accounts, the stress moved to issues of production, in particular when a series of price crises hit agriculture in the 1920s and 1930s. This time funds were provided by the landed elites of the Po Valley. Although the new alliance with the regime allowed Serpieri to create a stable institutional framework for research into agricultural economics (the INEA and its local Observatories), it did not encourage the degree of orderly participation that the experience of SBV required. In the end, the agreement between Serpieri, Federconsorzi, and the government proved unstable.[60]

The controversies over what was called the *Bonifica Integrale*, the project of total reclamation of land from marshes, the showcase of Fascist policies for

Corrado Gini and Luigi Galvani, 'Di una applicazione del metodo rappresentativo all'ultimo censimento italiano della popolazione 1 dicembre 1921', *Annali di Statistica,* 6th series, 4 (1929)) seems to have something in common with the stress that agricultural economists put on the study of typical individual farms, see Alain Desrosières, *La politique des grandes nombres: Histoire de la raison statistique* (Paris: La Découverte, 1993).

58 On the Italian Società degli agricoltori italiani from a European perspective: Maria Malatesta, 'Une nouvelle stratégie reproduction: les organisations patronales agraires européennes (1868–1914)', *Histoire, économie et société* 16.2 (1997).

59 On Serpieri's politics see Antonio Prampolini, 'La formazione di A. Serpieri ed i problemi dell'agricoltura lombarda', *Studi Storici* 17.2 (1976), pp. 171–209; Lea D'Antone, 'Politica e cultura agraria: Arrigo Serpieri', *Studi Storici* 20.3 (1979), pp. 609–42; and Mauro Stampacchia, *Ruralizzare l'Italia! Agricoltura e bonifiche tra Mussolini e Serpieri, 1928–1943,* Franco Angeli Storia 274 (Milano: Franco Angeli, 2000); when he died in 1944, Tassinari was the Minister of Agriculture of the Fascist Salò Republic.

60 See again Adorno, 'L'Italia agricola e il suo avvenire', p. 99ff. on the divergences between Serpieri's group and other groups of agriculturalists within the regime; and Zaganella, *Dal fascismo alla DC* for the contrast between Serpieri and Tassinari. The two converged precisely on the use of farm surveys, although Tassinari's pupil were more consistent in the survey of farm budgets.

agriculture, showed the isolation of Serpieri and of the agricultural experts. Land reclamation was promoted by Serpieri as the solution to the lack of land for peasants. It was intended – on the basis of an analysis similar to that of Laur on the social income of farms – to create medium-sized farms that could absorb daily workers and increase production (at least in part).[61] The development of agriculture implied farms that were both capital- and labour-intensive.[62] But, although the *Bonifica* progressed, Serpieri was ousted from the government.

The vows expressed at first by the General Assembly of the International Institute for Agriculture in 1922,[63] and then repeated at the Agricultural Congress of 1929 (and on both occasions welcomed by Italy's principal agrarian economists[64]), that all member countries might adopt standardized methods of accounting statistics on the Swiss model, remained almost without effect in Italy until the end of the Second World War. Still, the agricultural economists had successfully established themselves as the bearers of the analytical skills that any agricultural policy required.

61 Farms that were too small to remunerate work adequately should have been recombined following a model common in Germany: Giuseppe Tassinari, *Frammentazione e ricomposizione dei fondi rurali,* Pubblicazioni del R. Istituto Superiore Forestale Nazionale Firenze N. 8 (Firenze: Tip. M. Ricci, 1922).

62 Serpieri was not an isolated – nor the most extreme – supporter of a labour- and capital-intensive model: Čajanov's *Putešestvie moego brata Alekseya v stranu krest'yanskoj utopii* (1920) presents a future dominated by highly technological but labor intensive small farms (an English translation in Ivan Kremnev, 'The journey of my brother Alexei to the land of peasant Utopia', *Journal of Peasant Studies* 4.1 (1976), pp. 63–108).

63 'Rien ne serait plus susceptible de susciter de part et d'autre un jugement plus objectif qu'une comptabilité bien comprise qui, d'une part, renseignerait sur ce qui gagnent l'agriculteur et les autres producteurs ainsi que sur le cout de leur activité, et qui, d'autre part permettrait de se faire une idée exacte de ce que consomment et épargnent les ouvriers et les fonctionnaires. Il n'est donc pas exagéré de dire qu'en contribuant à la généralisation de la comptabilité agricole, nous collaborons en même temps à l'atténuation des antagonismes sociaux', the Spanish delegate to the IIA claimed on that occasion referring to the conflicts of opposing agriculturalists and urban dwellers, Institut International d'Agriculture, *Les offices de comptabilité agricole dans les divers pays*, pp. vii–viii.

64 See Laur's letter to 'MM. les chefs des offices de comptabilité agricole' (15 August 1929), Archivio dell'Accademia dei Georgofili, fondo Tassinari, 6.6.1.

8 Epilogue

In this book I have tried – the reader may judge how successfully – to discuss, together, different stories that – although potentially autonomous dimensions of the same story (and sometimes being given different disciplinary labels) – seemed to me so intrinsically connected that they would have been impossible to understand separately. My main characters have been the three forms of investigation that Salvioni and Valenti introduced: enquiry, statistics, and monographs. The first task was to give some substance to these three names. I had to clarify what agricultural economists had in mind when they were thinking of agricultural statistics, agricultural enquiries, and farm monographs. This was especially important for enquiries, since the core notion of the enquiry, as a way of observing agriculture, was more uncertain and less familiar to us. All the three forms of investigation, however, included relatively different practices whose content changed over time. The effort to define and describe these three forms of investigation explains why this book has so little diachronic depth (it covers less than 30 years and ends more or less with the establishment of ICS and INEA) and so much more synchronic breadth.

I decided therefore that the best way to tell the stories of my three main characters was to dedicate separate chapters to each of them. I identified the key elements of enquiries in the combination of questionnaires and inspections, in the qualitative rather than quantitative character of the observations, and in the importance that the positions of the observers had in making observation relevant and trustworthy (Chapter 3); statistics, instead, had an exclusively quantitative character and supplied large masses of data, collected as impersonally as possible (Chapters 4 and 5); monographs and budget investigations (Chapters 6 and 7) began with the study of individual farms, taken as typical instances of a kind. Each of those groups of chapters followed the evolution of a form of investigation through both Liberal and Fascist periods of Italy's history. Although I confined them in rigidly divided chapters, the three forms of investigation continuously combined and intersected: they were all different ways of observing the same object, agriculture. In practice, agricultural economists, and agricultural policymakers always combined them.

Acceptable observations

The fundamental question was which observations to consider acceptable. In the case of nineteenth-century enquiries, the strategy adopted to tackle this issue was to translate the original question into a different one: whose observations are acceptable? This was not the only strategy adopted, and different criteria of consistency were applied, but classical liberalism offered a general framework to answer it. Classical liberalism legitimized the parliamentary enquiries of the nineteenth century, as well as the role of *comizi agrari* in the collection of statistical data. First, none was in a better position to observe agriculture than agriculturalists themselves. Agriculture was as differentiated as landscape, and valid observations should acknowledge this differentiation. Agriculturalists, like Jacini or Cantoni, possessed the expertise, because they had the experience. Only agriculturalists would be able to appreciate the subtleties of such variety of farms. Second, among agriculturalists those most interested in knowing the truth were those who had at least some substantial property at stake. Owners were the nation, they were the 'universal class', and reliable contributors to the state budget. In theory, enquiries would guide deliberation, and true information would lead to right decisions, ultimately beneficial for the nation and for the landed elites that represented the nation in the utmost degree. The electoral system for parliament and the membership fees of the *comizi agrari* guaranteed that they would supervise investigations. Third, the public at large was supposed to verify the likelihood of the information collected. The results of enquiries were published in heavy volumes so that they entered, at least theoretically, the public debate, the 'bourgeois public sphere' of Jürgen Habermas.[1]

The Faina Enquiry and Valenti's Bureau of Agricultural Statistics demonstrate both the resilience of this particular strategy of information gathering, and its eventual loss of methodological credibility at the beginning of the twentieth century. We know that the Jacini Enquiry had already relied on the collaboration of economists and scientists, like Bordiga and Valenti himself (although Valenti was primarily a wealthy landowner, and not an academic). But the contribution of experts to the Faina Enquiry was broader and more apparent. The separation of the scientific and political parts was more radical, and the reports of the technical delegates were published separately, accounting for the most substantial part of the enquiry (the exception that confirms the rule was Nitti's report, which merged political and scientific conclusions). There were a number of reasons for this change. On the one hand, the 'universal class' ceased to exert the same degree of dominance, and the contrast of interests forced landed elites to make appeal to a different kind of rhetoric. On the other, as the discipline became more specialized and technical, agricultural

1 Juergen Habermas, *Strukturwandel der Oeffentlichkeit: Untersuchungen zu einer Kategorie der Buergerlichen Gesellschaft* (5th edn, Muenchen: Lucherhand, 1971).

economics and agricultural statistics entered academia. Finally, the kind of data required changed as well, becoming more demanding.

The lack of technical competency and the required discipline of observation made it impossible for the organizations of landowners and the unspecialized branches of the state administration to deal with statistical data. The landed elites were ill-suited to sustain alone the effort of a protracted collection of data year after year. The failure of the *comizi agrari* as statistical offices in the nineteenth century, and the limited functionality of provincial statistical offices demonstrate this point *ad abundantiam*.

Statistics required a persistent structure for the collection and elaboration of data. From outside the administration, Ghino Valenti, a former collaborator of the SAI, was summoned to direct what we can call a network of statistical observatories. This network consisted of a Bureau of Agricultural Statistics in Rome, and a variety of different institutions that collected and elaborated the data at local level. In the 1900s, Valenti resolved in this way the dialectic between centralization and decentralization that is characteristic of the organization of statistical offices, as underlined by Beaud and Prevost in their article of 1997.[2] In practice, landowners and large tenants still supervised the work of agricultural economists, who engaged in the actual collection of data, but the approach differed substantially from the statistics of the notables of the nineteenth century.[3] Thanks to this decentralized model, Valenti managed to produce modern statistics, and preserve the control of the landed elites over the final figures.[4] The reference to the theory of corporate social responsibility is somewhat ironic, but not out of place: the most important stakeholders of agricultural policies, the landowners, participated with the government in the making of statistics. This is consistent with what historians of the administration and of statistics have written about this period. Interest groups were included in the administration, by means of 'special bureaux', 'thanks to combination of exceptional circumstances held: the charisma of the office leaders, the quality of functionaries, the limited dimension, the clear identification of tasks, [. . .], the presence – outside the government – of conspicuous economic interests that assumed such bureaux as their privileged contact point within the state apparatus'.[5]

2 Jean-Pierre Beaud and Jean-Guy Prévost, 'La forme est le fond la structuration des appareils statistiques nationaux (1800–1945)', *Revue de synthèse* 118.4 (1997).

3 In southern Italy, instead, the role of public administration was still strong. Although the itinerant chairs had contributed decisively to the statistics since 1908, the *prefetti* preserved their centrality.

4 Significantly enough, statistics of agricultural output and acreage under crops are nowadays done to a great extent at local level, more or less for the same reasons put forward by Valenti: 'The rationale of devolution is to improve the quality of the final data, since the recording and possible corrections of data can be done not far from the place and time of their collection', Massimo Greco and Niccolò Mattaliano, eds, *Istruzioni per la rilevazione dei dati: Indagine sulla struttura e produzioni delle aziende agricole e principali coltivazioni legnose agrari* (Soveria Mannelli: Rubbettino, 2007), p. 12.

5 Guido Melis, 'Amministrazione e mediazione degli interessi: le origini delle amministrazioni parallele', in Istituto per la scienza dell'amministrazione pubblica, ed., *L'Amministrazione nella storia moderna*, Archivio (2 vols, Giuffrè editore) (Milano: Per i tipi dell'editore Giuffrè, 1985), II, p. 1437.

Statistics, I think it is important to stress, had to withstand international comparisons. If the International Institute of Statistics had provided a forum for methodological discussion since the nineteenth century, the importance of the International Institute of Agriculture, the first international governmental organization, should not be underestimated. The cases of farm surveys and of output statistics are particularly significant of the complex interplay between national scientific communities, international organizations, and global economic cycles. The nature of statistics, which lent itself so well to international comparison, led to harmonized methods across the European continent long before Eurostat was established. Agricultural statistics, since they concerned an important component of the world trade, were a core element of 'world connecting' in the first globalization.[6] The International Institute of Agriculture, with its *Statistical Yearbook*, had played a leading role in this effort of harmonization, since its inception in 1905. But it was in the wake of the Treaty of Versailles that figures acquired a crucial importance, when international organization such as the International Labour Office, and the League of Nations extended international cooperation to the economy.[7]

The First World Agricultural Census of 1929 became the IIA's single most significant contribution to the debates around the restoration of international trade after the disruption of the First World War. Moreover, the institute promoted the diffusion and standardization of farm surveys foreshadowing the integrated European network of agricultural accounting.[8] This effort was not fostered through arrangements between national statistical institutes of the different countries. It relied instead on the scientific prestige of the Swiss Ernst Laur, on the international network of agricultural economists, as well as on a number of agricultural organizations in the different countries of Europe and the Americas, most notably those affiliated with the Congress of Agriculture. It was, therefore, part of the process of the 'emergence of international society'.[9]

6 On the first globalization see Emily S. Rosenberg, ed., *A world connecting, 1870–1945* (Cambridge Mass: Belknap Press of Harvard University Press, 2012), especially parts 4 and 5.

7 On the role acquired by the League of Nations and the ILO during the interwar period, see Patricia Clavin, *Securing the world economy the reinvention of the League of Nations, 1920–1946* (Oxford: Oxford University Press, 2013), Sandrine Kott and Joelle Droux, eds, *Globalizing social rights: the international labour organization and beyond* (Basingstoke: Palgrave Macmillan, 2013), Amalia Ribi Forclaz, *Humanitarian imperialism the politics of anti-slavery activism, 1880–1940* (2015).

8 The European Economic Community launched a network of accounting observatories in 1965, see Roland Carles, 'Nouvel instrument d'observation pour la statistique agricole le réseau d'information comptable', *Economie et statistique* 6.1 (1969), pp. 62–6.

9 It should be remarked that the International Institute of Agriculture, from its inception, constantly tried to involve associations of agriculturalists from the different countries in its activities, and during the 1920s established the Comité Internationale Permanent des Associations Agricoles, with the involvement of Ernst Laur and the Marquis de Vogué the leaders of the Commission Internationale des Agriculteurs (eventually European Confederation of Agriculture). The role of non-governmental associations in international organizations during the interwar period has been the object of the studies collected in Daniel Laqua, *Internationalism reconfigured transnational ideas and movements between the World Wars* (London, New York, New York: I.B. Tauris, 2011), and of Daniel Gorman, *The emergence of international society in the 1920s* (2012).

The expert's gaze

What characterized this period was the ubiquitous reference to 'typicality'. This problematic concept runs as a red thread through all chapters. The literature on this concept is scarce, but it was a fundamental tool of observation.[10] The statistical definition of typical as the mode or average of the sample did not really correspond to a practice that agricultural economists shared with land surveyors, and land valuators. Features of typicality, such as ordinariness, were clear to the trained eye of an expert. The seemingly impersonal statistics relied in fact on such trained eyes, and the tacit expertise of the beholders. If there is a gap between the monographic method and the metrological ideal of statistics, as Desrosieres argued, typicality was then an attempt at filling the gap, enabling economists to generalize individual cases studied in depth.[11] Many of the things that statisticians did by invoking the idea of typicality, statisticians nowadays do by means of random sampling. But sampling was not familiar to Italian agricultural economists because they operated within a conceptual grid of essentially different *zone agrarie*. They believed in the theory of 'economic place' and the existence of typological differences appeared evident to them. In this sense, the failure to employ random sampling was indeed due to the lack of 'a coherent national system'.[12] However, we cannot overlook that random sampling made relatively little sense before the population was known. Emmanuel Didier showed how complicated it was for American statisticians to create the first samples of consumers. In Italy, the first census of farms was compiled only at the end of the period considered here, in 1929. It was published in 1930, together with the first World Agricultural Census of the IIA.[13]

To a great extent, it was precisely the importance of typicality that preserved agricultural statistics from the general process of 'deskilling' that invested in this period other areas of statistics, and which has been described by both Stapleford and Didier.[14] Statistics were not a contradiction of expert judgement: experts really needed them. The role of experts manifested itself on three different levels: they were acquainted with local conditions, they were familiar with the techniques of farming, and they were able to translate the operations of the farm into a universal and countable language, through accounting. The ubiquity of

10 Literature mostly relates to the use of typicality in ethnography, as in Talal Asad, 'Ethnographic Representation, Statistics and Modern Power', *Social Research* 61.1 (1994), pp. 55–88.

11 Alain Desrosières, 'How real are statistics?', *Social Research* 68.2 (2001), p. 342.

12 Alain Desrosières, 'Du singulier au général: l'argument statistique entre la science et l'État', in Bernard Conein and Laurent Thévenot, eds, *Cognition et information en société* (*Raison Pratiques* special issue 8, 1997), p. 274.

13 International Institute of Agriculture, *The first world agriculture census (1930)*, 1–5 (Rome: International Institute of Agriculture, 1939).

14 Thomas A. Stapleford, *The cost of living in America: A political history of economic statistics, 1880–2000* (Cambridge: Cambridge University Press, 2009), Emmanuel Didier, *En quoi consiste l'Amérique? Les statistiques, le new deal et la démocratie*, Série Anthropologie des sciences et des techniques (Paris: Éd. La Découverte, 2009).

accounting is a very important theme, strictly linked to that of typicality in this book. Accounting was a technology for the management of the farm, for increasing efficiency. The movement of farm accounting services that began with Howard in Germany popularized the technology between the nineteenth and twentieth century, as Taylorism did with cost accounting in industry. We can see a parallel between the extension of Taylorism to the management of society and the use of an accounting framework for observing the whole economy. At the beginning of the twentieth century, though, this did not mean the use of national accounting. Instead, it meant looking at the whole economy as the emerging property of individual businesses. The accounting books of firms showed therefore the way the gross product of society was divided between the factors of production. The macro was observed through the micro.

Alfredo Salsano underlined the difference between Keynesianism and previous forms of 'scientific management', identifying it in the diverging attitude to the macro- and micro-level of the economy.[15] Early twentieth-century scientific management, derived from Taylorism, imagined the economy as the extension of a factory, where social engineers should supervise production in order to use inputs more productively, and reduce waste. Keynesiansm, instead, began with aggregate data on national income, the balance of trade, inflation, and monetary mass, and mused over the productivity of 'wasted' resources.[16] Italian agricultural economists of the 1930s, although not necessarily infatuated with Taylorism and 'scientific management', clearly belonged to the older kind of state interventionists. Industrial farming was the most efficient way of using soil, labour, and capital (including costly industrial inputs, such as machines and fertilizers) only under specific geographic and economic conditions, which aggregate macro-data was not enable to assess.

This explains why, after the tensions of the period 1908–10 and then the strikes and land occupations of 1911 (which undermined Valenti's network of observatories), the Federazione Italiana Consorzi Agrari began financing research into the private economy of agricultural businesses, as a scientific approach to disputes. Farm surveys became the technique for umpiring the disputes between labour and capital, putting agricultural economists – just like Taylorist engineers – at the forefront in the struggle against class struggle.[17] This role they preserved when the war, and the vitality acquired by mass parties,

15 Alfredo Salsano, *Ingegneri e politici: Dalla razionalizzazione alla 'rivoluzione manageriale'*, Nuovo politecnico 0157 (Torino: Einaudi, 1987), p. 3.

16 Charles S. Maier, *In Search of Stability: Explorations in Historical Political Economy,* Cambridge Studies in Modern Political Economies (Cambridge: Cambridge University Press, 1988) often refers to 'waste' as a keyword of Taylorism, for example on p. 57; see, again, J. Adam Tooze, *Statistics and the German State, 1900–1945: The Making of Modern Economic Knowledge,* Cambridge Studies in Modern Economic History (Cambridge: Cambridge University Press, 2001), 'Introduction', passim.

17 Although the introduction of Taylorist methods was very much resisted by workers, Taylorism preached scientifically based social peace, see, *inter alia,* Richard K. Fleischman, 'Completing the triangle: Taylorism and the paradigms', *Accounting, Auditing & Accountability Journal* 13.5 (2000), pp. 597–623.

exasperated social conflicts. The war inflation favoured a large transfer of land from estate owners to peasants. State policies were forced to target great masses of peasants (smallholders, sharecroppers, small tenants). Agricultural economists were then asked to define the 'area of profitability of small farms' and how to spread smallholdings. Smallholdings – in Italy – seemed the solution for rural poverty and deficient production. Based on data from farm surveys, latifundia seemed to be a deviation from good agronomic practices.[18]

Market failure: the rationale for state intervention

Interventionism was linked to the shortcomings of market forces that enquiries, statistics, and farm surveys revealed. Agricultural economists were engaged in a modernizing project parallel to that of the Taylorist and Fordist industrial engineers, but they certainly embodied the ideal of the rule of the experts and shared some of the technocratic tendencies of the period. Just like engineers, they also valued knowledge, the bits of information they collected, as an instrument for transforming systems of production, and society at large.[19] In Italy, great emphasis has been placed on Francesco Saverio Nitti, but real technocratic tendencies have been attributed especially to the early and late periods of the Fascist regime.[20] In all these cases, the role of experts was closely linked to state interventionism and to an accumulated perception of market failures.

Although market failure became a dominant topic around the time of the First World War, and especially with the economic slumps of the interwar years, it had been a topic of discussion in the decade before the war. In Italy, the concern with market failures did not relate to gaps or lags between supply and demand, but was linked mainly to the topic of investment and to the role of monopolies. Nitti's insistence on the nationalization of hydroelectric power through a sort of *ante literam* project financing is of course the best-known example of this attitude. He insisted that the production of hydroelectric power benefited from economies of scale and had decreasing costs per unit of product after the initial investment (the terminology I am using here is not

18 In Italian, 'area di convenienza economia'; for the enquiry of 1917–22, and the role of Bordiga and Serpieri, see Ministero dell'Agricoltura – Direzione generale dell'agricoltura, *Per la piccola proprietà rurale e montana,* 2 vols (Roma: Tip. L. Cecchini, 1921–22).

19 This attitude was similar to what Howard Brick, *Transcending Capitalism: Visions of a New Society in Modern American Thought* (Ithaca and London, 2006) named 'visions of post-capitalism'.

20 Salsano, *Ingegneri e politici*, for general context; Alfredo Salsano, *L'altro corporativismo: Tecnocrazia e managerialismo tra le due guerre* (Torino: Il Segnalibro, 2003) for an interesting discussion of the French case; Emilio Gentile, *Le origini dell'ideologia fascista (1918–1925),* Biblioteca storica (Bologna: Il mulino, 1996) contains an interesting discussion of fascist *revisionisti*, while the essays collected in Emily Braun and Emilio Gentile, eds, *Modernità totalitaria: Il fascismo italiano*, 1. ed., Storia e società (Roma-Bari: Laterza, 2008) paradoxically ignore economic policies and focus on aesthetics; for the late policies of fascism Simone Misiani, *La Via Dei 'Tecnici': Dalla Rsi Alla Ricostruzione: Il Caso Di Paolo Albertario,* Studi e ricerche storiche (Milano: Franco Angeli, 1998).

Nitti's), and concluded that the state should actively promote the substitution of electricity to coal.[21]

Quite naturally, historians saw Serpieri's prestigious appointment in 1911 to the Forestry Institute of Vallombrosa-Firenze, on Nitti's order, as a demonstration of Nitti's desire to create a group of interventionist technocrats.[22] Forestry was a strategic resource. On the one hand, Nitti's obsession with hydroelectric power led him to focus on the hydrogeological situation in the mountains, and therefore on reforestation.[23] On the other, mountain agriculture was in a precarious condition at the beginning of the twentieth century, plagued by emigration and the overexploitation of workers and land, which made the hydrogeological situation only worse. Only the intervention of the state could solve a situation that was intolerable for peasants and damaging for society.

Stressing the importance of market failures can help to resolve the often-remarked contradiction beteween a young Serpieri and an older, *ruralist* Serpieri. The early Serpieri had a Schumpeterian confidence in the entrepreneur. In 1908, commenting on the rapid development of Italian agriculture, he wrote enthusiastically that 'the agriculturalist is turning, in this way, into a businessman'.[24] In the 1920s, instead, he turned to Pareto's sociology to say that agriculture, in contrast to industry and finance, was not 'the world of fast and rewarding gains, of quick innovations and combinations'.[25] At the same time, historians have often contrasted the old Serpieri with his pupil Giuseppe Tassinari. While Serpieri remained cautious about state intervention, Tassinari was much more enthusiastic about it.[26]

Serpieri's caution on state intervention and his increasing scepticism about the entrepreneurial future of agriculture have different origins. Fundamentally, Serpieri remained convinced of the benefits of the market. But over time he developed a clear awareness, rooted in the study of farms' accounting books, that entire generations of forward-thinking farmers could be wiped out by wrong investments, with heavy social costs. The state – he often claimed – had the task of intervening in order to foster social utility whenever the pursuit of mere economic utility failed to deliver, but also when other social mechanisms

21 Francesco S. Nitti, *La conquista della forza, Il capitale straniero in Italia,* Edizione Nazionale delle Opere di Francesco Saverio Nitti 3.2 (Bari, 1968).

22 Nitti was then Minister of Agriculture, Industry, and Trade. Lea D'Antone, 'Politica e cultura agraria: Arrigo Serpieri', *Studi Storici* 20.3 (1979), pp. 609–42; Antonio Prampolini, 'La formazione di A. Serpieri ed i problemi dell'agricoltura lombarda', *Studi Storici* 17.2 (1976), pp. 171–209. The connection between Serpieri and Nitti should not be overly stressed. While certainly Nitti thought he could rely on Serpieri as expert, Serpieri was, as Chapter 5 documents, well entrenched into different, more conservative, networks of experts and interest groups.

23 Nitti, *La conquista della forza, Il capitale straniero in Italia*, p. 90.

24 Arrigo Serpieri, 'La fase presente dell'agricoltura italiana', *L'Italia Economica* 2 (1908), p. 43.

25 Arrigo Serpieri, *Fra politica ed economia rurale*, Biblioteca di coltura per i rurali (2nd edn, Firenze: G. Barbera, 1937), p. 67.

26 Marco Zaganella, *Dal fascismo alla DC: Tassinari, Medici e la bonifica nell'Italia tra gli anni Trenta e Cinquanta,* I fatti e la storia 4 (Siena: Cantagalli, 2010).

forced economic agents to behave against economic rationality, with disastrous consequences.

If we focus on the first case, namely the failure of economic optima to deliver social optima, we see that in the aftermath of the Great War Serpieri identified the main reason for this in the specificity of agriculture. Building on his own 'Marshallian' theory of land valuation, and noticing the low level of returns on investment (in land), Serpieri worriedly argued that projects of land transformation and land reclamation could not be entirely funded by private investors, seeking market-level returns on investment and profit. Land reclamation and land transformation, although not viable for mere profit-seeking entities, were socially desirable, not just because they implied more occupation and a healthier life in the countryside (by eradicating malaria, for instance), but also because they would help rebalance Italy's problematic trade balance by intensifying the use of land.[27]

The second case, namely the hindrances to economic development that originated in the legal and social framework, was more complicated and depended on the peculiar nature of the farm (*azienda agricola*), which was at the same time a business and a way of life. There were at least two examples of this kind that were familiar to agricultural economists all over Europe. One risk farmers often ran was to over-invest: in contrast to profit-seeking companies that invested less than socially desirable, peasants and small owners often burdened themselves with debts that were difficult to repay and therefore subtracted precious resources that would have otherwise been available for the improvement of the land. In his writings of the 1920s and 1930s, Serpieri stressed in particular the psychological reasons that lay behind this behaviour, building upon Pareto's sociology: agriculturalists were not financiers who followed profit, they were deeply attached to the land. But it was very clear to him (as to other agricultural economists) that the industrial sector was not ready to absorb vast masses of peasants, and that this kind of over-investment was, to an extent, as much a rational behaviour for peasants, as a desirable tendency for the Italian state. Agricultural economists, therefore, were to find the right balance in this delicate trade-off.

An instance of the second case had attracted a great deal of attention since the nineteenth century. The inheritance law that was generalized to most of Europe during the Napolenic era imposed the division of land among the heirs. This was one of factors (allegedly one of the main factors) that created

27 The discussions that took place within the League of Nations during the 1920s made the problems of Italy's trade balance evident: Italy was neither a powerful industrial exporter, nor a suitable member for the Eastern European Agrarian Bloc, nor a massive exporter of agricultural commodities such as Argentina, Australia, or Canada; on the economists' perception of these problems, Fabrizio Bientinesi, *La parziale eccezione: Costi comparati e teorie del commercio internazionale in Italia dalla metà dell'Ottocento alla Seconda Guerra mondiale,* Biblioteca storica degli economisti italiani 242 (Milano: Franco Angeli, 2011).

a general tendency for farms to grow smaller and smaller.[28] This problem had long seemed to require the intervention of the state for consolidation of land plots into farms of a decent size. Conversely, the structure of land ownership could be such as to prevent the purchase of land by small farmers. This was the case of the latifundia that dominated (or so the public opinion thought) southern Italy and Sicily. Latifundia seemed to involve a number of shortcomings, including the creation of a vast mass of seasonal workers without any specific attachment to property, but also a kind of land use that was less intensive than technically desirable.[29]

Moreover, agricultural economists were fully aware that short-sighted exploitation of land would deplete the soil and result in long-term damage to agricultural productivity. Specific contracts were to blame: the short-term lease, most of all. The market, by itself, did not fully account for long-term costs of agriculture. The market does not pay sufficient attention to 'the way in which the stream of goods is distributed through time, taking into consideration not just the life of individuals, but the life of the Nation that runs perpetually across the generations'.[30]

For all these different pathologies, Serpieri invoked different degrees of state intervention, ranging from the state directly taking over private properties and substituting land owners (a disputed point of his land reclamation law, which actually cost him his position in the ministry), to softer forms of intervention, such as the establishment of advisory centres (within the INEA's provincial observatories) for prospective owner-farmers.

As we said, Serpieri entered the cabinet as vice-minister for agriculture only with the Fascist regime, but his ideas about state intervention had been formed long before, when he was close to the Catholic Partito Popolare. The recipe that Italian agricultural economists devised for the balanced modernization of agriculture between the 1910s and the 1940s relied on sharecropping, family farms, and cooperatives as a way to overcome the shortcomings of small farms. Agricultural economists, in Serpieri's understanding, had to supervise the development of agriculture. The Fascist state, with its emphasis on coordination, provided a new, seemingly more effective, framework for the enforcement of proposals and ideas that agricultural experts had been developing over a long time. It is probably for this reason that Serpieri declared himself a 'true corporativist', although, in

28 The demographic origins of inequality had long been a contested issue; for a reconstruction of this debate in the Italian context, Giovanni Favero, 'I quartieri di Firenze: la costruzione statistica dello spazio urbano', *Città e Storia* 8.2 (2013), pp. 433f.

29 On the economic viability of latifundia, though, the debate was intense, with *meridionalisti* underlining the impact of a tough environment, what Guido Dorso defined as 'the bone' of southern Italy: but see also the retrospective analysis of Manlio Rossi-Doria on Eugenio Azimonti in Manlio Rossi-Doria, *La gioia tranquilla del ricordo: memorie, 1905–1934,* Storia-memoria (Bologna: Mulino, 1991); for the debates on *latifondo*, see also Marta Petrusewicz, *Latifondo: economia morale e vita materiale in una periferia dell'Ottocento,* Saggi Marsilio (Venezia: Marsilio, 1989).

30 Arrigo Serpieri, 'La bonifica integrale', *Annali di Economia* 12 (1937), p. 126.

contrast with other agricultural economists, including some of his pupils, he maintained a deep respect for the virtue of private property.[31]

The paradigm of agricultural economists

The creation of the ICS in 1926 imposed on the field of statistics the centralizing will of the regime. The jealous conception of statistics held by ICS director Gini imposed a sharp separation between the activities of agricultural economists and those of statisticians. Agricultural economists were absorbed in the administration, by the 'bureaucratic-cooperative mantle' that was imposed on Italian agriculture during the 1930s.[32] Their scientific activities and empirical research were centralized in Serpieri's INEA, and the character of their activity remained clearly distinct from the *modus operandi* of statisticians. The INEA took over the study of farm budgets and the statistics of business.

The INEA served the rhetoric of the regime, giving scientific support to the image of the virtuous toiling peasant ready to invest their labour and capital in slowly making the landscape a 'handmade product'. INEA followed Serpieri's agenda, investigating the pathologies of the farm and the psychology of peasants. Serpieri's *Guida a ricerche di economia agraria* became the reference textbook for INEA research. The relationship between statistics, enquiries, and surveys that the *Guida* displayed was surprisingly similar to what Coletti and Valenti had already proposed in the 1900s, in a striking example of methodological continuity. The *Guida* moves from the general to the particular. It begins with the 720 *zone agrarie* of Valenti's CA and moves to the study of typical farms and typical peasant families. This required, as we have seen, the use of monographs.[33] INEA's work reflects in part this preference, as Tolaini recalled, and wavered between economics and sociology.

Tassinari and his pupils instead adopted a different strategy. There was no real conflict between the two approaches, but they clearly reveal diverging options. Tassinari decided to study the consequences of the agricultural crisis of the 1920s on the economic situation of farms. In the beginning, Tassinari had to rely on typicality, like Serpieri did, but this was not a deliberate methodological choice, only the result of the difficulties encountered in enlarging the sample. Actually, Tassinari had been clear from the beginning that the study of the economic conjuncture could not rely on incomparable typical

31 He stated this, in 1947, as a witness to the Constitutional Assembly. See also ibid., which lists three points of view on the economy: the quantity of goods made available, their distribution among the members of society, and their distribution across generations, the latter two certainly requiring the 'direction' of the state; Serpieri also wrote a handbook of economics inspired by *corporativismo*: Arrigo Serpieri, *Principi di economia corporativa* (Firenze: Barbera, 1938).

32 Carlo Fumian, 'I tecnici tra agricoltura e Stato. 1930–1950', *Mélanges de l'Ecole française de Rome. Italie et Méditerranée* 95.2 (1983), p. 211.

33 Arrigo Serpieri, *Guida a ricerche di economia agraria,* Studi e monografie / Istituto Nazionale di Economia Agraria 1 (Roma: Treves Dell'Ali, 1929).

farms. His preferred option was the sheer increase of the number of farms observed, ideally aiming at the whole population.[34] But his networks and connections did not make him strong enough to do that until the beginning of the 1930s.

The example to be followed was Ernst Laur's well-functioning observatory of agriculture, where observations were repeated in longitudinal samples, with a hundreds of individuals observed, and the trends of costs, products and financial results constantly monitored. Paradoxically, while cost accounting in industry exalted standardization and scale economies, Laur's studies of farm accounting went in a totally different direction. He used his data to shape the Swiss political debate on foreign trade and small properties, and obtained protectionist policies, support for the export of dairy products, and a law that privileged only one of the heirs of an agricultural property (*Anerbenrecht*). The International Institute of Agriculture and the Agricultural Congresses favoured the spread of Laur's methods internationally alongside his praise of smallholdings, and farm cooperatives.

Although Serpieri and Tassinari clashed violently over agricultural policies, especially during the 1930s, their divergences emerged within the same paradigm of modernizing agrarianism. The methodological framework of their arguments was also very similar, since they shared a farm-centred methodology of observation in which the basic tool was farm accounting. This methodology translated into a farm-centred 'ontology' that shaped decisively the way in which social and production problems were understood. Giuseppe Medici and Manlio Rossi Doria, the two most prominent agricultural economists of the post-war generation, shared this fundamental paradigm, which survived the Second World War and inspired the land reform of the 1950s.

34 INEA still carries out the survey of farm budgets for ISTAT. This approach was not exclusively Italian. When the League of Nations asked the International Institute of Agriculture for a report on the economic problems of agriculture in international perspective for the economic conference of Geneva, the IIA described the agricultural conjuncture in terms of aggregate supply of farming costs and revenues. This report shows the persistence of the old methods, alongside the new one, centred on aggregate data, International Institute of Agriculture, *Agricultural problems in their international aspect* (Rome: Printing office of the International Institute of Agriculture, 1927).

Bibliography

Adorno, Salvatore, 'L'Italia agricola e il suo avvenire: Note sul ruolo della Commissione di studi tecnici ed economici della Federconsorzi', in Fontana, ed., *La Federconsorzi tra stato liberale e fascismo*, pp. 61–108.

Albertario, Paolo, 'Le "fattorie" dell'Italia centrale', *Annali di Statistica* III (Serie VII) (1939), pp. 103–91.

Alberti, Manfredi, *La scoperta dei disoccupati: Alle origini dell'indagine statistica sulla disoccupazione nell'Italia liberale, 1893–1915,* Premio tesi di dottorato 34 (Firenze: Firenze University Press, 2013).

Asad, Talal, 'Ethnographic Representation, Statistics and Modern Power', *Social Research* 61.1 (1994), pp. 55–88.

Associazione Agraria Ravennate, *Condizioni del lavoro e della produzione nell'agro ravennate e l'agitazione agraria del 1910: Memoriale presentato dall'Associazione Agraria Ravennate all'On. Commissione d'Inchiesta nominate da S.E. il Presidente del Consiglio* (Bologna, 1910).

Aubin, David, Charlotte Bigg, and Heinz O. Sibum, *The heavens on earth: Observatories and astronomy in nineteenth-century science and culture,* Science and cultural theory (Durham: Duke University Press, 2010).

Augé-Laribé, Michel, 'Les statistiques agricoles', *Annales de Géographie* 54.294 (1945), pp. 81–92.

Azimonti, Eugenio, *Basilicata: Relazione del delegato tecnico,* Atti della giunta parlmentare di inchiesta sulle condizioni dei contadini nelle province meridionali e in Sicilia 5.1 (Roma: Bertero, 1909).

———, *Il Mezzogiorno agrario quale è: relazioni e scritti* (Bari: G. Laterza & figli, 1919).

Baffigi, Alberto, *Cultura statistica e cultura politica: L'Italia nei primi decenni unitari,* Quaderni dell'Ufficio Ricerche Storiche / Banca d'Italia 15 (Roma, 2007).

Baglioni, Guido, *L'ideologia della borghesia industriale nell'Italia liberale* (Torino: Einaudi, 1977).

Banti, Alberto M.,'Organizzazioni di agrari in Prussia e nella Valle Padana, 1880–1914', *Annali dell'Istituto Alcide Cervi* 14–15 (1993), pp. 421–40.

Barbagallo, Francesco, *Francesco S. Nitti,* La Vita sociale della nuova Italia 33 (Torino: UTET, 1984).

Barberi, Benedetto, 'Indagine statistica sulle disponibilità alimentari della popolazione italiana dal 1922 al 1937', *Annali di Statistica* III (serie VII) (1939), pp. 5–98.

Baumann, Werner, *Bauernstand und Bürgerblock: Ernst Laur und der Schweizerische Bauernverband, 1897–1918* (Zürich: Orell Füssli Verlag, 1993).

Baumann, Werner, and Peter Moser, *Bauern im Industriestaat: agrarpolitische Konzeptionen und bäuerliche Bewegungen in der Schweiz, 1918–1968* (Zürich: Orell Füssli Verlag, 1999).

Beaud, Jean-Pierre, and Jean-Guy Prévost, 'La forme est le fond la structuration des appareils statistiques nationaux (1800–1945)', *Revue de synthèse* 118.4 (1997), pp. 419–56.

Behrisch, Lars, *Vermessen, Zählen, Berechnen: Die politische Ordnung des Raums im 18, Jahrhundert,* Historische Politikforschung Bd, 6, Frankfurt am Main (New York: Campus, 2006).

Belgium, Ministère de l'agriculture, *Monographies agricoles,* 1–4, Brussels: Ministère de l'agriculture, 1899–1901.

Benini, Rodolfo, 'Sei anni di protezionismo o dodici anni di sgoverno?', *Giornale degli economisti* 10 (1895), pp. 283–326.

———, *Principi di statistica metodologica* (Torino: UTET, 1906).

Bergmann, Denis R.,'Les études d'économie rurale', *Économie rurale* 39–40 (1959), pp. 259–68.

Bevilacqua, Piero, ed., *Storia dell'agricoltura italiana in età contemporanea: Mercati e istituzioni* (Venezia: Marsilio, 1990).

———, 'La "storia economica" e l'economia', in Ciocca and Toniolo, eds, *Storia economica d'Italia,* pp. 159–98.

Biagioli, Giuliana and Rossano Pazzagli, eds, *Agricoltura come manifattura: Istruzione agraria, professionalizzazione e sviluppo agricolo nell'Ottocento* (Firenze: Leo S. Olschki, 2004).

Bientinesi, Fabrizio, *La parziale eccezione: Costi comparati e teorie del commercio internazionale in Italia dalla metà dell'Ottocento alla Seconda Guerra mondiale,* Biblioteca storica degli economisti italiani 242 (Milano: Franco Angeli, 2011).

Bordiga, Oreste, *L'agricoltura e gli agricoltori del Novarese, memoria distinta col premio massimo di lire 500 dall'Onorevole giunta parlamentare per la Inchiesta agraria* (Novara: Tipografia della Rivista di contabilità, 1882).

Boumans, M.,'Observations in a Hostile Environment: Morgenstern on the Accuracy of Economic Observations', *History of Political Economy* 44, Supplement 1 (2012), pp. 114–36.

Bourguet, Marie N.,*Déchiffrer la France: la statistique départementale à l'époque napoléonienne,* Ordres sociaux (Paris: Editions des archives contemporaines, 1988).

Bourguinat, Nicolas, 'Libre-commerce du blé et représentations de l'espace français.: Les crises frumentaires au début du XIXe siècle', *Annales, Histoire, Sciences Sociales* 56.1 (2001), pp. 125–52.

Brassley, Paul, David Harvey, Matt Lobley, and Michael Winter, 'Accounting for agriculture: The origins of the Farm Management Survey', *Agricultural History Review* 61.1 (2013), pp. 135–53.

Braun, Emily and Emilio Gentile, eds, *Modernità totalitaria: Il fascismo italiano,* Storia e società (Roma-Bari: Laterza, 2008).

Brick, Howard, *Transcending Capitalism: Visions of a New Society in Modern American Thought* (Ithaca and London: Cornell University Press, 2006).

Brizi, Alessandro, IIA, Comité économique agricole, Ière Session, 1–3 Octobre 1929, Enquetes complémentaires sur les conditions générales de l'Agriculture et documentation ordinaire de l'Institut, partie IIème, FAO Archive.

Brizi, Alessandro, and Alfredo De Polzer, *L'Ufficio di contabilità agraria e l'Ufficio di estimo rurale dell'Unione svizzera dei contadini,* Studi e monografie (Roma: INEA, 1938).

Bruisch, Katja, *Als das Dorf noch Zukunft war: Agrarismus und Expertise zwischen Zarenreich und Sowjetunion,* Beiträge zur Geschichte Osteuropas 47 (Köln: Böhlau Köln, 2014).

Byerlee, Derek et al., *World development report 2008: agriculture for development,* World Development Report 30 (Washington, DC: World Bank Group, 2008).

Čajanov, Aleksandr V., *A.V. Chayanov on the theory of peasant economy,* ed. D. Thorner, B. H. Kerblay, and R. E. F. Smith (Manchester: Manchester University Press, 1986).

Čajanov, Aleksandr V.,*O budžetnikh issledovanjakh* (Moskva: Izdatel'skij Dom Tonču, 2006).

Camera dei Deputati, *Atti del Parlamento del Regno d'Italia: Legislatura XXVI, Sessione 1, 2a Tornata del 23 Giugno 1922* (Roma, 1922).

Canali, Massimo, Giancarlo Di Sandro, Bernardino Farolfi, and Massimo Fornasari, eds, *L'agricoltura e gli economisti agrari in Italia dall'Ottocento al Novecento* (Milano: Franco Angeli, 2011).

Cantoni, Gaetano., *Trattato completo teorico- pratico di agricoltura del dott, Gaetano Cantoni, professore d'agronomia al R. Museo Industriale Italiano in Torino*, I (2nd edn, Milano: Vallardi, 1866).

———, *L'agricoltura in Italia: Dieci anni di sperienze agrarie eseguite presso la R. Scuola Superiore di Agricoltura di Milano dal direttore Prof, Gaetano Cantoni,* Ars et labor (Milano: Lampi di Stampa, 2010).

Caprotti, Federico, 'Internal colonisation, hegemony and coercion: Investigating migration to Southern Lazio, Italy, in the 1930s', *Geoforum* 39.2 (2008), pp. 942–57.

Caracciolo, Alberto, *L'inchiesta agraria Jacini* (Torino: Einaudi, 1959).

Cardoza, Anthony L.,*Agrarian elites and Italian fascism: the Province of Bologna, 1901–1926* (Princeton University Press, 1982).

Carles, Roland, 'Nouvel instrument d'observation pour la statistique agricole le réseau d'information comptable', *Economie et statistique* 6.1 (1969), pp. 62–6.

Carli, Gian R., *Il censimento di Milano* (Milano: Giovanni Silvestri, 1815).

Casciani, Paolo, 'Relazione del la Giunta generale del bilancio sul disegno di legge "Provvedimenti per la statistica agraria", presentata al la Camera dei deputati nel la seduta del 15 Maggio 1908', in MAIC, ed., *Esperimenti di statistica agraria in alcune province del Regno*, fasc. II, pp. 28f.

Catizzone, Antonio and Sabatino Di Filippo, eds, *Un tesoro ritrovato: Dal rilievo alla rappresentazione* (Roma: Gangemi, 2009).

Catolfi, Carla, *L'inchiesta Jacini in Romagna: I materiali inediti del Riminese* (Rimini: Maggioli, 1990).

Cattaneo, Carlo, *Saggi di economia rurale*, ed. Luigi Einaudi (Torino: Einaudi, 1939).

Cattedra di Agricoltura per la Provincia di Milano, *Annuario della cattedra di agricoltura per la provincia di Milano, anno 1902–1903* (Milano: Tipografia agraria, 1904).

———, *Annuario della cattedra di agricoltura per la provincia di Milano, anno 1908* (Milano: Tipografia agraria, 1909).

———, *Annuario della cattedra di agricoltura per la provincia di Milano, anno 1916* (Milano: Tipografia agraria, 1917).

Cavaglieri, Guido, 'Le statistiche agrarie in Italia', *Bollettino quindicinale della Società degli Agricoltori Italiani* 5.24 (1900), pp. 892–910.

CESET, ed., *Aspetti evolutivi della scienza estimativa: Seminario in onore di Ernesto Marenghi* (Firenze: Florence University Press, 1995).

Ciocca, Pierluigi and Gianni Toniolo, eds, *Storia economica d'Italia,* I (Roma/Bari: Laterza, 2004).

Ciuffoletti, Zeffiro, 'Dirigenti e ideologie del movimento cooperativo', in Sapelli, ed., *Il movimento cooperativo in Italia: Storia e problemi*, pp. 89–190.

Clavin, Patricia, *Securing the world economy: the reinvention of the League of Nations, 1920–1946* (Oxford: Oxford University Press, 2013).

Cohen, Jon S., and Giovanni Federico, *The growth of the Italian economy, 1820–1960,* New studies in economic and social history (Cambridge, New York: Cambridge University Press, 2001).

Cohen, Jon S., and Francesco L. Galassi, 'Sharecropping and productivity:'feudal residues'in Italian agriculture, 1911', *Economic History Review* 43.4 (1990), pp. 646–56.

Coletti, Francesco, 'I contratti agrari e il contratto di lavoro agricolo in Italia: Inchiesta intorno ai disegni di legge presentati alla Camera dai Ministri competenti il 26 novembre 1902, Relazione del prof. dott. Francesco Coletti, Segretario generale della Società degli agricoltori italiani', *Bollettino quindicinale della Società degli Agricoltori Italiani* VIII, 4–5–6, 30 Aprile 1903 (1903), pp. 91–175.

———, *Come si compilano le monografie di famiglia: Estratto dallo Cheysson e Focillon* (Roma: Bertero, 1906).

———, *Programma questionario dell'inchiesta per i delegati tecnici* (Roma: Bertero, 1906).

Collins, H. M., and R. Evans, 'The Third Wave of Science Studies: Studies of Expertise and Experience', *Social Studies of Science* 32.2 (2002), pp. 235–96.

Comizio Agrario di Bologna, *Monografia del podere bolognese* (Bologna: Società tip. già compositori, 1881).

Conein, Bernard and Laurent Thévenot, eds, 'Cognition et information en société', Special issue, *Raison Pratiques* 8 (1997).

Corner, Paul, *Contadini e industrializzazione: società rurale e impresa in Italia dal 1840 al 1940*, Quadrante (Roma: Laterza, 1993).

Corti, Paola, 'I comizi agrari dopo l'Unità (1866–91)', *Ricerche di storia sociale e religiosa* 3 (1973), pp. 247–301.

———, *Inchiesta Zanardelli sulla Basicicata,* Piccola biblioteca Einaudi (Torino: Einaudi, 1976).

Cottini-Agostinelli, Giacinto, *L'Istituto Internazionale di Agricoltura: l'affermazione integrale delle sue attività* (Terni: Alterocca, 1933).

Craigie, Patrick G.,'Memorandum on the methods employed in the collection of the annual Agricultural Statistics of Great Britain', *Bulletin de l'Institut international de statistique* 13.2 (1903), pp. 322–4.

Cullather, Nick, *The hungry world America's Cold War battle against poverty in Asia* (Cambridge, MA: Harvard University Press, 2010).

Cuppari, Pietro, 'Spese e proventi di una famiglia colonica', *Giornale agrario toscano* 3 (1860), pp. 298–304.

———, 'Studi di economia rurale italiana, Territorio Bolognese (Tipo di pianura)', *Giornale agrario toscano* XI (1864), pp. 117–30.

———, *Manuale dell'agricoltore* (Firenze: Barbera, 1869).

D'Agostino, Peter, 'Craniums, Criminals, and the "Cursed Race": Italian Anthropology in American Racial Thought, 1861–1924', *Comparative Studies in Society and History* 44.2 (2002), pp. 319–43.

Daniele, Vittorio, and Paolo Malanima, 'Il prodotto delle regioni e il divario Nord-Sud in Italia (1861–2004)', *Rivista di politica economica*, 3–4 (2007), pp. 267–316.

D'Antone, Lea, 'Politica e cultura agraria: Arrigo Serpieri', *Studi Storici* 20.3 (1979), pp. 609–42.

———, 'La modernizzazione dell'agricoltura italiana negli anni Trenta', *Studi Storici* 22.3 (1981), pp. 603–29.

———, 'L'intelligenza dell'agricoltura: Istruzione superiore, profili intellettuali e identità professionale', in Bevilacqua, ed., *Storia dell'agricoltura italiana in età contemporanea: Mercati e istituzioni*, pp. 391–426.

Daston, Lorraine, and Peter Galison, *Objectivity* (Cambridge, MA: Zone Books, 2007).

Daston, Lorraine and Elizabeth Lunbeck, eds, *Histories of Scientific Observation* (Chicago: University of Chicago Press, 2011).

D'Attorre, Pier P., *Novecento padano: l'universo rurale e la 'grande trasformazione,* Saggi: Storia e scienze sociali (Donzelli, 1998).

D'Attorre, Pier P. and A.D Bernardi, eds, *Studi sull'agricoltura italiana: società rurale e modernizzazione,* Annali (Fondazione Giangiacomo Feltrinelli) (Milano: Feltrinelli, 1994).

D'Autilia, Maria L., *L'amministrazione della statistica nell'Italia fascista: Il caso dell'agricoltura* (Roma: Gangemi, 1992).

———, *Il cittadino senza burocrazia Società umanitaria e amministrazione pubblica nell'Italia liberale* (Milano: Giuffrè, 1995).

———, 'Statistics. Giovanni Montemartini's ideas and actions', Paper presented at the European Business History Association, Glasgow, 27 August 2010' (unpubl.), http://www.gla.ac.uk/media/media_169409_en.pdf.

David, Eduard, 'Oekonomische Verschiedenheiten zwischen Landwirthschaft und Industrie', *Die neue Zeit Revue des geistigen und öffentlichen Lebens* 2.41 (1895), pp. 449–55.

Delors, Jacques, 'Déclaration sur les orientations de la Commission: faite devant le Parlement européen . . . Strasbourg, 17 et 18 janvier 1989', Bulletin des Communautés européennes Supplément 1/89 (1989).

Demangeon, Albert,'La statistique agricole de la France', *Annales de Géographie* 37.210 (1928), pp. 554.

Desideri, Carlo, *L'amministrazione dell'Agricoltura (1910–1980),* Paperback/Officina 9 (Roma: Officina, 1981).

Desrosières, Alain, 'La partie pour le tout: comment généraliser? La prehistoire de la contrainte de représentativité', *Statistique et analyse des données* 13.2 (1988), pp. 93–112.

———, *La politique des grandes nombres: Histoire de la raison statistique* (Paris: La Découverte, 1993).

———, 'Du singulier au général: l'argument statistique entre la science et l'État', in Conein and Thévenot, eds, 'Cognition et information en société', pp. 267–82.

———, 'How real are statistics?' *Social Research* 68.2 (2001), pp. 339–55.

———, *Pour une sociologie historique de la quantification: L'argument statistique* I (Paris: Presses de l'Ecole des Mines, 2008).

Dettweiler, Friederich, *Die Handarbeit in der Landwirtschaft* (Jena: Fischer, 1905).

Di Sandro, Giancarlo, *Gli economisti agrari italiani tra Otto e Novecento,* Collana di economia applicata 6 (Bologna: Clueb, 1995).

———, 'La manualistica di economia agraria da Cuppari a Serpieri', *Il pensiero economico italiano* 14.1 (2006), pp. 173–212.

———, 'Il pensiero economico-agrario in Italia (1800–1980)', in Canali et al., eds, *L'agricoltura e gli economisti agrari in Italia dall'Ottocento al Novecento*, pp. 173–370.

Didier, Emmanuel, *En quoi consiste l'Amérique? Les statistiques, le new deal et la démocratie,* Série Anthropologie des sciences et des techniques (Paris: Éd, La Découverte, 2009).

Dilio, Mario, *Il viaggio di Zanardelli in Basilicata* (Bari: Adriatica Editrice, 1970).

D'Onofrio, Federico, 'Making variety simple: agricultural economists in Southern Italy, 1907–1909', *History of Political Economy* 44.5 (2012), pp. 93–113.

———, 'Les statistiques agricoles . . . ', in Fraboulet et al., eds, *Les organisations patronales et la sphère publique*, pp. 143–52.

Einaudi, Luigi, *La terra e l'imposta,* Nuova Universale Einaudi 155 (Torino: Einaudi, 1974).

Engel, Ernst, 'Die Lebenskosten belgischer Arbeiter-Familien früher und jetzt, Ermittelt aus Familien-Haushaltrechnungen und vergleichend zusammengestellt', *Bulletin de l'Institut International de Statistique* 9.1 (1895), pp. 1–124.

Engstrom, Eric J. et al., eds, *Figurationen des Experten. Ambivalenzen der wissenschaftlichen Expertise im ausgehenden 18. und frühen 19. Jahrhundert* (Frankfurt a. M.: Peter Lang Verlag, 2004).

———, 'Figurationen des Experten', in Engstrom, Eric J. et al., eds, *Figurationen des Experten. Ambivalenzen der wissenschaftlichen Expertise im ausgehenden 18. und frühen 19. Jahrhundert*, pp. 7–77.

Facchini, Fabio, *La famiglia Faina: tre secoli di storia* (Todi: Publimedia, 2000).

Failla, Osvaldo and Giampiero Fumi, eds, *Gli agronomi in Lombardia: dalle cattedre ambulanti ad oggi* (Milano: Franco Angeli, 2006).

Farinelli, Franco, 'La cartografia della campagna nel Novecento', in *Storia d'Italia*, pp. 626–54.

Farneti, Paolo, *Sistema politico e società civile: saggi di teoria e ricerca politica*, Pubblicazioni dell'Istituto di scienze politiche dell'Università di Torino (Torino: Giappichelli, 1971).

Farolfi, Bernardino, and Massimo Fornasari, 'Agricoltura e sviluppo economico: il caso italiano (secoli XVIII–XX)', in Canali et al., eds, *L'agricoltura e gli economisti agrari in Italia dall'Ottocento al Novecento*, pp. 13–70.

Faucci, Riccardo, *L'economia politica in Italia: Dal Cinquecento ai nostri giorni*, Collana di storia dell'economia politica (Torino: UTET Libreria, 2000).

Favero, Giovanni, *Le misure del regno: Direzione di statistica e municipi nell'Italia liberale*, Ricerche 19 (Padova: Poligrafo, 2001).

———, 'Business Attitudes Toward Statistical Investigation in Late Nineteenth Century Italy: A Wool Industrialist from Reticence to Influence', *Enterprise and Society* 12.2 (2011), pp. 265–316.

———, 'I quartieri di Firenze: la costruzione statistica dello spazio urbano', *Città e Storia* 8.2 (2013), pp. 429–51.

Federico, Giovanni, 'Per una valutazione critica delle statistiche della produzione agricola italiana dopo l'Unità (1860–1913)', *Società e Storia* 15 (1982), pp. 87–130.

———, 'Italy, 1860–1940: A Little-Known Success Story', *Economic History Review* 49.4 (1996), pp. 764–86.

———, 'Le nuove stime della produzione agricola italiana, 1860–1910: primi risultati e implicazioni', *Rivista di storia economica* 3 (2003), pp. 359–82.

———, 'Not Guilty? Agriculture in the 1920s and the Great Depression', *Journal of Economic History* 65.04 (2005), pp. 949–76.

———, 'Ma l'agricoltura meridionale era davvero arretrata?', *Rivista di politica economica* 97.3 and 4 (2007), pp. 317–40.

Federico, Giovanni, Sandra Natoli, Giuseppe Tattara, and Michelangelo Vasta, *Il commercio estero italiano, 1862–1950*, Collana storica della Banca d'Italia, Statistiche storiche 4 (Roma-Bari: Laterza, 2012).

Federico, Giovanni, and Antonio Tena, 'Was Italy a protectionist country?', *European Review of Economic History* 2 (1998), pp. 73–97.

Federico, Giovanni, and Nikolaus Wolf, *Comparative Advantages in Italy: A Long-Run Perspective*, Economic History Working Papers, 2011 9.

Feinstein, C. H., Peter Temin, and Gianni Toniolo, *The world economy between the world wars* (New York: Oxford University Press, 2008).

Fernández-Prieto, Lourenzo, Juan Pan-Montojo, and Miguel Cabo, eds, *Agriculture in the age of fascism: Authoritarian technocracy and rural modernization, 1922–1945*, Rural history in Europe 13 (Turnhout: Brepols, 2014).

Ferraris, Carlo F., *Saggi di economia, statistica e scienza dell'amministrazione* (Torino-Roma: E. Loescher, 1880).

Fettarappa, Giulio, *Nozioni di economia politica: intorno alla produzione, allo scambio, al valore, al capitale ed all'interesse: Come introduzione a un corso d'estimo ad uso degl'ingegneri, geometri e periti catastali* (Torino: Camilla e Bertolero, 1887).

Fileni, Enrico, 'Cattedra ambulante di agricoltura in Enciclopedia Italiana', http://www.treccani.it/enciclopedia/cattedra-ambulante-di-agricoltura_(Enciclopedia-Italiana)/.

Fleischman, Richard K., 'Completing the triangle: Taylorism and the paradigms', *Accounting, Auditing & Accountability Journal* 13.5 (2000), pp. 597–623.

Fontana, Severina, ed., *La Federconsorzi tra stato liberale e fascismo*, Biblioteca di cultura moderna 1084 (Roma, Bari: Laterza, 1995).

———, 'Les associations agraires et industrielles en Italie entre la fin du XIXe siècle et le début du XXe siècle', *Histoire, économie et société* 16.2 (1997), pp. 221–36.

Forte, Francesco, 'Cesare Jarach e Achille Necco', in Marchionatti and Becchio, eds, *La scuola di economia di Torino: Da Cognetti de Martiis a Einaudi*, pp. 149–63.

Foucault, Michel, *Sécurité, territoire, population: cours au Collège de France, 1977–1978,* Hautes études (Paris: Gallimard, 2004).

Fraboulet, Danielle, Clotilde Druelle-Korn, and Pierre Vernus, eds, *Les organisations patronales et la sphère publique* (Rennes: Presses Universitaires de Rennes, 2013).

Franchetti, Leopoldo, and Sydney Sonnino, *La Sicilia nel 1876* (2nd edn, Firenze: Vallecchi, 1926).

Frankel, Oz, *States of Inquiry: Social Investigations and Print Culture in Nineteenth-Century Britain and the United States* (Baltimore: Johns Hopkins University Press, 2006).

Fumian, Carlo, 'I tecnici tra agricoltura e Stato, 1930–1950', *Mélanges de l'Ecole française de Rome, Italie et* Méditerranée 95.2 (1983), pp. 209–17.

Fumian, Carlo, 'Gli agronomi da ceto a mestiere', in Bevilacqua, ed., *Storia dell'agricoltura italiana in età contemporanea: Mercati e istituzioni*, pp. 345–89.

Gabba, Alberto, 'L'opera di Ernesto Marenghi', in CESET, ed., *Aspetti evolutivi della scienza estimativa*, pp. 5–14.

———, '"Lo studio di un'azienda rurale", in una lettera di Pietro Cuppari a Francesco Brioschi', *Aestimum* 39 (2000), pp. 163–67.

Galassi, Francesco, and Vera Zamagni, 'L'azienda agraria: un problema storiografico aperto, 1860–1940', in D'Attorre and Bernardi, eds, *Studi sull'agricoltura italiana: società rurale e modernizzazione*, pp. 3–17.

Galassi, Francesco L., and Jon S. Cohen, 'The Economics of Tenancy in Early Twentieth-Century Southern Italy', *Economic History Review* 47.3 (1994), pp. 585–600.

Galasso, Giuseppe, *Passato e presente del meridionalismo,* I Tascabili (2 vols, Napoli: Guida, 1978).

Gambi, Lucio, 'Le "statistiche" di un prefetto del regno', *Quaderni storici* 15.45 (1980), pp. 823–66.

Garelli, Alessandro, *La rappresentanza dell'agricoltura al Congresso dei comizi agrari in Cuneo, 17 settembre 1905* (Cuneo: Tip. Oggero, 1905).

Garstenauer, Rita, Ernst Langthaler, and Sophie Tod, 'Wachsen, Weichen, Weitermachen: Familienbetriebliche Agrarsysteme in zwei Regionen Niederoesterreich 1945–1985', *Historische Anthropologie* 20.3 (2010), pp. 346–82.

Garstenauer, Rita, Ulrich Schwarz, and Sophie Tod, 'Alles unter einen Hut bringen: Baeurliche Wirtschaftsstile in zwei Regionen Niederoesterreichs 1945–1980', *Historische Anthropologie* 20.3 (2010), pp. 382–426.

Gentile, Emilio, *Le origini dell'ideologia fascista (1918–1925),* Biblioteca storica (Bologna: Il mulino, 1996).

Giaconi, Daniela, 'Dall'inchiesta agraria agli studi sulla proprietà: Le radici del pensiero di Ghino Valenti e l'affermazione di un metodo d'indagine', *Quaderni Fiorentini* XXXII (2003), pp. 375–460.

Gilbert, Jess, and S. M. Brown, 'Alternative Land Reform Proposals in the 1930s: The Nashville Agrarians and the Southern Tenant Farmers' Union', *Agricultural History* 55 (1981), pp. 351–69.

Gill, Desmond, 'Tuscan sharecropping in United Italy: The myth of class collaboration destroyed', *Journal of Peasant Studies* 10, 2–3 (1983), pp. 146–69.

Gini, Corrado, *L'ammontare e la composizione della ricchezza delle nazioni* (Torino: Fratelli Bocca, 1914).

Gini, Corrado, and Luigi Galvani, 'Di una applicazione del metodo rappresentativo all'ultimo censimento italiano della popolazione 1 dicembre 1921', *Annali di Statistica,* 6th series, 4 (1929).

Gioia, Vitantonio and Stefano Spalletti, eds, *Etica ed economia: La vita, le opere e il pensiero di Giovanni Lorenzoni* (Soveria Mannelli: Rubbettino, 2005).

Giuva, Linda, and M. Guercio, 'I ministeri economici', in Melis, ed., *L'amministrazione centrale dall'Unità alla Repubblica, Le strutture e i dirigenti*, pp. 69–213.

Gorman, Daniel, *The emergence of international society in the 1920s*, 2012.

Gramsci, Antonio, *Selections from the Prison Notebooks* (New York: International Publishers, 1971).

———, *Quaderni del carcere,* Einaudi tascabili, Saggi 835 (4 vols, Torino: Einaudi, 2001).

Granata, Ivano, *In difesa della terra: l'Ufficio agrario della Società Umanitaria 1905–1923* (Milano: Franco Angeli, 2003).

Greco, Massimo and Niccolò Mattaliano, eds, *Istruzioni per la rilevazione dei dati: Indagine sulla struttura e produzioni delle aziende agricole e principali coltivazioni legnose agrari* (Soveria Mannelli: Rubbettino, 2007).

Guidi, Marco E., 'Cooperazione, socialismo ed economia agraria: note su Ghino Valenti', in Guidi and Michelini, eds, *Marginalismo e socialismo nell'Italia liberale, 1870–1825,* pp. 327–56.

Guidi, Marco E. and Luca Michelini, eds, *Marginalismo e socialismo nell'Italia liberale, 1870–1825*, Annali (Fondazione Giangiacomo Feltrinelli) (Milano: Feltrinelli, 2001).

Habermas, Juergen, *Strukturwandel der Oeffentlichkeit: Untersuchungen zu einer Kategorie der Buergerlichen Gesellschaft* (5th edn, Muenchen: Lucherhand, 1971).

Herf, Jeffrey, *Reactionary modernism: Technology, culture, and politics in Weimar and the Third Reich* (Cambridge: Cambridge University Press, 1984).

Hitier, Henri, 'La statistique agricole de la France', *Annales de Géographie* 8.40 (1899), pp. 350–57.

Howald, Oskar, and Schweizerischer Bauernverband, *Der Schweizerische Bauernverband, 1897–1922: Festschrift herausgegeben zum 25jährigen Jubiläum des Schweizerischen Bauernverbandes* (Schweizerischer Bauernverband, 1922).

Howlett, Peter and Mary S. Morgan, eds, *How Well Do Facts Travel? The Dissemination of Reliable Knowledge* (Cambridge: Cambridge University Press, 2010).

Institut International d'Agriculture, *Les offices de comptabilité agricole dans les divers pays* (3 vols, Rome: Institut International d'Agriculture, 1920–24).

Institut National de la Statistique et des Études Économiques, ed., *Pour une histoire de la statistique: Matériaux,* (Paris: Institut national de la statistique et des études économiques, 1977).

International Institute of Agriculture, *Agricultural problems in their international aspect* (Rome: Printing office of the International Institute of Agriculture, 1927).

———, *The first World Agriculture Census (1930)* (5 vols, Rome: International Institute of Agriculture, 1939).

Ipsen, Carl, *Dictating Demography: The Problem of Population in Fascist Italy,* Cambridge Studies in Population, Economy and Society in Past Time 28 (Cambridge: Cambridge University Press, 1996).

Istituto centrale di statistica, *Catasto agrario 1929*, Roma, 1929–1939.

———, 'Il progettato trasferimento degli uffici di statistica agraria', *Annali di Statistica: Atti del Consiglio superiore di statistica* VI (1930), pp. 238–45.

———, *Le rilevazioni statistiche in Italia dal 1861 al 1956 modelli di rilevazione* (Roma, 1959).

Istituto per la scienza dell'amministrazione pubblica, ed., *L'Amministrazione nella storia moderna,* Archivio (2 vols, Milano: Giuffrè, 1985).

Jaberg, Karl et al., *Sprach- und Sachatlas Italiens und der Südschweiz* (Zofingen: Ringier, 1928).

Jacini, Stefano, *I risultati dell'inchiesta agraria.* (1885; 3rd edn, Torino: Einaudi, 1976).

Johnson, Riccardo, 'Amministrazione e organizzazione delle informazioni: Il ministero dell'agricoltura e i problemi del lavoro', in Istituto per la scienza dell'amministrazione pubblica, ed., *L'Amministrazione nella storia moderna, 2.*

Kalaora, Bernard, and Antoine Savoye, *Les Inventeurs oubliés: Le Play et ses continuateurs aux origines des sciences sociales,* Collection Milieux (Paris: Champ Vallon, 1989).

Kerblay, Basile, 'A. V. Chayanov: Life, career, works', in Čajanov, Aleksandr V., *A.V. Chayanov on the theory of peasant economy*, p. xxxiv.

Klatzmann, M., 'La statistique agricole aux Pays-Bas', *Etudes et conjuncture* 10.12 (1955), pp. 1057–67.

Klotz, Gérard, 'L'Économie saisie par la statistique', *Romantisme* 36.133 (2006), pp. 59–69.

Kott, Sandrine and Joelle Droux, eds, *Globalizing social rights: the international labour organization and beyond* (Basingstoke: Palgrave Macmillan, 2013).

Kremnev, Ivan, 'The journey of my brother Alexei to the land of peasant Utopia', *Journal of Peasant Studies* 4.1 (1976), pp. 63–108.

Krugman, Paul, *Increasing Returns and Economic Geography* (Cambridge, MA: National Bureau of Economic Research, 1990).

Kürschners, Joseph, *Handbuch der Presse: Für Schriftsteller, Redaktionen, Verleger, überhaupt für alle, die mit der Presse in Beziehung stehen* (Berlin: Hillger, 1902).

Labrousse, Ernest, Ruggero Romano, and F.-G. Dreyfus, *Le prix du froment en France au temps de la monnaie stable (1726–1913)* (Paris: S.E.V.P.E.N, 1970).

Lacey, Micheal J. and Mary O. Furner, eds, *The State and Social Investigation in Britain and the United States* (Cambridge: Cambridge University Press, 1993).

Langthaler, Ernst, *Schlachtfelder: Alltägliches Wirtschaften in der nationalsozialistischen Agrargesellschaft, 1938–1945* (Wien-Koeln-Weimar: Böhlau Verlag, 2016).

Laqua, Daniel, *Internationalism reconfigured transnational ideas and movements between the World Wars* (London, New York: I.B. Tauris, 2011).

Latour, Bruno., *Science in action: How to follow scientists and engineers through society* (Cambridge, MA: Harvard University Press, 1987).

Laur, Ernst, 'Die Schaetzung des Ertragswertes von Landguetern nach dem Rohertrage des landw, Betriebes', *Archiv fuer exakte Wirtschaftsforschung* IV.2 (1912), pp. 231–60.

———, *Landwirtschaftliche Betriebslehre für bäuerliche Verhältnisse: Lehrbuch für den Unterricht an landwirtschaftlichen Schulen un für den praktischen Landwirt* (8th edn, Aarau: Wirz, 1927).

———, IIA, Comité économique agricole, Ière Session, 1–3 Octobre 1929, Directives générales pour les travaux de l'Institut International d'Agriculture rapport presenté par M. le Prof, Laur, FAO Archive.

———, *Einführung in die Wirtschaftslehre des Landbaus: Unter besonderer Berücksichtigung der Landarbeitslehre* (2nd rev. Berlin: Parey, 1930).

———, *Erinnerungen eines schweizerischen Bauernführers: ein Beitrag zur Wirtschaftsgeschichte* (Bern: Buchverlag Verbandsdruckerei, 1943).

Lavoisier, Antoine-Laurent, *De la richesse territoriale du royaume de France*, ed. Jean-Claude Perrot (Paris: Comité des travaux historiques et scientifiques, 1988).

Lechi, Francesco, 'Réflexions sur l'évolution de la pensée économique agricole en Italie', *Économie rurale* 200 (1990), pp. 36–39.

Legnani, Massimo, 'Battaglia del grano e istituzionalizzazione del regime reazionario di massa nelle campagne', in Legnani et al., eds, *Le campagne emiliane in periodo fascista*, pp. 15–26.

Legnani, Massimo, Domenico Preti, and Giorgio Rochat, eds, *Le campagne emiliane in periodo fascista: Materiali e ricerche sulla battaglia del grano* (Bologna: Clueb, 1982).

Levasseur, Émil M., 'La statistique graphique', in Statistical Society of London, ed., *Jubilee Volume*, pp. 218–50.

———, 'Les procédés de la statistique agricole', *Bulletin de l'Institut international de statistique* 13.2 (1903), pp. 1–85.

Levi, Carlo, *Christ stopped at Eboli: The story of a year* (New York: Farrar, Straus and Giroux, 2006).

Longobardi, Cesare, *Land-reclamation in Italy* (London: King, 1936).

Lorenzo, Renata de, ed., *L'organizzazione dello Stato al tramonto dell'Antico Regime*, Collana di storia (Napoli: Morano editore, 1990).

Lorenzo, Renata de, 'Strategie del territoria e indagini statistiche nel Mezzogiorno fra Settecento e Ottocento', in Lorenzo, Renata de, ed., *L'organizzazione dello Stato al tramonto dell'Antico Regime*, pp. 129–85.

Lorenzoni, Giovanni, *Le inchieste statistiche dell'ufficio del lavoro* (Milano: Ufficio del lavoro, 1903).

———, *Sicilia: Relazione del delegato tecnico,* Atti della giunta parlmentare di inchiesta sulle condizioni dei contadini nelle province meridionali e in Sicilia (Roma: Bertero, 1911).

———, *Introduzione e guida ad un'inchiesta sulla piccola proprietà coltivatrice postbellica in Italia,* Studi e monografie / Istituto Nazionale di Economia Agraria 5 (Roma: Treves Dell' Ali, 1929).

Maas, Harro, and Mary S. Morgan, 'Observing the Economy: Historical Perspectives', *History of Political Economy* 44 (2012), pp. 1–24.

Macry, Paolo, 'Rethinking a stereotype: Territorial differences and family models in the modernization of Italy', *Journal of Modern Italian Studies* 2.2 (2008), pp. 188–214.

Magnarelli, Paola, *L'agricoltura italiana fra politica e cultura,* Studi e ricerche di scienze sociali (Edizioni di Comunità, 1981).

———, 'Francesco Coletti' in *Dizionario Biografico degli Italiani* 26 (1982), http://www.treccani.it/enciclopedia/francesco-coletti.

MAIC, and Direzione Generale di agricoltura, *Notizie e studi sulla agricoltura* (Roma: Tip. eredi Botta, 1876–98).

MAIC, and divisione di agricoltura, *Relazione intorno alle condizioni dell'agricoltura nel quinquennio 1870–1874* (3 vols, Roma: G. Barbera 1876–79).

MAIC, ed., *Esperimenti di statistica agraria in alcune province del Regno* (Roma: Bertero, 1907).

———, *L'azione del Ministero nell'ultimo triennio* (Roma: Tip. G. Civelli, 1909).

———, *Valutazione della produzione lorda della agricoltura italiana* (Roma: Tip. Luzzatti, 1925).

MAIC, Direzione generale statistica e. del lavoro, *Catasto agrario del Regno d'Italia: Compartimento del Lazio* (Roma: Bertero, 1911).

MAIC-Ispettorato del bonificamento agrario e della colonizzazione, *Attività delle Regie cattedre ambulanti di agricoltura della Basilicata e Calabria durante il 1908* (Roma: Bertero, 1910).

MAIC Ufficio di Statistica Agraria, *Norme e istruzioni pel servizio di statistica agraria* (Roma: Tip. ditta L. Cecchini, 1914).

Maier, Charles S., 'Between Taylorism and Technocracy: European Ideologies and the Vision of Industrial Productivity in the 1920s', *Journal of Contemporary History* 5.2 (1970), pp. 27–61.

———, *Recasting bourgeois Europe: Stabilization in France, Germany, and Italy in the decade after World War I* (Princeton, NJ: Princeton University Press, 1975).

———, *In Search of Stability: Explorations in Historical Political Economy,* Cambridge Studies in Modern Political Economies (Cambridge: Cambridge University Press, 1988).

Malatesta, Maria, *I signori della terra: l'organizzazione degli interessi agrari padani (1860–1914),* Democrazia, stato e società industriale (Milano: Franco Angeli, 1989).

———, 'Une nouvelle stratégie reproduction: les organisations patronales agraires européennes (1868–1914)', *Histoire, économie et société* 16.2 (1997), pp. 203–19.

———, *Le aristocrazie terriere nell'Europa contemporanea*, Quadrante (Roma: Laterza, 1999).

Marchionatti, Roberto and Giandomenica Becchio, eds, *La scuola di economia di Torino: Da Cognetti de Martiis a Einaudi* (Torino: Leo S. Olschki, 2005).

Marenghi, Ernesto, *Calabria: Relazione del delegato tecnico,* Atti della giunta parlamentare di inchiesta sulle condizioni dei contadini nelle province meridionali e in Sicilia (Roma: Bertero, 1909).

———, 'Organizzazione ed importanza degli Uffici di contabilità per lo studio dell'economia dell'azienda agraria', *Rivista Italiana di Ragioneria*, n, 4, pp. 162–175; n, 5, pp. 201–204; n, pp. 6, pp. 241–246; n, 7, pp. 289–301; n, 8, pp. 329–338; n, 9, pp. 386–390; (1914).

———, *Lezioni di contabilità agraria* (Milano: Libreria editrice Politecnica, 1922).

Marsili Libelli, Marco, 'La provincia di Firenze e il nuovo catasto', *Atti della reale Accademia economico-agraria dei Georgofili di Firenze* XC (IX della V serie) (1912).

Martinelli, Pablo, *Latifundia Revisited: Market Power, Land Inequality and Efficiency in Interwar Italian Agriculture*, 2012, Working Paper 020.

Marucco, Dora, *L' amministrazione della statistica nell'Italia unita* (Roma-Bari: Laterza, 1996).

Mayer, Arno J., *The persistence of the Old Regime: Europe to the Great War* (Pantheon Books, 1981).

McCloskey, Deirdre N., *The Bourgeois Virtues: Ethics for an Age of Commerce* (Chicago: University of Chicago Press, 2010).

Medici, Giuseppe, *Richerche intorno all'azienda agraria tipica* (Faenza: F.lli Lega, 1933).

———, *L'azienda agraria tipica: Nuove ricerche* (Faenza: F.lli Lega, 1945).

———, 'Stato e problemi degli studi di economia agraria in Italia', *Rivista di Economia Agraria* 1.2 (1946), pp. 124–34.

Medici, Giuseppe, and William G Murray, *Principles of appraisal* (Ames, Iowa: the Iowa state college press, 1953).

Melis, Guido, ed., *L'amministrazione centrale dall'Unità alla Repubblica, Le strutture e i dirigenti* (Bologna: Il mulino, 1992).

———, 'Amministrazione e mediazione degli interessi: le origini delle amministrazioni parallele', in Istituto per la scienza dell'amministrazione pubblica, *L'Amministrazione nella storia moderna*, pp. 1434–41.

Mendelsohn, J. A., 'The World on a Page: Making a General Observation in the Eighteenth Century', in Daston and Lunbeck, eds, *Histories of Scientific Observation*, pp. 396–420.

Mespoulet, Martine, 'Statisticiens des zemstva', *Cahiers du monde russe Russie, Empire russe, Union soviétique, États indépendants* 40.4 (1999), pp. 573–624.

———, *Statistique et révolution en Russie un compromis impossible, 1880–1930* (Rennes: Presses Universitaires de Rennes, 2001).

Messedaglia, Angelo, *Il Catasto e la perequazione: Relazione parlamentare, nuova edizione a cura di Luigi Messedaglia, pref, di Giuseppe Tassinari* (Bologna: Licinio Cappelli, 1936).

'Miliani, Giambattista', in *I Senatori d'Italia: A cura dell'Archivio Storico del Senato della Repubblica*, http://notes9.senato.it/Web/senregno.NSF/1dbf7f5088956bebc125703d004d5ffb/074d5fa43da04f204125646f005d8415?OpenDocument.

Miller, Peter, and Ted O'Leary, 'Accounting and the construction of the governable person', *Accounting, Organizations and Society* 12.3 (1987), pp. 235–65.

Ministero dell'Agricoltura – Direzione generale dell'agricoltura, *Per la piccola proprietà rurale e montana* (2 vols, Roma: Tip. L. Cecchini, 1921–22).

Misiani, Simone, *La Via Dei 'Tecnici': Dalla Rsi Alla Ricostruzione: Il Caso Di Paolo Albertario,* Studi e ricerche storiche (Milano: Franco Angeli, 1998).

Monclus, Javier, and José L. Oyon, *Politicas y tecnicas en la ordenacion del espacio rural* (Madrid: I.E.A.L, 1988).

Moore, Barrington, *Social origins of dictatorship and democracy: Lord and peasant in the making of the modern world* (2nd edn, Boston: Beacon Press, 1993).

Morgan, Mary, 'Experimental Farming and Ricardo's Political Arithmetic of Distribution', *Amsterdam WP Series* 3 (2008).

———, 'Seeking parts, looking for wholes', in Daston and Lunbeck, eds, *Histories of Scientific Observation*, pp. 326–48.

Mortara, Giorgio, 'Italian Economic Statistics: A Reply to Professor Salvemini', *Political Science Quarterly* 46.4 (1931), pp. 593–5.

Mozzarelli, Cesare, and Stefano Nespor, 'Amministrazione e mediazione degli interessi: le Camere di Commercio', in Istituto per la scienza dell'amministrazione pubblica, *L'Amministrazione nella storia moderna*, pp. 1649–709.

Mozzarelli, Cesare, and Stefano Nespor, *Giuristi e scienze sociali nell'Italia liberale: il dibattito sulla scienza dell'amministrazione e l'organizzazione dello stato*, Saggi Marsilio (Venezia: Marsilio, 1981).

Musella, Luigi, *Proprietà e politica agraria in Italia, 1861–1914*, Storia 23 (Napoli: Guida, 1984).

———, 'Oreste Bordiga e l'agricoltura meridionale, 1884–1914', in D'Attorre and Bernardi, eds, *Studi sull'agricoltura italiana: società rurale e modernizzazione*, pp. 123–38.

———, 'Il Mezzogiorno agrario di Eugenio Azimonti', in Fontana, ed., *La Federconsorzi tra stato liberale e fascismo*, pp. 108–29.

Niccoli, Vittorio, *Bibliografia dell'estimo ordinario in Italia fino al 1856* (Verona-Padova: Drucker e Tedeschi, 1889).

———, *Prontuario dell'agricoltore: Manuale di agricoltura, economia, estimo e costruzioni rurali* (Torino: UTET, 1897).

———, *Economia rurale, estimo e computisteria agraria* (Torino: UTET, 1898).

———, *Economia rurale, agrotimesia e computisteria agraria* (Torino: UTET, 1927).

Niceforo, Alfredo, *Antropologia delle classi povere, Trattato di medicina sociale* (Milano: Vallardi, 1910).

———, *Il metodo statistico: Teoria e applicazioni alle Scienze naturali, alle Scienze sociali, e all'Arte* (Messina: Casa Editrice Giuseppe Principato, 1923).

Nitti, Francesco S., *La conquista della forza, Il capitale straniero in Italia*, Edizione Nazionale delle Opere di Francesco Saverio Nitti 3.2 (Bari, 1968).

Nõu, Joosep, *Studies in the development of agricultural economics in Europe*, Lantbrukshögskolans annaler, v, 33, nr, 1 (Uppsala, 1967).

Nützenadel, Alexander, 'Economic Crisis and Agriculture in Fascist Italy, 1927–1935, Some New Considerations', *Rivista di Storia Economica* 18.3 (2001), pp. 289–312.

Orlando, Giuseppe, *Storia della politica agraria in Italia dal 1848 a oggi*, Storia e società (Roma-Bari: Laterza, 1984).

Pallot, Judith, 'Imagining the rational landscape in late imperial Russia', *Journal of Historical Geography* 26.2 (2000), pp. 273–91.

Pansini, Valeria, 'Pour une histoire concrète du "talent": les sélections méritocratiques et le coup d'oeil du topographe', *Annales Historiques de la Révolution Française* 354 (2008), pp. 5–27.

Patriarca, Silvana, *Numbers and nationhood: Writing statistics in nineteenth-century Italy*, Cambridge studies in Italian history and culture (Cambridge: Cambridge University Press, 1996).

———, 'How many Italies? Representing the South in official statistics', in Schneider, ed., *Italy's 'Southern Question': Orientalism in one country*, pp. 77–97.

Patrizi, Ugo, 'La discussione del bilancio di agricoltura', *Bollettino dell'Associazione delle cattedre ambulanti di agricoltura* 2.6 (1910), p. 1.

Pazzagli, Rossano., *Il sapere dell'agricoltura: Istruzione, cultura, economia nell'Italia dell'Ottocento*, Temi di storia 120 (Milano: Franco Angeli, 2008).

Pederzani, Ivana, *Dall'antico regime alla restaurazione: Profili di storia costituzionale in area lombarda tra Sette e Ottocento*, Scienze storiche, filosofiche, pedagogiche e psicologiche 315 (Roma: Aracne, 2008).

Penati, Beatrice, 'On the Soviet discovery of rural Central Asia. The Karp commission in context', *Monde(s),Histoire, Espaces, Relations* no. 4 (2013), pp. 105–25.

Perdisa, Luigi, 'I redditi dell'agricoltura emiliana: I risultati economici di 40 aziende nel settennio 1925–1931', *Annali dell'Osservatorio di economia agraria per l'Emilia* (1933).

Perini, Dario, *Risultati economici di aziende agrarie,* Studi e monografie 18 (Roma: Treves Dell'Ali, 1932).

Petrusewicz, Marta, *Latifondo: economia morale e vita materiale in una periferia dell'Ottocento*, Saggi Marsilio (Venezia: Marsilio, 1989).

———, *Come il Meridione divenne una questione, Rappresentazione del Sud prima e dopo il Quarantotto* (Soveria Mannelli: Rubbettino, 1998).

Peytavin, Mireille, 'Le calendrier de l'administrateur: Périodisation de la domination espagnole en Italie suivant les visites générales', *Mélanges de l'Ecole française de Rome, Italie et Méditerranée* 106.1 (1994), pp. 263–332.

Pilat, Theodore M., 'Rapport sur la statistique agricole', *Bulletin de l'Institut international de statistique*, 11.2 (1899), pp. 86–104.

Placanica, Augusto, 'La capitale, il passato il paesaggio: I viaggiatori come 'fonte' della storia meridionale', *Meridiana* 1 (1987), pp. 165–79.

Polelli, Mario, and Guidi Sali, 'La valutazione dei capitali fondiari', in CESET, ed., *Aspetti evolutivi della scienza estimativa*, pp. 89–101.

Polzer, Alfredo de, *Statistiche agrarie* (Milano: Giuffrè, 1942).

Porter, Theodore M., *The Rise of Statistical Thinking, 1820–1900,* Princeton paperbacks (Princeton: Princeton University Press, 1986).

———, *Trust in Numbers: The Pursuit of Objectivity in Science and Public Life* (Princeton: Princeton University Press, 1996).

———, 'The statistical office as a social observatory', *Centaurus* 49 (2007), pp. 258–60.

———, 'The engineer and the sage: Le Play's quest for social renewal and the reconstruction of observation', *History of Observation in Economics Working Paper Series* 2 (2009).

Prampolini, Antonio, 'La formazione di A. Serpieri ed i problemi dell'agricoltura lombarda', *Studi Storici* 17.2 (1976), pp. 171–209.

———, *Agricoltura e società rurale nel Mezzogiorno agli inizi del '900: L'inchiesta parlamentare sulle condizioni dei contadini nelle provincie meridionali e nella Sicilia*, La societa' italiana moderna e contemporanea 7 (Milano: Franco Angeli, 1981).

Preti, Domenico, 'Per una storia agraria e del malessere agrario nell'Italia fascista: la battaglia del grano', in Legnani et al., eds, *Le campagne emiliane in periodo fascista*, pp. 27–77.

Prévost, Jean-Guy, *Total Science: Statistics in Liberal and Fascist Italy* (Montreal: MQUP, 2009).

Prévost, Jean-Guy, and Jean P. Beaud, *Statistics, Public Debate and the State, 1800–1945: A Social, Political and Intellectual History of Numbers* (London: Pickering & Chatto Publishers, 2012).

Protasi, Maria R., 'Tra scienza e riforma sociale: Il pensiero e il metodo d'indagine sociale di F. Le Play e dei suoi continuatori in Italia (1857–1914)', *Studi Storici* 37.3 (1996), pp. 813–45.

Puccini, Sandra, *L'itala gente dalle molte vite: Lamberto Loria e la Mostra di etnografia italiana del 1911* (Roma: Meltemi, 2005).

Putnam, Robert D., and R. Leonardi, *Making Democracy Work* (Princeton: Princeton University Press, 2002).

R. Accademia Dei Lincei, ed., *Cinquanta anni di storia italiana* (3 vols, Roma: Tip. della R. Accademia Dei Lincei, 1911).

Rabinow, Paul, *French Modern: Norms and Forms of the Social Environment* (Chicago: University of Chicago Press, 1995).

Raffaelli, Tiziano., 'The Role of Intelligence, Institutions, and Place in Carlo Cattaneo's Economics', *History of Political Economy* 46.2 (2014), pp. 265–80.

Randeraad, Nico, *Authority in search of liberty: The prefects in liberal Italy*, Scrinium 7 (Amsterdam: Thesis Publ, 1993).

Ribi Forclaz, Amalia, *Humanitarian imperialism the politics of anti-slavery activism, 1880–1940* (Oxford: Oxford University Press, 2015).

Ricci, Umberto, *Les bases théoriques de la statistique agricole internationale* (Rome: Imprimerie de l'Institute International d'Agriculture, 1914).

Rogari, Sandro, *Ruralismo e anti-industrialismo di fine secolo: Neofisiocrazia e movimento neocorporativo cattolico* (Firenze: Felice Le Monnier, 1984).

———, 'La Società degli agricoltori italiani', in D'Attorre and Bernardi, eds, *Studi sull'agricoltura italiana: società rurale e modernizzazione*, pp. 139–56.

———, *Proprietà fondiaria e modernizzazione: La Società degli Agricoltori Italiani 1895–1920,* La società moderna e contemporanea Analisi e contributi 40 (Milano: Franco Angeli, 1994).

———, *Rappresentanza corporazione conflitto: ceti e figure dell'Italia rurale fra Otto e Novecento,* Politica e storia (Firenze: Centro editoriale toscano, 1998).

Rogari, Sandro, and Eugenio Faina, *Mezzogiorno ed emigrazione: L'inchiesta Faina sulle condizioni dei contadini nelle province meridionali e nella Sicilia 1906–1911* (Firenze: Centro editoriale toscano, 2002).

Romani, Mario, *Storia economica d'Italia nel secolo XIX* (Bologna: Il mulino, 1982).

Romeo, Rosario, *Risorgimento e capitalismo,* Economica Laterza (Laterza, 1998).

Rosenberg, Emily S., ed., *A world connecting, 1870–1945* (Cambridge Mass: Belknap Press of Harvard University Press, 2012).

Rossi-Doria, Manlio, *La gioia tranquilla del ricordo: memorie, 1905–1934,* Storia-memoria (Bologna: Il mulino, 1991).

Roth, Walter J., 'Farm accounting in Switzerland', *Journal of Farm Economics* 13.4 (1931), pp. 554–72.

Roveri, Antonio, *Le origini del fascismo a Ferrara, 1918–1921,* I Fatti e le idee, saggi e biografie (Milano: Feltrinelli, 1974).

Salsano, Alfredo, *Ingegneri e politici: Dalla razionalizzazione alla 'rivoluzione manageriale',* Nuovo politecnico 0157 (Torino: Einaudi, 1987).

———, *L'altro corporativismo: Tecnocrazia e managerialismo tra le due guerre* (Torino: Il Segnalibro, 2003).

Salvemini, Gaetano, 'Mussolini's Battle of Wheat', *Political Science Quarterly* 46.1 (1931), pp. 25–40.

Salvioni, Giovanni B., 'Ai confini della statistica', *Rassegna di scienze sociali e politiche* 217 (1892), pp. 25–42.

———, 'Ai confini della statistica', *Rassegna di scienze sociali e politiche* 218 (1892), pp. 95–107.

Sapelli, Giulio, ed., *Il movimento cooperativo in Italia: Storia e problemi*, (Torino: Einaudi, 1981).

Saraiva, Tiago, and M. Norton Wise, 'Autarky/Autarchy: Genetics, Food Production, and the Building of Fascism', *Historical Studies in the Natural Sciences* 40.4 (2010), pp. 419–28.

Saraiva, Tiago, 'Fascist Labscapes: Geneticists, Wheat, and the Landscapes of Fascism in Italy and Portugal', *Historical Studies in the Natural Sciences* 40.4 (2010), pp. 457–98.

Schneider, Jane, ed., *Italy's 'Southern Question': Orientalism in one country* (Oxford and New York, 1998).

Schultz, Helga and Angela Harre, eds, *Bauerngesellschaften auf dem Weg in die Moderne: Agrarismus in Ostmitteleuropa 1880 bis 1960,* Frankfurter Studien zur Wirtschafts- und Sozialgeschichte Ostmitteleuropas (Harrassowitz Verlag, 2010).

Schutter, Olivier de, 'Submission to the G20 Development Group Food Security Review' (last modified 9 Sept., 2014), http://www.srfood.org/images/stories/pdf/otherdocuments/20140404_UNSR%20RTF_G20%20DWG%20Food%20Security%20Review.pdf.

Scott, James C., *Seeing like a state: How certain schemes to improve the human condition have failed,* Yale ISPS series (New Haven: Yale university press, 1998).

Šebesta, Giuseppe, 'Fotografia e disegno nella ricerca etnografica', *La Ricerca Folklorica* 2 (1980), pp. 37–44.

Sen, Amartya, 'Positional Objectivity', *Philosophy & Public Affairs* 22.2 (1993), pp. 126–45.

Sereni, Emilio, *Il capitalismo nelle campagne (1860–1900),* Piccola biblioteca Einaudi (Torino: Einaudi, 1968).

Sering, Max, *Die innere Kolonisation im östlichen Deutschland,* Schriften des Vereins für Socialpolitik (Duncker & Humblot, 1893).

Serpieri, Arrigo, *Sui metodi di determinazione del profitto nelle imprese rurali: Analisi di stima e conti colturali* (Milano: tipo-litografia agraria, 1901).

———, 'La fase presente dell'agricoltura italiana', *L'Italia Economica* 2 (1908), pp. 42–47.

———, *Il contratto agrario e le condizioni dei contadini nell'Alto milanese* (Milano: Ufficio agrario della Società Umanitaria, 1910).

———, 'Il metodo di stima dei beni fondiari', *Annali del R. Ist, Superiore Forestale Nazionale* II (1916–17).

———, *La politica agraria in Italia e i recenti provvedimenti legislativi* (Piacenza: Federazione italiana dei consorzi agrari, 1925).

———, 'Giuseppe Zattini', *Studi e Notizie Rassegna trimestrale dell'Istituto di Economia e Statistica Agraria* (1926), pp. 5–9.

———, *Guida a ricerche di economia agraria,* Studi e monografie / Istituto Nazionale di Economia Agraria 1 (Roma: Treves Dell' Ali, 1929).

———, *La guerra e le classi rurali italiane,* Carrnegie endowment for international peace, Division of economics and history, Storia economica e sociale della guerra mondiale, Serie italiana (Bari, New Haven: G. Laterza & figli; Yale university press, 1930).

———, *Fra politica ed economia rurale,* 2 edition, Biblioteca di coltura per i rurali (Firenze: G. Barbera, 1937).

———, 'La bonifica integrale', *Annali di Economia* 12 (1937), pp. 125–41.

———, *Principi di economia corporativa* (Firenze: Barbera, 1938).

———, *L'azienda agraria* (Bologna: Edagricole, 1946).

———, 'Sui concetti di impresa marginale, impresa ordinaria e azienda tipo', *Rivista di Economia Agraria* 2.2 (1948).

———, *Istituzioni di economia agraria* (2nd edn, Bologna: Edizioni agricole, 1950).

Sismondi, Jean C. L., *Tableau de l'agriculture toscane* (Genève: Paschaud, 1801).

Smit, Jan G., 'Laendliche Neusiedlung in Mitteleuropa vom Ende des 19, Jahrhunderts bis zur Gegenwart als nationalpolitisches Instrument: Ziele, zeitgenoessische Stellungnahmen und Ergebnisse', *Erdkunde* 40.3 (1986), pp. 165–74.

Società Agraria di Lombardia, *La Società agraria di Lombardia: la storia e l'anima* (Milano: Società Agraria di Lombardia, 1998).

Sofia, Francesca, *Una scienza per l'amministrazione* (Quaderni di Clio, Carucci, 1988).

Soresina, Marco, *Conoscere per amministrare: Luigi Bodio: statistica, economia e pubblica amministrazione,* Studi e ricerche storiche (Milano: Franco Angeli, 2001).

———, 'Cesare Correnti ministro della cultura', *Società e Storia* 114 (2006), pp. 675–729.

Speich, Daniel, 'Travelling with the GDP through early Development Economics' History', Working Papers on The Nature of Evidence: How well do Facts Travel 33 Unpublished manuscript,

Stampacchia, Mauro, *Ruralizzare l'Italia! Agricoltura e bonifiche tra Mussolini e Serpieri, 1928–1943,* Franco Angeli Storia 274 (Milano: Franco Angeli, 2000).

Stanziani, Alessandro, 'Les statistiques des récoltes en Russie, 1905–1928', *Histoire & Mesure* 7.1 (1992), pp. 73–98.

Stapleford, Thomas A., *The cost of living in America: A political history of economic statistics, 1880–2000* (Cambridge: Cambridge University Press, 2009).

Strangio, Donatella, 'The Policy of Stockpiling Grain and its Costs to the Italian State after World War II', *Rivista di storia economica,* 3/2012 (2012), pp. 453–86.

Statistical Society of London, ed., *Jubilee Volume of the Statistical Society of London* (London, 1885).

Storia d'Italia (Torino: Einaudi, 1976).

Tassinari, Giuseppe, *Frammentazione e ricomposizione dei fondi rurali,* Pubblicazioni del R. Istituto Superiore Forestale Nazionale Firenze N. 8 (Firenze: Tip. M. Ricci, 1922).

———, *Saggio intorno alla distribuzione del reddito nell'agricoltura italiana* (Piacenza: Federazione italiana dei consorzi agrari, 1926).

———, *La distribuzione dell reddito nell'agricoltura italiana* (Piacenza: Federazione Ital. dei Consorzi Agrari, 1931).

Tedeschi, Paolo, 'Notes sur les enquêtes agraires en Lombardie au XIXe siècle', in Vivier and Marache, eds, *L'État et les sociétés rurales*, pp. 525–41.

Teodori, Marco, and Andrea Zanini, 'Institutions publiques et associations patronales: le cas de l'Associations italienne des hoteliers (1899–1943)', in Fraboulet et al., eds, *Les organisations patronales et la sphère publique*, pp. 171–82.

Thaer, Albrecht, *Einleitung zur Kenntniß der englischen Landwirthschaft und ihrer neueren practischen und theoretischen Fortschritte in Rücksicht auf Vervollkommnung deutscher Landwirtschaft* (Hannover: Gebrüder Hahn, 1804).

Theodore, Gérard, and Michel Volle, 'Les statistiques agricoles', in Institut National de la Statistique et des Études Économiques, ed., *Pour une histoire de la statistique: Matériaux*, pp. 501–32.

Théré, Christine, and Loïc Charles, 'The Writing Workshop of François Quesnay and the Making of Physiocracy', *History of Political Economy* 40.1 (2008), pp. 1–42.

Thom, Martin, '"Liberty and truth" or "the sovereignty of reason": Carlo Cattaneo and the place of politics in the modern world', *Journal of Modern Italian Studies* 6.2 (2001), pp. 178–94.

Thünen, Johann Heinrich von, *Der isolierte Staat in Beziehung auf Landwirtschaft und Nationalökonomie, oder, Untersuchungen über den Einfluss, den die Getreidepreise, der Reichthum des bodens und die Abgaben auf den Ackerbau ausüben* (Hamburg: Verlag Wirtschaft und Finanzen, 1826).

Tolaini, Roberto, *Contadini toscani negli anni Trenta: Monografie di famiglie dell'INEA 1931–1938,* Collana del Centro di documentazione e ricerca sulla storia dell'agricoltura e della società contadina 0002, Ospedaletto (Pisa: Pacini, 2005).

Tommasina, Cesare, *Corso di estimo civile industriale rurale: Teoria dell'estimo razionale e tecnica estimativa con esercizi numerici, esempi di stima e tavole finanziarie,* Grande biblioteca tecnica 10 (Torino: S.T.E.N, 1912).

Toniolo, Gianni, *An economic history of liberal Italy, 1850–1918* (London, New York: Routledge, 1990).

Tooze, J.A., *Statistics and the German State, 1900–1945: The Making of Modern Economic Knowledge,* Cambridge Studies in Modern Economic History (Cambridge: Cambridge University Press, 2001).

Tosi, Luciano, *Alle origini della FAO: Le relazioni tra l'Istituto Internazionale di Agricoltura e la Società delle Nazioni,* Storia (Milano: Franco Angeli, 1989).

Uekötter, Frank, *Die Wahrheit ist auf dem Feld: Eine Wissensgeschichte der deutschen Landwirtschaft,* Umwelt und Gesellschaft 1 (Göttingen: Vandenhoeck & Ruprecht, 2010).

Valenti, Ghino, 'Per l'ordinamento della statistica agraria in Italia', *Bollettino Ufficiale del Ministero dell'Agricoltura, Industria e Commercio* II (1907).

———, 'L'Italia agricola dal 1861 al 1911', in R. Accademia Dei Lincei, ed., *Cinquanta anni di storia italiana,* II, pp. 1–147.

———, *Studi di politica agraria* (Roma: Athenaeum, 1914).

———, ed., *L'agricoltura e la politica commerciale dell'Italia,* Comitato nazionale per le tariffe doganali e per i trattati di commercio (Roma: Bertero, 1917).

———, 'La statistica agraria quale rappresentazione dell'economia rurale italiana', in Valenti, ed., *L'Italia agricola e il suo avvenire.*

———, ed., *L'Italia agricola e il suo avvenire* (Roma, 1919).

———, *Per la riforma della pubblica amministrazione: studi* (Unitas: Milano, 1919).

van de Grift, Liesbeth, 'On New Land a New Society.: Internal Colonisation in the Netherlands, 1918–1940', *Contemporary European History* 22.04 (2013), pp. 609–26.

van der Ploeg, Jan D. and Ann Long, eds, *Born from Within: Practice and Perspectives of Endogenous Rural Development,* European perspectives on rural development (Assen: van Gorcum, 1994).

van der Ploeg, Jan D., 'An Introductory Note on Concepts and Methodology', in van der Ploeg, Jan D. and Ann Long, eds, *Born from Within,* pp. 7–30.

Vanclay, Frank, Peter Howden, Luciano Mesiti, and Scott Glyde, 'The Social and Intellectual Construction of Farming Styles: Testing Dutch Ideas in Australian Agriculture', *Sociologia Ruralis* 46.1 (2006), pp. 61–82.

Vaquero Pineiro, Manuel, *Da fattori a periti agrari.: Formazione professionale e modernizzazione dell'agricoltura in Umbria (1884–1929)* (Foligno: Editoriale Umbra, 2011).

Villari, Lucio, *Il capitalismo italiano del Novecento* (Roma-Bari: Laterza, 1975).

Vivarelli, Roberto, *Il fallimento del liberalismo: Studi sull'origine del fascimo* (Bologna: Il mulino, 1981).

Vivier, Nadine and Corinne Marache, eds, *L'État et les sociétés rurales: Enquêtes agricoles, enquêteurs et enquêtés aux XIXe et XXe siècles* (*Annales du Midi* special issue, 284, 2013)

Weber, Maximilian, *Die Verhältnisse der Landarbeiter im ostelbischen Deutschland (Preussische Provinzen Ost- und Westpreussen, Pommern, Posen, Schlesien, Brandenburg, Grossherzogtümer Mecklenburg, Kreis Herzogtum Lauenburg),* Schriften des Vereins für Socialpolitik (Duncker & Humblot, 1892).

Zaganella, Marco, *Dal fascismo alla DC: Tassinari, Medici e la bonifica nell'Italia tra gli anni Trenta e Cinquanta,* I fatti e la storia 4 (Siena: Cantagalli, 2010).

Zaninelli, Sergio, ed., *Le conoscenze agrarie e la loro diffusione in Italia nell'Ottocento* (Torino: G. Giappichelli, 1990).

Zannoni, Ilario, 'La colonizzazione interna', *L'Italia Economica* 2 (1908), pp. 50–6.

Zeri, Federico, *I francobolli italiani: grafica e ideologia dalle origini al 1948* (Genova: Il melangolo, 1993).

Zucchini, Mario, *Le cattedre ambulanti di agricoltura* (Roma: G. Volpe, 1970).

Index

Abruzzo 61n56, 84n49
Accademia dei Georgofili 21, 29, 99, 110n, 154n
Accademia dei Lincei 12, 13n38
Adorno, Salvatore 40
Adriatic Sea 39
Aereboe, Friederich xi
Albertario, Paolo 21–2, 46n92, 148n47
Alpe, Vittorio xv, 98n26, 99, 103, 104n46, 109
Antinori, Raffaelo x, 28
Apulia 61n56
Associazione Agraria Friulana 29, 98, 101
Associazione Agraria Ravennate 97, 145n37
Aubin, David 3
Austria, consolidation of plots 121n24, Hofkarte 8
Austria-Hungary xi, 5, 57
Austrian Cadastre of Milan 80
Azimonti, Eugenio x, 57, 61–7, 99, 131n54, 164n29

Basilicata x, 57, 6–67; cattedre d'agricoltura 33–5, 62; extensive farm 54; Zanardelli's journey 52
Basso, Luigi 97, 99–100, 103–5
Belgium, statistics of harvest 5, 59, 78; farm surveys 123
Beneduce, Alberto 106
Benini, Rodolfo 30n26, 104n48, 136n14, 149n49
Bernstein, Eduard 19n57
Bigg, Charlotte 3
Bodio, Luigi 70–2, 76, 88n57, 91, 104–5, 109, 124n31
Bologna 28, 38, 39, 107, 145–7; Osservatorio provinciale di economia agraria 15, 147–8; University 144
Bonaparte, Napoleon 2, 5, 6n19, 80
Bordiga, Oreste 50, 57, 99, 102n40, 105, 109, 115, 161
Borio, Giuseppe 120–1
Braudel, Fernand 1
Brighton 48n5
Brizi, Alessandro 148n45
Brugg xv, 140, 143, 147, 153
Bruisch, Katja vi, 11
Budapest, ISI Congress 72n6
Bund der Landwirte 31–2, 32n32, 39n58

Cagliari 36
Čajanov, Alesksandr Vasilevič 8, 8n26, 114n4, 141–2n27, 154n62
Calabria xi, 61, 67 129; cattedre d'agricoltura 34–5
Canada 163n27
Canepa, Giuseppe 37
Cantoni, Gaetano xv, 11, 28–9, 156
Cappelli, Raffaele xiv, 31, 37, 95–6, 143
Carcano, Paolo 94n12, 105
Casciani, Paolo 94–5, 104
Cattaneo, Carlo 20–1
Cavaglieri, Guido 73–4
Cavalieri, Enea xiii, 32, 47, 52
Cavalieri San Bortolo, Nicola 120
Cavani, Francesco 102n40, 105
Cavour, Camillo Benso di 25
Cheysson, Emile, 8, 60, 123–6, 131, 148
Cobden, Richard, 21

Cocco-Ortu, Francesco 36–7, 53, 75–7, 81–2, 84, 91, 94, 96n19, 98–9, 104–5, 114, 123–4
Colajanni, Napoleone 104n48
Coletti, Francesco x, 12, 31–2, 39, 51–2, 54, 56–61, 65, 69, 79n30, 104n48, 125–8, 134, 136, 141, 148, 165
Colonna, Francesco 94n
Comitato Nazionale per le Tariffe Doganali 110n
Compans, Carlo 31
Confederazione Generale dell'Agricoltura Italiana xv
Confederazione Nazionale Agraria xv, 39
Congress of Agriculture 11, 147n45, 154, 158, 166
Correnti, Cesare 73
Corte Palasio, school of agriculture 28
Crispi, Francesco 30–1
Cuppari, Pietro 29, 64n61, 115–17, 124n31, 144

D'Attorre, Paolo 42, 46
D'Autilia, Maria Letizia 6, 12n37, 45n90, 76n19, 91n2, 104n48, 108, 136n9
Daston, Lorraine 3, 134
David, Eduard 19
De Capitani D'Arzago, Giuseppe 42n72
De Gasperi, Alcide 148
De Polzer, Alfredo 71, 71n3, 74n12, 78n27, 88n57, 141n23, 142n29
De Viti De Marco, Antonio 82n41, 104, 109
Delors, Jacques 1
Depretis, Agostino 30
Desio, competition of peasants 139
Desrosières, Alain 60, 159
Dettweiler, Friederich 7, 126n38, 136
Devincenzi, Giuseppe xiv, 30
di Collobiano Arborio, Luigi Avogadro 94n12
Didier, Emanuel 6n18, 67n73, 78n25, 134n6, 159
Direzione Generale della Statistica see Ministero di Agricoltura, Industria e Commercio, General Directorate of Statistics
Dragoni, Carlo 95n16, 108

Einaudi, Luigi 81n39, 104n48, 127, 145
Elbe 7
Ellena, Vittorio, industrial enquiry 55
Emilia 75, 145; cattedre di agricoltura 33; Osservatorio di economia agraria 148n46, 150; repression 41; strikes 38–9
Engel, Ernst 117, 133–4
England, agricultural statistics 79; high farming 26
Europe 5–7, 13, 16, 19, 21, 44, 80, 97n23, 116, 119, 133, 163
European Communities 1, 158n8

Fabbroni, Adamo 120
Faina, Eugenio x, 9n, 55–8, 95–6, 108
Faina Enquiry (Parliamentary Enquiry on the conditions of peasants in the southern Provinces and Sicily) ix–xi, 10, 15, 24–6, 48, 61, 53–5, 62, 67–8, 70, 84, 125–6, 128–9, 136, 156
Federazione Italiana dei Consorzi Agrari xi, xiii, 32, 39, 46, 95, 106–8, 145, 160
Federzoni, Luigi, 41
Ferrara 99, 150
Ferraris, Carlo Francesco 48–9, 51, 53, 70
Ferraris, Maggiorino 93n10
Fileni, Enrico 33n37
Florence 29, 99, 100, 108n, 144; agricultural cadastre 85–7
Food and Agriculture Organization 95, 148
Forlì 50n9
forms of observation 4, 10, 23, 112, 114
Foucault, Michel, 1
France xi, xiv, 5–6, 8, 15n44, 30, 74, 128n45; French agricultural statistics 73
Franchetti, Leopoldo 26, 47, 52
Fusco, Ludovico 31

Galanti, Giuseppe Maria 48n5
Galison, Peter 3n9, 134
Gallarate 99
Garelli, Alessandro 93n10, 95n14
General observation 54
Germany x, xi, 7–8, 15, 57, 116, 126n38, 154n61, 160
Gervaso, Pietro 95n14, 103

Gini, Corrado xiii, 71, 95n14, 108, 112, 152n57, 153, 165
Gioia, Melchiorre 120
Giolitti, Giovanni x, xi, 14, 24, 32, 35–42, 51, 76, 103, 106–7, 133–5, 153
Gramsci, Antonio 17–18, 31
Great Britain xiv, 2n5, 6, 7n23, 15; agricultural statistics 78–9, 102, 126n38
Guicciardini, Francesco 74

Helen of Sparta 117
Herf, Jeffrey 17

Institut national de la statistique et des études économiques 1
International Institute for Agriculture viii, x, xi, xiii, xiv, 6, 11, 57–8, 95–6, 143, 147, 154, 158–9, 166
International Labour Office 158n7
International Statistical Institute viii, 11, 71n4, 72n6, 76–8, 104n49, 133n2, 158
Ireland 20n60, 21
Istituto Centrale di Statistica viii, xiii, 72n6, 85n50, 92, 106n55, 108, 109n65, 113, 135n7, 141n25, 155, 165; ISTAT vi, viii, 71, 92–3, 108, 166n34
Istituto di Economia e Statistica Agraria xiv, 45, 112, 147
Istituto forestale di Vallombrosa xi, 29, 108n62, 162
Istituto Geografico Militare viii, xiii, 85, 109
Istituto Nazionale di Economia Agraria viii, xi, xii, xiv, 8, 11, 45, 69–70, 112–13, 129, 132, 135, 145n36, 147–8, 153, 155, 164–6
Istituto per la Ricostruzione Industriale 106
Italy ix, x, xiii, xiv, 4, 12–13, 17–18, 23, 26–7, 31, 35, 42, 47, 66, 73, 94–8, 112, 118, 130, 132–3, 135, 145, 147, 154, 155, 157, 161, 163; agricultural economists 11; agricultural statistics 5, 70, 72–5, 77, 79, 87–8, 101; cadastres 80–1, 84; central Italy x, 13, 26–7, 29, 131; enquiries 10, 48n, 50; interregional gap 35; land valuation 119; many Italies 25, 123n29; northern Italy 13, 29, 33, 37–8; southern Italy x, 26, 52, 54, 55, 67, 129–30, 157n3, 164; surveys 8, 116, 132, 140, 145–7

Jacini, Stefano x, xv, 13, 25, 26, 28, 47–50, 93, 123n29, 156
Jacini enquiry xi, xii, 10–13, 23, 30, 50–1, 53, 55, 76–7, 80
Jarach, Cesare 57, 61

Keynesian revolution 4, 30, 160
Kiaer, Anders N. 71n4, 152n57
Kroton 117

Latium 44
Latour, Bruno 53n21, 66, 90
Laur, Ernst x, xv, 8, 15, 19, 129n48, 135, 140–4, 147–8, 152–4, 158, 166
Lavoisier, Antonie-Laurent 5n14
Le Play, Frederic 8, 59, 60, 66, 114–15, 117, 123–5, 127, 133
League of Nations, xv, 6n20, 43n80, 158, 163n27, 166n34
Levasseur, Emile 78n26, 79, 88n60
Levi, Carlo 53
Liguria 75, 89
Lombardy x, xv, 13, 20–1, 26, 33, 49n8, 75, 89, 99, 118, 145, 148
Lombroso, Cesare 129
Longobardi, Cesare 17, 20n59, 44
Lorenzoni, Giovanni Giuseppe xi, 11, 40, 52, 57, 58n41, 61, 67–8, 136
Loria, Lamberto 129n47
Loria, Prospero Moisè xv, 136
Lubin, David xv, 136
Luzzatti, Luigi 76n19, 107

Maas, Henricus B. J. B. vi, 4
Macerata 76, 97
Maestri, Pietro 73
MAIC see Ministero di Agricoltura, Industria e Commercio
Maier, Charles S. 15, 16n, 111, 134n3, 160n16
Mantua 102
Marche, agricultural statistics 88, 106; Jacini enquiry 76, 80
Maremma 118
Marenghi, Ernesto xi, 34n43, 52, 57, 61, 64, 67, 121n22, 129, 135, 141n21, 143–4
Maria Theresa of Habsburg, Holy Roman Empress 20

Marshall, Alfred 115, 121–2, 150–1, 163
Marx, Karl 19
Mayr, Georg 88
Mazzocchi Alamanni, Nallo 72, 108, 109n65
Medici, Giuseppe 15, 148–52, 162n26, 166
Meklemburgische Patriotische Verein 7
Melis, Guido 12n35, 24n4, 92n4, 103n42, 108, 111n70, 157n5
Messedaglia, Angelo 49, 81, 92n5
Milan xiv, xv, 17, 28–9, 34, 64–5, 80, 97, 103–4, 121n24, 143; cattedra d'agricoltura 34–5, 99; Higher School of Agriculture x, xi, 38, 57, 99–100, 107n60, 144; University of Milan xi
Miliani, Giovanni Battista xv, 31, 37, 39, 41, 94–5
Ministero delle Corporazioni 45
Ministero di Agricoltura, Industria e Commercio (MAIC) vii, xiv, 24, 25, 29, 35–8, 40n61, 45, 72–6, 82n41, 83–9, 91–4, 97–8, 100–5, 107, 108n64, 118; Bureau of Agricultural Statistics xii, 11–13, 24, 38, 45, 73–5, 78, 87, 91–3, 96–8, 102–6, 107n59, 111–12, 156–7; Bureau of Labour 24, 124; cattedre 35; General Directorate of Statistics xiv, 70, 91, 97–8, 104; politica produttivista 35
Ministry of Agriculture xiv, 40n61
Ministry of Agriculture and Forests vi, xiv, 108, 110
Ministry of Finance 36, 72, 81–2
Ministry of Industry xiv
Ministry of National Economy 44, 108n64
Ministry of War 36
Miraglia, Nicola 31n, 49n, 99, 109
Montemartini, Giovanni 12n, 104, 124n31
Morelli, Bartolomeo 104
Murat, Gioacchino 48n5
Mussolini, Benito x, xi, xiii, 14, 42–3, 45, 108, 147, 153

Naples xiv, 28, 99; Kingdom of 5, 48n5, 50n13
Narduzzi, Oreste 103
Netherlands vi, vii, 5, 19n58
Niccoli, Vittorio xi, 11, 64, 65n63, 85–7, 99, 100, 102n40, 105, 109, 115n6, 116, 118–19, 125, 144–5
Niceforo, Alfredo 125n33, 129–30, 149n49
Nitti, Francesco Saverio xi, 20, 24, 36, 38–9, 56n34, 57, 65, 103n42, 106–8, 111, 156, 161–2
Nobili Vitelleschi, Francesco 76

Ottavi, Edoardo xiv, 31, 37, 107

Padua xi, xii, 29, 81–5, 97–103, 123; University of Padua 76, 81
Pallot, Judith 52
Pantaleoni, Maffeo 38, 104, 105n52, 109
Pantano, Edoardo 107, 123–4
Pareto, Vilfredo 121, 162–3
Partito Socialista Italiano 40–1
Peglion, Vittorio 109
Perdisa, Stefano 150
Perini, Dario 115n6, 147–8
Perugia xi, xii, 57
Pestelli, Tito 87
Piacenza xi, xiii, 32
Piedmont 26, 75, 89, 145
Pilat, Theodore 78n26, 79
Pisa xi, 28, 85; University of Pisa 28–9, 44
Pistoia 89
Po Valley 18, 26, 32, 35, 38–9, 46, 153
Poggi, Tito 31, 33
Porter, Theodore M. 2n5, 3, 66, 68n77, 92n7, 134n5
Portici, Higher School of Agriculture 57
Potenza 35, 57, 62
Presutti, Enrico 57
Preti, Dario 42, 43n79

Quételet, Adolphe 53n23, 59–60, 104n48, 123n28, 124–5, 141

Raineri, Giovanni xi, xiii, 31–2, 37, 39, 95
Rava, Luigi xiv
Ravenna 97, 107
Repubblica Sociale Italiana xii
Ricasoli, Bettino 25
Ricci, Umberto 75n18, 95n16, 103–4
Ridolfi, Cosimo 28–9
Rogari, Sandro 9n30, 25, 30n25 and n27, 31n29, 32, 37n51 and n52, 39n56 and

n60, 43n82, 55n29, 93n10, 95n16, 145n37
Romagna 38, 39, 41, 75
Romani, Oddo 35
Rome vi, vii, xiii, xiv, 12, 58, 60, 81, 84, 97–8, 102–3, 105n51, 109; Universal exhibition 1911 12, 129n47
Rossi, Alessandro 71
Rossi-Doria, Manlio 164n29, 166
Rovigo 33
Russia 11, 15, 18, 40, 52; agricultural statistics 6

Salvemini, Gaetano 14n42, 31n28
Salvioni, Giovanni Battista 4, 7, 69–70, 77, 125, 133, 155
Sanjust di Teulada, Edmondo 62
Sankt Petersburg, ISI congress 72n6
Sardinia 55; cattedre d'agricoltura 35
Sassari, university 56
Saxony 133
Schanzer, Carlo 94n12
Schlözer, August Ludwig 2
Schmoller, Gustav xi
Schweizerischer Bauernverband viii, xv, 31, 135, 140–3, 153
Scott, James F. 2, 19n56, 66n72
Scuola Superiore di Agricoltura di Milano *see* Milan, Higher school of agriculture
Scuola Superiore di Agricoltura di Portici *see* Portici, Higher school of agriculture
Sereni, Emilio 18, 31n28
Sering, Max xi, 7, 20n58
Serpieri, Arrigo x-xiv, 11, 15–18, 21–2, 34, 39n, 40, 44–6, 65, 69, 89n61, 98n26, 99–100, 107–9, 112, 113n1, 115n6, 117n13 and n14, 118n17, 121–2, 126, 131, 161–6; land valuation 150–4; Upper milanese 135–40, 144, 146–7
Sibum, Otto 3
Sicily x, xi, 47, 55, 164; Faina enquiry 51, 61, 126; plantations 13, 26
Siena xii
Sismondi, Jean Charles Léonard Simonde de 21, 116, 144n36
Società Agraria di Bologna 29, 147
Società Agraria di Lombardia vii, viii, xv, 29, 30n23, 34, 93, 96n19, 98–105
Società degli Agricoltori Italiani viii, x, xii, xiv, xv, 31–2, 37–9, 41, 57, 73, 95, 97–108, 110n67, 157
Società dei Proprietarii e Agricoltori 99
Società dei Viticultori see Society of Viticulturalists xiv, 30
Società dell'Orticoltura 99
Società Subalpina 29
Società Umanitaria di Milano viii, xv, 58, 92, 99, 135–6
Sonnino, Sidney 21, 26, 39, 47, 52, 55, 76n19, 94n12, 144n36
Soresi, Giuseppe 98n26, 99, 100, 103
Soresina 146
Stabilini, Carlo 99, 100
Stapelford, Thomas 10
Stolypin, Pietr Arkadievič 52
Svorenčik, Andrej vi
Switzerland x, xv, 15, 129n48, 140–2

Tanari, Luigi 50n
Tassinari, Giuseppe xii, 11, 15–16, 46, 121n24, 144–8, 150, 152–3, 154n61, 162, 165–6
Tedeschi, Paolo 49n8, 50
Thaer, Albrecht 54n27, 65n63, 116
Thünen, Johan Heinrich von 54, 116
Tooze, Adam 1, 2, 3–4, 160n16
Trapani 101
Trinci, Cosimo 119
Turin 29, 99, 145
Tuscany 20–1, 28, 41, 75, 87, 144, 145n36, 146

Udine 29, 98–9, 101–3
Ufficio del Lavoro *see* Ministero di Agricoltura, Industria e Commercio, Bureau of Labour
Ufficio di Statistica Agraria *see* Ministero di Agricoltura, Industria e Commercio, Bureau of Agricultural Statistics
Umbria 24n5, 88, 106
Union of Soviet Socialist Republics xiv, 11, 18; surveys 8, 15
United States of America 5–6, 14, 16, 18–19, 78

Val d'Elsa 118
Valenti, Gioacchino (Ghino) x–xii, 12–14, 38, 45n88, 71–2, 76–81, 85–6, 95, 100–10, 112, 114, 123–5, 155–7, 160, 165; and discentramento 93, 96–8; Jacini enquiry 53n24, 76; at SAI 31–2; in Padua 81–3; zone agrarie 87
Veneto 75, 89
Verein für Sozial Politik 7, 48, 126n38
Vittorio Emanuele III xiii, 36, 87, 95, 105
Vivier, Nadine 9, 48n5, 49n8
Volpi di Misurata, Giuseppe 42

Walras, Léon 121–2, 150
Weber, Max 7
World Bank (International Bank for Reconstruction and Development) 22

Young, Arthur 8n26, 65n63, 116

Zanardelli, Giuseppe ix, 33–4, 52
Zanoni, Umberto 99
Zattini, Giuseppe 96n20, 102–3, 105, 107–9, 112
Zeuxis 117

For Product Safety Concerns and Information please contact our EU representative GPSR@taylorandfrancis.com
Taylor & Francis Verlag GmbH, Kaufingerstraße 24, 80331 München, Germany

www.ingramcontent.com/pod-product-compliance
Ingram Content Group UK Ltd.
Pitfield, Milton Keynes, MK11 3LW, UK
UKHW011012180926
475701UK00004B/708
* 9 7 8 1 0 3 2 4 0 2 4 8 2 *